International Business English
Teacher's Book

International Business English

Communication skills
in English for
business purposes

Teacher's Book

Leo Jones
Richard Alexander

CAMBRIDGE
UNIVERSITY PRESS

Published by the Press Syndicate of the University of Cambridge
The Pitt Building, Trumpington Street, Cambridge CB2 1RP
40 West 20th Street, New York, NY 10011–4211, USA
10 Stamford Road, Oakleigh, Victoria 3166, Australia

© Cambridge University Press 1989

First published 1989
Third printing 1992

Printed in Great Britain
at the University Press, Cambridge

ISBN 0 521 36959 2 Teacher's Book
ISBN 0 521 36957 6 Student's Book
ISBN 0 521 36958 4 Workbook
ISBN 0 521 36149 4 Student's Cassettes
ISBN 0 521 36148 6 Set of 3 Cassettes
ISBN 0 521 427320 Video (VHS PAL)
ISBN 0 521 427339 Video (VHS SECAM)
ISBN 0 521 427347 Video (VHS NTSC)
ISBN 0 521 427355 Video Teacher's Guide

CE

Contents

Thanks vi

Introduction 1

1 **Face to face** 22

2 **Letters, telexes and memos** 43

3 **On the phone** 58

4 **Reports and summaries** 75

5 **The place of work** 99

6 **Import and export** 120

7 **Money matters** 136

8 **Delivery and after-sales** 162

9 **Visits and travel** 181

10 **Marketing and sales** 204

11 **Meetings** 221

12 **Operations and processes** 232

13 **A new job** 252

14 **Working together** 267

15 **A special project** 284

Acknowledgements 313

Thanks

In preparing this book we've had generous help and advice from a large number of teachers and business people: our thanks to all of them.

In particular, we'd like to thank the following for their assistance during the research for this book, for using and evaluating the pilot edition and for contributing detailed comments and suggestions:

Sue Gosling
Lesley Stéphan in Lyon
Sandra Bennett-Hartnagel at Hewlett Packard in Böblingen
Pauline Bramall-Stephany at Braun AG in Karlsruhe
the British School of Monza
Business English Programmes in San Sebastian
CAVILAM in Vichy, France
the staff of Calor S.A. in Lyon, France
the English School of Osaka
Christine Frank at Sennheiser in Hanover
Eileen Fryer
Stephen Hagen at Newcastle Polytechnic
International House Executive Courses in London
ITCS 'Dell'Acqua' in Legnano, Milan
ITCS PACLE 'G. Maggiolini' in Parabiago, Milan
Christine Johnson
Peter Kirchhoff
Des O'Sullivan
PERKS Enseñanza de Idiomas in Barcelona
Francis Pithon of SETARAM in Lyon
Nic Underhill
the VHS Language Centre in Nuremberg.

RA would also like to thank Gerlinde for her support and sustenance while the book was being written.

Last but not least, special thanks to Peter Donovan, Peter Taylor and Avril Price-Budgen for their patience, good humour and expertise whilst *International Business English* was being planned, written, recorded and edited.

Introduction

About the course

International Business English is a course in communication skills in English for intermediate and more advanced students who need, or will soon need, to use English in their work. There are 15 units, each centred around a different business situation, designed to involve students in a variety of task-oriented 'integrated activities'. The situations reflect the kind of standard business practice that most students of business English are likely to encounter in their working environments.

We have called this course *International Business English* because English is the major means of communication between business people in different countries. This may involve a Swede talking to a German, a Japanese talking to an Italian and not just foreigners talking to British and American people. As there is no international standard form of English, we have incorporated both British and American usage into the book. The cassettes include recordings of a very wide variety of different speakers, not all of whom are native speakers of English.

The standard business situations covered in the course are ones that are common to all businesses. We have ensured that even in an activity that seems to focus on a special skill like, for example, taking an order over the phone, the kind of language practice that students are getting will also be relevant and useful to students who are less likely to need to use the phone in this particular way. Similarly, in role plays that involve buying and selling (a central part of any business), even a student who is a professional salesperson will benefit from playing the role of buyer and seeing a familiar process from a different point of view.

'Business English'

Business English is not a special language – it is simply English used in business situations. If there is a special language of business, it tends to consist of the specialized terms used by, say, freight forwarders or arbitrage dealers. In fact, every trade and every firm has its own jargon and its own ways of doing business. Every department within a company may use its own special terms. This course does not cover this kind of technical or specialist vocabulary, but it does cover the basic business or commercial terms that most business people use in

1

the course of their work. Any specialist or technical vocabulary that your students require they will either know already or will have to research for themselves, using a technical dictionary or by consulting colleagues at work. We assume that students already know (or can be relied upon to learn) all the English terms they need to talk about their own firm's product or services. These terms are best learned 'on the job'.

Active focus on business

The emphasis of *International Business English* is on carrying out activities, not just discussing what you would do. Students should be aware that they should be using their judgement, business knowledge and skills as they participate in the activities. In speaking and using English in business settings, students are encouraged to be creative in both their actions and their thoughts. Students will not only be improving their English, adding to their vocabulary and language skills, but actually *using* their English throughout the course. The course thus aims to be both stimulating and motivating.

The course aims to improve students' English so that they can use English effectively and confidently in their work. Using English in business always involves using both business skills and language skills – someone whose English is excellent, for example, may not be able to make a phone call complaining about poor service as effectively as someone who has the appropriate knowledge and experience. Using English in business involves both knowing how to use English and knowing how to do business.

While the course does not presuppose any previous business experience, students who do have work experience are encouraged to apply their business knowledge and experience as they work through the book. In its conception, the course draws on the insights of management training techniques as well as the communicative approach in language learning. Students with less work experience will benefit from the opportunity to practise and rehearse the kinds of business skills required in a wide range of professions and business organizations.

Many sections are devoted to language skills and revision of language points: grammar, punctuation, functions, reading aloud, etc. However, particularly in the integrated activities, students will have the opportunity to sharpen their business and management skills – we have incorporated this element into the course because we want students' work in class to be both challenging and interesting. We believe that students who are using their intelligence, imagination and knowledge, as well as their knowledge of English, are more likely to remain highly motivated throughout a long course. We have also included a lot of discussion in the course – we believe that one of the main benefits students get from working in a class is exchanging ideas with other students and learning from *each other* – not just sitting attentively, trying to absorb all their teacher's knowledge.

Who the course is for

International Business English is suitable for a wide range of students: from those with no work experience up to managers and executives, and from early intermediate up to more advanced levels. This may seem an extravagant claim, but as so many of the activities are open-ended, students can perform them according to their abilities. As we discovered when the material was piloted, *International Business English* does work in a surprisingly wide range of classes. Of course, the teacher will need to adapt material to suit particular students' needs – this may involve selecting particular activities and leaving out others and it may sometimes involve supplementing this book with material from other sources or with your own material.

International Business English is extremely flexible. It is designed to be used with all kinds of people who need to be able to use English effectively in their work. It can be used with business people who:

- all work in the same field *or* in entirely different fields
- work within the same company *or* in different firms
- are managers *or* who hold more lowly jobs

and with:
- students who are still studying business and who have little or no practical experience of business practice
- people who intend to take an examination in business English (such as the ICC English for Business Purposes examination in Europe, or a London Chamber of Commerce examination).
- people from different walks of life who need to improve their English, and who will appreciate a highly practical and purposeful approach that a 'general English' course may not offer.

How the course is organized

The Student's Book contains 15 units. Units 1 to 4 introduce the basic business skills, Units 5 to 14 are centred on integrated skills, each organized round a different business situation. Units 1 to 14 contain a functions or reading aloud section, a grammar section, a vocabulary section, discussion opportunities and reading and listening material. The way that the different types of section work is explained below.

To complete the material in a typical unit will take about four 90-minute lessons (a total of roughly sixty 90-minute periods). The exact time required depends on the length of the unit and the level of your class. If your class has less time available, you will need to select the units and activities that will be most useful for your students. The material is designed to be used selectively in this way.

Unit 15 is different and special: it takes the form of a full-scale simulation and revises the skills introduced and practised in the earlier units. The simulation can be spread over 2 to 4 90-minute lessons. The procedure for the simulation is described in detail in the teaching notes for Unit 15 on page 284. No special equipment or facilities are required for the simulation, but some documents will have to be photocopied from the Teacher's Book and given to selected participants. If you can manage to requisition an extra room for the simulation, the scenario may seem more realistic; if there is another class in your college or institute doing *International Business English* you could arrange to combine the two classes at that stage and use both rooms.

The first four units

These units introduce the 'basic business English skills' that students are expected to have some experience in before they embark on the work in Unit 5 onwards: Talking to people in business, Writing letters, memos and telexes, Using the telephone and Writing reports and notes. These are skills that are fundamental to all business contexts where English is used, and will be practised throughout the course.

Students who already actually use these skills in English in their work will not need to spend so long on these units as students with less experience of using English at work. We recommend, however, that *all* students should do some of the work in these units – it will help to refresh their minds about the skills they use and build up confidence for the more demanding activities they will be doing in later units. If your students are finding a particular section in the first four units very easy, or if you anticipate that they will, we recommend that they do the section quickly rather than leave it out altogether. If your students are having difficulty with a particular basic business English skill in a later unit, you may decide to return to one of the first four units to do some remedial work.

The first four units also contain grammar, vocabulary and functions or reading aloud sections that all students need to cover. These should not be omitted.

Types of activities and exercises

In *International Business English*, the various language skills are integrated into task-directed and communicative activities, wherever possible. In many of the speaking, writing, reading and listening activities students are expected to work together in pairs or groups. They are encouraged to play roles and to co-operate purposefully in solving a problem or performing a task.

Integrated activities

In these activities a variety of skills are used: for example, after reading a short text, students listen to a recorded phone message, discuss what they should do and then role-play a telephone call or draft a letter, fax or telex, and then receive further information which will lead to further discussion, role playing or writing.

These activities contain tasks that are similar to the kind of tasks students will have to perform in business life, where they will be using a wide range of skills (language skills as well as business skills and knowledge) to operate effectively in English.

Each SECTION is subdivided into several STEPS (**A**, **B**, **C** and so on) and sometimes the steps are themselves divided into smaller steps (1, 2, 3 and so on). A recommended procedure for each activity is given briefly in the Student's Book and, in more detail, in the Teacher's Book. If you decide to diverge from this procedure and skip a step, for example, make sure that everyone is fully aware of what they have to do and what step you're asking them to ignore.

A real life setting involves very detailed knowledge of the product, circumstances and personalities involved – the scenarios we have used are deliberately general and idealized, so that they can be swiftly understood and then discussed and dealt with. Any missing information that students request for the case or the activity may have to be sorted out by mutual agreement before work starts. We can't supply a full set of recent sales figures, complete customer files or personnel records! But in real life such information would be available *plus* a whole range of other documents and data, colleagues with special knowledge to be consulted and background knowledge of company policy and practice. In real life, clearly, an enormous amount of information from all kinds of sources would be taken into account in reaching a decision. So, find out if members of your class have specialist knowledge to contribute. If, for example, a knowledgeable member of the class says 'I think we need to know whether the firm's cashflow is healthy before we can reach a decision' or 'I need to know what the warehouse capacity is and whether the goods will deteriorate during storage', then be prepared to reach a consensus on this and perhaps make a ruling before resuming the activity. The alternative is for you to say 'You can assume this aspect of the scenario works in the same way as it would in your own company'.

Role play

Many of the activities in *International Business English* involve students taking on specified ROLES in pairs. These are shown in the Student's Book with this symbol: ▉. These include fairly simple activities, such as acting out face-to-face visits in 2.11, as well as more elaborate tasks, such as explaining how to do something in 12.3. The roles are explained in the main text of the Student's Book or explained in the Files (see below). When students are asked to play a role this simulates the kind of situations in which they may find themselves in business life.

Some of the role plays involve TELEPHONE CONVERSATIONS. These are shown in the Student's Book with this symbol: ☎. Students should be encouraged to sit back-to-back for such role plays, to simulate the essential fact that we aren't able to see the person we're talking to on the phone. During a role play, you should go round the class, listening in to what is going on and offering individual advice and vocabulary suggestions. Make a note of the errors you overhear so that you can draw everyone's attention to them in the feedback / follow-up session at the very end of the activity or section.

If you have a video camera and recorder available, many of these role plays can be recorded for playback, analysis and discussion later. This will enable students to 'see themselves as others see them', which may be very beneficial in the long run. If you are going to do this, keep a copy of one of the recordings you make at the beginning of the course – then you will be able to play it again later in the course to show your students how much progress they have made. An audio cassette recorder (with a good microphone) can be used in the same way.

Files

Many of the role play activities involve an 'information gap'. Here students are directed to separate sections at the back of the book, called 'FILES', where each person is given different information and can't see the other's information. Their purpose is then to find out what their partners know and to tell them what they know.

The Files are on pages 195 to 235 of the Student's Book. As you will see, they are jumbled up in random order, so that it is not possible to find your way through them easily and so students are unable to 'cheat' and look at each other's information.

In these information gap activities two or three students are each given different information, such as two halves of a price list or different role descriptions, and then have to bridge the gap in a conversation or phone call: the Files work in the same sort of way as role cards. An example of this is in section 6.1, where one member of each pair looks at File 17 while the other looks at File 42: by asking each other questions they build up a complete picture of the price list.

Some of the Files contain information that students do not need to see until they have completed a certain number of steps in an activity. An example of this is in section 8.1, where students are only given the information required for step 3 (in File 99) when they have completed step 2.

Some of the Files provide model answers to written tasks, which students are not supposed to look at until they·have completed the task. An example of this is in section 2.10 where students see a model telex in File 108 after they have attempted the task themselves. Model answers to all the other tasks are given in the Teacher's Book and you may photocopy these if you think your students will find it helpful to see them.

The Teacher's Book contains a brief summary of each activity where the Files are involved and a description of what will happen. There is also an overview of all the Files on page 19 of the Teacher's Book.

Listening

Within the integrated activities, recorded information is given to provide input or stimulus for the discussion or role play, shown by

in the Student's Book text. This may be a message recorded on an answerphone, or an overheard telephone call or conversation. These are not 'listening comprehension exercises' with questions to answer, but essential components of the activity. An example of this is the telephone message in 8.1, where further information is supplied for the second step in the activity.

You may well need to play a recording to the class two or three times, while they take notes and concentrate on understanding the information given in the recording. In most cases, they will not need to understand every word that is spoken. If students listen to the recordings in pairs, rather than as individuals, they can help each other to understand. You may decide to introduce a few helpful questions to guide your students towards recognizing the relevant information and we have suggested such questions in the teaching notes.

In the recordings of *International Business English* you will hear a wide variety of speakers – both British and American accents are heard and some of the speakers are non-native speakers with foreign accents.

Most of the recordings are simulated authentic conversations. Some of these recordings were improvised, some are loosely scripted and others are more closely scripted – though all the features of real conversations, telephone calls or messages (hesitation, false starts, slightly unclear phraseology or pronunciation, etc) have been retained and not 'edited out'.

There are also some self-contained listening comprehension exercises in the Student's Book, with accompanying tasks. The procedure for these usually involves a pre-listening step to prepare students for the text and establish certain expectations about its content, followed by a main task, then followed by a post-listening step where students compare notes with a partner or discuss the topic in a larger group.

In the Workbook and on its accompanying cassettes, there are further listening tasks, some of which you may like to use in class.

These introduce a different aspect of the theme of the unit and may be used as a lead-in for a discussion, for example.

Reading

Reading is integrated into the texts as an intrinsic part of the activity. For example, extracts from letters, telexes, news articles or information on record cards may provide necessary reading input for a speaking or writing activity. Alternatively, students may be expected to use checklists or to arrange items in order of priority as preparation for a listening task or a pairwork activity involving the Files. These are not 'reading comprehension texts' with questions to answer but sources of information that will help students to cope with the task they are involved in. An example of this is in section 6.4 where the advertisement provides essential information for the steps that follow.

Clearly, in such activities, a skill like reading does not play an isolated role. Nor is this the case in most business situations: participants in a business situation switch from the spoken medium to the written medium and vice versa with little or no conscious focusing on the medium they are using. It is communication purpose that affects which skill is being used. Hence it is a tenet of this course that the practising of such skills needs to be as organic as the classroom situation allows.

At the same time, *International Business English* also contains a number of individual reading exercises. Here different aspects of the reading skill are focused on: reading for gist, extracting specific information and reading to find particular details.

At the same time, we have included a number of longer reading texts, involving aspects of the business world, which are of interest in themselves and relevant to the topics dealt with in the unit. An example of this is in section 12.9. These texts are accompanied by tasks, which are fully explained in the Teacher's Book. There are three basic types of tasks in these exercises:

- Reading for gist: to get the basic information from the text
- Scanning: looking through the text to find specific information as quickly as possible
- Reading for detail: understanding more detailed information in the text.

In some units reading tasks are integrated into discussion activities (see also below). Here the reading of the text – it may be an advertisement or a longer passage – provides input for a subsequent discussion.

Writing

The integrated activities contain all kinds of writing tasks, including making notes and drafting memos, letters, telexes, faxes and short reports. Students are usually asked to '*draft* a letter or telex...' rather than 'write' one, since a first draft may be the most that students can realistically achieve in class. However, for homework, students can be asked to produce a revised final draft – perhaps word-processed or typed. The writing that they will do within an activity is communicative and an integral part of the activity: what they have written is usually 'delivered' to another pair who have to reply or react to it.

Students are often expected to do their written drafts in pairs, so that they can help each other, and the completed draft can be shown to another pair for their comments. The purpose of this is to encourage co-operation within the class and to give students a chance to benefit from each other's ideas and experience. Usually such written drafts would then be collected and marked by you. Alternatively, students may be asked to prepare revised drafts for homework, and these are what you would collect and mark.

Depending on your students' line of business, the use of telexes may be 'on its way out' and faxes or electronic mail may be a more usual way of communicating rapidly in writing, when an exchange of letters would take too long. We have made no assumptions about this and usually we have left it to students to decide whether they will draft a letter, fax or telex when a written communication is required in an activity. This decision will presumably be based on their real life needs, but students who are taking an examination may need to be encouraged to write letters more often than telexes, as telexes tend to be shorter and obey fewer rules of style and layout. Moreover, with telexes the tolerance of error is much higher – business people are often quite surprised if they get a telex from another country with no mistakes in it!

Over the past twenty years or so, business letter-writing in English has undergone something of a transformation: the traditional Dickensian style of business letters, using a multitude of formulae and clichés ('We are in receipt of your esteemed favour of the 14th inst....'), has been replaced by a much more straightforward style of writing. Moreover, many firms have come to realize that even a telex or fax message is a personal as well as a corporate piece of communication: a brief personal greeting often helps to maintain a relationship between two people in different parts of the world – and the closer the relationship, the more likely it is that the customer will remain loyal or that the supplier will do his or her best to satisfy the customer.

In some activities, there is a letter or telex to read or reply to, which itself becomes the *model* for a letter or telex that the students will have to write later in the same activity, an example of this is in section 7.4, where the students read a 'first reminder' letter from a supplier on page 77 for the information it contains and later use it as a model for their own letter to their own customer.

Model versions of the letter, memo or telex-writing tasks are given in the Teacher's Book. You may photocopy some of these to give your students further ideas. If there is an overhead projector in your classroom, you could photocopy these model versions onto OHP transparencies (most modern photocopying machines can do this impressively well) and project them for the whole class to see.

In some cases, where it is essential for students to see a model version, this is hidden among the Files, so that students do not get to see the model until after they have completed the task.

Discussion and follow-up

At the end of every section, you should allow enough time to discuss with the class how they got on in the activities and give them time to raise any problems or queries they may have. This is a significant activity in its own right and can contribute much to the learning process. It may sometimes be better to skip the final step of an activity so as to allow time for this before the lesson ends.

Where an integrated activity contains a large number of steps or raises any controversial issues, there are detailed notes in the Teacher's Book for a FOLLOW-UP DISCUSSION. This will involve giving feedback to the class on their performance in the activity and allow them to step outside their roles and consider the value of the tasks and how their own business situations are different to (and usually more complex than) the simplified or idealised scenario they have enacted. A real-life setting involves very detailed knowledge of the product and situation one is in, whereas the scenarios we have used are more general, so that they are more easy to understand and deal with. Like case studies in a training course, the issues that are raised must be localized to students' own circumstances.

Towards the end of some units there are special discussion sections. Many of these discussions are provoked or led into by short recorded texts or interviews, shown by [cassette icon] in the Student's Book, or by short reading passages. The discussions are in several steps, with different aspects of a topic being covered. The discussions are designed to work best in small groups – though if your whole class is small, a whole-class discussion may be best. An example of this is 8.7, where the value of good customer relations is discussed.

Students should be encouraged to reflect on the issues and activities they have been dealing with. One reason why this is particularly important is that the language required in a discussion to express opinions, evaluate ideas, agree and disagree and so on is fundamental to much business interaction, as well as contributing to one's broader educational development. You will find that discussion naturally arises after many of the activities throughout this course, such as reading a text, and particularly after students have taken part in an integrated activity.

Discussion about business topics is a regular feature of *International*

Business English. Participation in a language class gives everyone a valuable opportunity to exchange ideas with other people who may be in similar or in very different situations and this will perhaps encourage them to re-examine their own ideas and prejudices. Discussion, particularly in small groups, also gives everyone a chance to use and consolidate the vocabulary that they have encountered in the unit.

At the end of each section of *International Business English* students should be given a chance to raise any queries or doubts they have. Sometimes it may be a good idea to ask them to explain how they benefited from doing a particular section. This may seem like asking for trouble (in some classes you might really be opening a can of worms by asking this kind of question!) but it is very reassuring to students to find out that the other people in the class have had similar difficulties and that others have found the activity useful.

You should also provide the students with feedback, pointing out errors you have noted down and congratulating them on the activities they have performed well.

In some sections we have suggested extra discussion ideas in the Teacher's Book, in the form of further questions you can present to the class.

Grammar

Each unit contains a grammar section, covering the main 'problem areas' of English grammar:

1.2	Asking questions	page	4
2.5	Joining sentences		14
3.5	Present tenses		27
4.5	Using the passive		35
5.5	Referring to the past		50
6.6	Looking into the future		66
7.1	Reported speech		70
8.4	Conditionals		93
9.5	Infinitives and gerunds		108
10.3	Comparison		122
11.5	Place and direction		142
12.4	Modal verbs		150
13.5	Relative clauses		169
14.6	Order of adverbs		185

The aim of these sections is not to provide a fully exhaustive treatment of English grammar: this would go far beyond the scope of *International Business English*.

Further problems that arise should be dealt with by correction and giving your class a brief summary of the 'rules'. If your students are particularly weak in grammar, we recommend that they do the exercises and activities in selected units from *Use of English* by Leo Jones (CUP). For reference, we recommend that students refer to *Basic English Usage* or the more advanced *Practical English Usage* by Michael Swan (OUP).

The grammar sections consist of several steps, the first of which is PRESENTATION. In this step some of the rules and problems are introduced, together with recorded examples on the cassette, shown by in the Student's Book. If possible, students should study this step before the lesson, to save more time in class for more active work.

The following steps consist of EXERCISES AND ACTIVITIES. First, students use the particular structures or grammatical forms to fill gaps in sentences or write endings to incomplete sentences. Then they have a chance to use the structures in a freer discussion activity. Most of these activities are best done by students in pairs or groups.

In the Teacher's Book we also suggest an EXTRA ACTIVITY that students can do if further work is required.

The Workbook contains follow-up exercises on all the grammar topics covered in the Student's Book. If your class are having a lot of difficulty with a grammar section, you could supplement their work by using one of the exercises from the Workbook in class.

In the Workbook there are also exercises on prepositions and phrasal verbs — a topic we feel is best dealt with by students working alone, though you may choose to do selected exercises from the Workbook in class.

Functions

Ten units contain a section dealing with functions. The following groups of functions are covered:

1.4	Meeting and greeting people	page	6
3.2	Getting people to do things		24
5.2	Agreeing and disagreeing		43
6.1	Getting and giving information		55
8.2	Complaining and apologizing		88
9.3	Narrating		103
10.10	Possibility, probability and certainty		134
11.1	Discussion techniques		137
12.3	Explaining, giving instructions		149
14.1	Asking for and giving advice		177

One major emphasis of these sections of *International Business English* is to make students aware of the need to select appropriate forms to fit in with the demands of the situations encountered. This may often mean choosing an exponent (and commensurate tone of voice) which matches up with the type of person one is dealing with — whether they are complete strangers, superiors, familiar colleagues, valued clients or acquaintances.

To a great extent, success in business depends on creating the right impression. Politeness and formality are often keys to achieving a desired communicative effect, whether one is apologizing for the late delivery of a product or attempting to sell something to a customer. The kind of language used also marks or characterizes the speaker as friendly or unfriendly, helpful or unhelpful. We are all aware of how such signals tend to aid (or hinder) the smooth running of everyday social interaction: in business situations this tendency may often be magnified. Unit 1 emphasizes various aspects of how to create the right impression.

As in the grammar sections, there is a PRESENTATION step with recorded examples (shown by ⬛ in the Student's Book text) in which the function and some typical exponents are introduced. Students are asked to look at the speech balloons and to listen to the recording. Here the cassette can also be used for pronunciation practice, using a play-pause-repeat technique: students hear each exponent on the tape, the tape is paused and the class repeat it, trying to copy the intonation and tone of voice. This may sound slightly demeaning for more advanced students, but it is an extremely effective way of focusing attention on aspects of phonology that are difficult to define, such as 'sounding polite' or 'being deferential'.

This is followed by a series of ACTIVITIES in which students practise using the exponents in role plays or a discussion. While they are doing these activities, you should go round the class eavesdropping and discreetly offering advice, making notes on any points that should be made to the whole class afterwards.

In the Teacher's Book we also suggest an EXTRA ACTIVITY to involve students in more communicative practice.

The Workbook contains follow-up exercises on all the functions covered in the Student's Book. If your class are having a lot of difficulty with a functions section, you could supplement their work by using an exercise from the Workbook in class. Some of these Workbook exercises are recorded on the Workbook cassettes.

Reading aloud

Four units of *International Business English* contain a section dealing with reading aloud. In business, people are often called upon to read out information from an article, letter or form or to relay information verbatim. Even such basic skills as spelling out names (and being able to understand other people dictating names to you) and reading out figures (and being able to write figures down quickly) are both skills that tend to cause difficulties for intermediate and more advanced students.

We have covered four important aspects of reading aloud:

2.2   Spelling out names and addresses   page   12
4.4   Stress and intonation   35
7.6   Reading out numbers   81
13.2 Joining up words (catenation)   164

The exercises provide students with practice in reading aloud by first letting them listen to a recording of a text as a model (shown by 📼 in the Student's Book), and then working in pairs to make the activity more realistic. Model readings of the pairwork texts are also given on the cassette, where this is relevant and helpful.

For the first part of the exercise, the technique of 'shadowing' can be used to help students to copy and assimilate stress and intonation patterns. 'Shadowing' (i.e. reading the text aloud softly at the same time as the model recording while they are listening to it) seems a strange thing to do at first, but it is a surprisingly effective technique that seems to work just as well in class as it does in private or in a language laboratory. Repetition practice, using the cassette and pausing it after each tone group is also helpful. There are further reading aloud exercises in the Workbook.

Vocabulary

Vocabulary that is special to a particular trade, industry or firm cannot be covered in a book of this type. What we have done is to identify vocabulary items that are common to all aspects of business, using the syllabus of the ICC Certificate in English for Business Purposes as one of our sources. The texts, instructions, exercises and situational dialogues contain much of the 'business' vocabulary that students will require, thus enhancing the active nature of the book. The majority of this vocabulary is assimilated as students carry out a task-related activity and should not be taught 'separately' out of context.

In addition, most units in *International Business English* contain at least one exercise on the vocabulary related to the particular theme of the unit. These exercises are designed to introduce business-related vocabulary and terms which have not occurred elsewhere in exercises or texts. Given that some of these exercises are to a certain extent test-like, they will appeal variously to different types of students. These exercises can be done at any stage in the unit where time allows and are useful when one activity has finished and there isn't quite enough time to begin another. They can be done by students working together in pairs but, if possible, students should prepare them before the lesson. An example of this is 8.5.

As we are dealing with English as an international language, we have tried to show no bias towards the British dialect of English. Both

British and American vocabulary items are used in the text, in the vocabulary exercises and on the tapes.

Students should be encouraged to use a general dictionary such as the *Collins COBUILD English Language Dictionary*, the *Longman Dictionary of Contemporary English*, the *Oxford Advanced Learner's Dictionary of Current English* or the *Chambers Universal Learners Dictionary* – or the less well-known but splendid *Penguin Wordmaster Dictionary*. A special dictionary of business English terms is probably unnecessary, as all the basic business vocabulary is covered in these dictionaries together with all the non-business vocabulary students are likely to come across. A pocket-size bilingual dictionary is likely to be more annoying than helpful, except perhaps when away from one's desk or travelling.

The important vocabulary that has come up in each unit is revised in further exercises in the Workbook. The Workbook also contains exercises on collocations and word-formation.

Background information for the non-business person

Many of the units in *International Business English* rely on a certain amount of knowledge about the business world or business practice. Where this is the case, we have included in the Teacher's Book a section of Background Information for teachers who are not specialists. (You may wish to photocopy some of these sections for any of your students who lack work experience.) Don't worry about your own lack of business knowledge: you are the *English language* specialist and your students are the business specialists. Don't be tempted to bluff them into thinking you know more than you do – be frank about your lack of knowledge of business, let the class explain to *you* how business works. Say things to them like: 'I've read that in business people often... – is that true in your experience?' rather than 'In business you should always...'. The Teacher's Book gives you enough information to understand the content of all the activities and exercises that your students will be doing – but remember that they are bringing to the activities and the discussion experience and knowledge that you, as language teacher, may lack.

Further background information can be found in readable non-specialist books like the following – all are inexpensive paperbacks and easily understood by the 'general reader':
- *Background to Business* by Terry Price (Pan Breakthrough Books, 1983)
- *So you think you're in business?* – a Video Arts Guide (Methuen, 1986)
- *So you think you can sell?* – a Video Arts Guide (Methuen, 1985)
- *So you think you can manage?* – a Video Arts Guide (Methuen, 1984)

- *Effective Management Skills* by John Scott and Arthur Rochester (Sphere/British Institute of Management, 1984).

And to keep in touch with developments in the business world, we recommend that you look regularly at the business section of *The Economist* and the financial and business section of one of the 'quality' newspapers (in the UK: *The Guardian, The Times, The Independent* or *The Daily Telegraph*).

Mistakes and correction

Although accuracy is an important aspect of language learning and should never be ignored, it is far more important for learners to be able to communicate effectively. To speak English fluently it is important to develop confidence and this is impossible if one is afraid of making mistakes. Students should not be corrected too often as this may have an inhibiting effect and make them 'mistake-conscious'. One cannot learn a language without making mistakes, and mistakes are a useful indicator of what students still need to learn. In real life, after all, people have to communicate with each other *in spite of* the mistakes they may be making and the limited amount of English they know.

Students should certainly be corrected when they make serious errors, but it is usually best to point out any mistakes that were made *after* the class have completed an activity, rather than interrupting during the activity. While students are working in pairs or groups, and you are going from group to group listening in, you may be able to make the occasional discreet correction without interrupting the flow of the conversation, but normally it is better to make a note of some of the errors you overhear and point them out later.

You may hear your students making mistakes in pronunciation, grammar, vocabulary or style, but rather than mentioning *every* mistake you have heard, it is more helpful to be selective and to draw attention to certain points that you think your students can improve. It may be less confusing to focus on just one type of error at a time by, for example, drawing attention to pronunciation errors after one activity and then to vocabulary errors after another. Accuracy is something that takes a long time to develop and it cannot be achieved overnight!

In writing, where errors are more noticeable, accuracy is much more important. When marking students' written work, you can't really overlook some of their mistakes as you might do if they were talking. However, it is helpful to show students which of their mistakes are more or less serious and to distinguish between different kinds of mistakes. Give students a chance to correct their own mistakes by underlining the relevant parts or showing in the margin whether there is a mistake in grammar (**G**), word order (**WO**), vocabulary (**V**), punctuation (**P**), spelling (**Sp**) or style (**ST**). A tick (✓) is a nice way of showing that an idea has been well expressed. And make sure that you show your appreciation by adding an encouraging comment at the end – seeing a page of corrections can be quite demoralizing!

Using *International Business English*

We recommend that you always read the teaching notes for each section and prepare ahead what you'll be covering in class. This is particularly important in the role plays and the integrated activities where you will need to know who's doing what and when. Many of the activities in *International Business English* are open-ended and hence unpredictable. A course full of predictable, controlled exercises would be much less exciting and challenging.

It is not possible for us to predict how long any activity will last in a particular class. The level and enthusiasm of the class as well as the time you have available will control this.

You may well find that there is more material in the book than you can cover in the time you have available, in which case you will need to **select** the units and sections within a unit that will be of most benefit to your students. Indeed, we recommend that you do select among the activities, since not everything in the book is likely to be equally relevant to every group of students. Many of the sections are 'free-standing' and don't depend on having done the work in a previous section. You may decide to deal with units in a different sequence from the way they are presented in the Student's Book and this will not affect the way that the course works. However the units do become progressively more difficult.

It is important to adjust the emphasis of the course to suit your students' level and their experience of the business world – as well as to suit their individual needs and interests. Using the Workbook will enable slower students to keep pace with their colleagues, and will provide extra practice in all the main language points dealt with in each unit. The Workbook is an integral part of the course, as explained below.

The teaching notes for Unit 1 explain the rationale behind the different types of activities you will be using and are rather more detailed than subsequent ones.

The Workbook

The Workbook and its self-study cassettes are an integral part of *International Business English*, consolidating and extending the work that is done in class using the Student's Book.

We have designed the Workbook to be helpful, stimulating and sometimes challenging. The exercises are all 'self-correcting', with an answer key at the back. The material in the Workbook provides:

1 **Follow-up exercises** to each unit in the Student's Book for students to do as homework. Each unit in the Workbook contains:
   - grammar exercises
   - functions or reading aloud exercises, with accompanying recorded material on the cassettes
   - exercises on the essential business vocabulary presented in the Student's Book

2 **Additional material** in the form of:
   - exercises on prepositions and word-building
   - supplementary tasks to practise the writing of letters, telexes, reports and the like
   - business-related recordings and listening comprehension tasks (on the cassettes). Listening to a broadcast or telephone message is often best done alone with a cassette recorder: students can hear and re-hear the recording as many times as they wish, without feeling embarrassed that they are wasting their colleagues' time in class.

Many exercises in the Workbook can be used in class to supplement the work in the Student's Book. We have not suggested a procedure for these, as the exercises are designed to be self-explanatory and easily usable by students working alone. We have mentioned any relevant exercises in the Workbook at the appropriate place in the Teacher's Book.

It is also useful and reassuring for students to share their experiences of using the Workbook with their class-mates, and we recommend that a little time be set aside on a regular basis for queries and discussion on what students have done in the Workbook.

The Workbook should be viewed as a means for sustaining interest and maintaining momentum in the learning process during the time in which the students are not in class. This also serves the purpose of helping students to grasp the importance of attaining a degree of autonomy in their language learning and of creating a motivation to persist.

Home study

We believe that in working with *International Business English*, however busy your students are, they must spend about as much time studying at home as they spend in class. Part of this work should be homework and preparation stemming from or leading to work in the Student's Book, some should be doing the self-correcting exercises in the Workbook, and some should be self-directed reading connected with the student's own trade or industry. Such material can be found in the trade press or in more general business (and non-business) weeklies like *The Economist, International Business Week, Time* or *Newsweek*. The kind of books, newspapers or magazines you recommend will, of course, depend on a particular student's interests and line of business.

Guide to the files in the Student's Book

As the Files are printed in the Student's Book in a random format, here is a 'map' to help you find your way through them, showing which sections have Files belonging to them.

Unit number	File content	File numbers			
1.4	meeting and greeting teams	A: 1	B: 7		
2.2	address labels	77			
	foreign addresses	A: 10	B: 3		
2.9	memo	97			
2.10	telexes:	108			
3.2	part one	A: 5	B: 11		
	part two	A: 20	B: 13		
3.7	phone calls				
	In groups of *three*:				
	stage 1	A: 16	B: 67	C: 2	
	stage 2	A: 91	B: 4	C: 31	
	stage 3	A: 85	B: 43	C: 50	
	stage 4	A: 6	B: 64	C: 73	
	In groups of *four*:				
	stage 1	A: 16	B: 67	C: 2	D: 2
	stage 2	A: 109	B: 109	C: 31	D: 36
	stage 3	A: 85	B: 43	C: 50	D: 85
	stage 4	A: 73	B: 64	C: 73	D: 6
3.9	part one	A: 18	B: 25		
	part two	A: 66	B: 51		
4.1	discussion	A: 21	B: 92		
4.2	model memo	78			
4.4	KfW company report	A: 41	B: 32		
4.5	price lists	A: 12	B: 106		
5.4	company organization	A: 19	B: 26		

Unit number	File content	File numbers		
5.6	Lucky-Goldstar ad	A: 23	B: 40	
6.1	price lists	A: 17	B: 42	
6.2	role information for Jim Dale	96		
6.4	printout of stock position	115		
	1st telephone enquiry	A: 59	B: 105	
	2nd telephone enquiry	A: 69	B: 45	
6.7	18 July telex	86		
	20 July telex	103		
	13 Sept telex	55		
	15 Nov note from Mr Richardson	48		
	23 Dec telex	33		
7.1	report of a phone call	A: 38	B: 57	
7.2	phone call to Mr Granger	A: 80	B: 74	
	telex from Mr Granger	56		
7.3	correct version of letter of credit document	98		
7.5	credit controllers	A: 113	B: 15	C: 52
7.6	waybills	A: 104	B: 79	
8.1	telex and files	99		
8.2	complaints and apologies	A: 24	B: 61	
8.6	telex from Mr Reynard	116		
9.1	Manchester Airport	A: 39	B: 60	
	Hotel Miramar	A: 58	B: 44	
9.6	hotels	A: 76	B: 68	
10.4	arranging a meeting	A: 114	B: 70	
10.5	sales talk			
	first part	A: 22	B: 8	
	second part	A: 8	B: 30	
10.6	questionnaires	A: 62	B: 28	C: 46
11.3	staff meeting	A: 14	B: 65	C: 100
	managers' meeting	A: 88	B: 9	C: 37
	notes for chairperson	47		

Unit number	*File content*	*File numbers*			
11.5	office layout	A: 90	B: 101		
12.1	diagram of table	112			
12.3	coffee machine	A: 94	B: 36		
13.1	career histories	A: 107	B: 111		
13.2	Help Wanted ads.	A: 63	B: 75	C: 35	
13.3	application letter	87			
13.8	progress interviews	A: 53	B: 81	C: 71	
13.9	checklist for interviewers	89			
14.1	giving advice, part one	A: 34	B: 29	C: 70	D: 27
	giving advice, part two	A: 83	B: 102	C: 93	D: 4
14.2	interview	A: 84	B: 54		
14.10	consultative meeting	A: 95	B: 49	C: 82	D: 110

1 Face to face

To some extent, this unit can be considered as a 'comfortable introduction' to the rest of the course – it also introduces the types of exercises and activities that students will be doing during the course and shows the degree of student autonomy expected. But this is not just a 'getting to know your class-mates' unit: the emphasis throughout is on encouraging students to consider and re-evaluate the social functions of English. In business, this is particularly important, as students may be dealing with all kinds of people in English: clients and colleagues, friends and strangers, superiors and subordinates – all of whom have to be talked to in different ways.

The whole of Unit 1 comprises material for two or at most three double lessons of $1\frac{1}{2}$ to 2 hours each. All subsequent units will take longer to do.

This and the other three introductory units would be compulsory for students without work experience, but work-experienced students should still go through them, perhaps more quickly, before they begin work on Unit 5. Many of the skills taken for granted in Units 5 onwards are introduced or revised and practised in Units 1 to 4.

The teaching notes for this unit are rather more detailed than subsequent units, as we are introducing some of the methods and ideas underlying the course. It is advisable to read the notes through before the lesson.

1.1 First impressions ...

This section introduces the idea that, in business life, it's important not just to be efficient and do your job but also to look and sound friendly, confident, sincere and helpful ... and not unfriendly, insincere, shy or unhelpful! People in different countries have different ideas of what sounds friendly, polite or sincere.

■ Students need to be made aware of how their 'natural' way of talking sounds to a British or American person – some nationalities (e.g. some Cantonese speakers and some German speakers) may sound rather abrupt or rude to other ears and such speakers may need to make a considerable effort to **smile** more than usual and be **extra-polite** to compensate for this!

First of all

If the members of the class are together for the first time, get everyone to introduce themselves, saying who they are, what name they like to be called by, where they work, where they come from, and so on. Introduce yourself in the same way too. Don't spend too long on this, as students will be talking in more detail about the kind of work they do in section 1.3. If everyone already knows everyone else, start straight in with the recording.

Procedure

A Play the recording. Perhaps point out that the people greeting the visitors are *not* all receptionists, some are people who happen to be in the office when the visitor arrives – a situation all members of the class may find themselves in. We suggest that you play the recording through three times, though you may wish to pause the tape between each interaction for your students to make comments and ask questions:

1. Play the recording all the way through so that students can imagine each of the situations, get used to the voices and get the gist of what is being said. Encourage them to close their eyes to cut out distractions.
2. Play the tape again and this time ask everyone to decide on their answers to the questions in the Student's Book. Then get everyone to discuss their answers. Why did some speakers sound more friendly or efficient than others? Was it the language they used or their tone of voice or what? (The man in extract 5 and the woman in extract 9 are particularly impolite.)
3. Play the tape for a third time and ask them to just sit back and listen. Maybe they could note down any questions they want to ask you at the end, or note down vocabulary or expressions that were used – or just relax and enjoy the conversations while soaking up ideas and vocabulary.

1
Woman: Good evening, Mr Green, how nice to see you again.
Man: Good evening, it's nice to be back. How are you?

2
Man: Good morning, madam, can I help you?
Woman: Yes, I've got an appointment with Mr Henry Robinson.

3
Woman: Good afternoon, sir.
Man: Good afternoon. I'd like to see Mr Ferguson please.

4
Man: Hello, madam, can I help at all?
Woman: Yes, I'd like to know what time...

5

1st man (brusque): Er ... good morning, sir. Do you have an appointment?

2nd man: Yes, I've arranged to see Ms Shapiro. I think I may be a bit early...

6

1st man (friendly, polite): Good morning, sir. Do you have an appointment?

2nd man: Yes, er ... I've arranged to see Ms Shapiro. I think I may be a bit early...

7

Woman: Good morning, Mr Rossi. How are you today?

Man: Just fine, thanks. Is Mr Grady in yet?

Woman: I'll just find out for you...

8

Man: Er ... hello, Miss Macdonald, I'm afraid ... er ... Mrs Sanderson isn't back from lunch yet.

Woman: Oh, that's OK, I'll sit and wait if that's all right.

Man: Oh, certainly, would you like some coffee?

Woman: Mm, that sounds a good idea, thanks.

9

Woman (off-hand): Yes?

Man: Good morning, my name's Martin. I'm here to see Mr Suzuki.

Woman: Who?

Man: Mr Suzuki.

Woman: Oh, he's busy I think.

Man: Could you let him know I'm here, please?

Woman: OK.

10

Woman (polite, friendly): Good morning, sir.

Man: Good morning, my name's Martin, I'm here to see Mr Suzuki.

Woman: If you'll just take a seat, Mr Martin, I'll let him know you're here.

Man: Fine, thanks.

Woman: Mr Suzuki, Mr Martin's in reception for you ... He's on his way down.

[Time: 2 minutes 25 seconds]

B Put the class into groups of three or four and get them to ask each other the questions in the Student's Book. At the end of the discussion (which could last between two and five minutes, depending on how much the groups have to say on the subject) ask each group to report its most interesting ideas to the rest of the class.

C For this step, the same groups should work together. When they have added some adjectives, ask the groups to tell the others what they wrote down. Be prepared to help with supplying unknown vocabulary here. Some possible additions to the 'try to be' list are:

alert, distinct, friendly, confident, calm, honest, skilful, intelligent, nice, helpful, polite,

and for the 'try not to be' list:

sleepy, unclear, lazy, dishonest, clumsy, stupid, prejudiced, inefficient, nasty, unhelpful, off-hand, rude,

Once you have decided as a class on the 'top five' or even 'top ten' adjectives, these can be written on the board in LARGE LETTERS and henceforth considered as 'Golden Rules of Speaking' that can be referred back to later in the unit.

D Again in the same groups, students should exchange ideas. If your class is very small, this may be best dealt with as a whole class. The conclusions they may come to are that giving a good impression reflects your company's image (no firm wants its customers to think it's unpleasant!) and that if you start off a relationship in a friendly, pleasant way it is likely to go on in the same way, which will be to everyone's advantage.

The answer to the last question on page 3 will depend partly on the established practice in a firm: usually 'Good morning/afternoon, can I help you?' or 'Good afternoon, Mr Brown...' are more common than 'Hello, can I help you?' or 'Hi, Mr Brown...'. But the most important thing is a nice smile and friendly eye contact.

If necessary, draw students' attention to the point we made above about smiling and being extra-polite.

Extra activity

If you have a smallish, fairly advanced class, you could ask everyone to record their own voices on a blank cassette. Once they have done this they should pass the cassette to another group who will then comment on the impression they get. Students who are judged to sound abrupt or unfriendly should be recommended to smile more and be extra-polite!

This activity may also be done by students working together in pairs as part of their homework, and would be suitable for a larger class in this case.

1.2 Asking questions   *Grammar*

One way to give someone a good impression is to talk without making too many grammatical errors! As asking questions is something people have to do a lot in business, we're going to look at this topic first.

The purpose of the exercises in this section is to diagnose what difficulties your students have with forming questions, so that you can draw their attention to points they should do more work on. They will all have 'done' question-formation in previous language courses, so this is clearly revision and not new information.

Exercises and activities

A Put everyone into pairs or groups of three. This apparently back-to-front, but quite straightforward exercise gives everyone a chance to find out some of their strengths and weaknesses in forming questions. Each pair should write down the questions and when ready compare what they've written with another pair. Encourage them to discuss the differences and decide which of them they prefer. Then go through with the whole class – draw attention to the need for the questions to be accurate (no mistakes) and plausible (making sense in the context).

Here are some suggested correct questions, though your students may have other equally plausible suggestions:
1. Did you have a good flight?
2. Who would you like to see?
3. Who did you speak to last time you came?
4. Who recommended this particular hotel to you?
5. When would you like to see round the factory?
6. Are you travelling alone?
7. How long are you planning to stay?
8. Has your husband been here before?

The complete dialogue, with those questions and the answers in the Student's Book, is recorded on the cassette. Play this *after* your students have suggested their own versions, otherwise this may take away their confidence.

B   Again students should work in pairs. Perhaps, to get things started, begin by asking everyone in the class to suggest just one interesting question they might ask a man from India: about life in his country, the differences between this country and his, the ways of doing business there, his journey, etc. Then each pair should write down their ten questions. Again, when the list of ten is complete the pairs should look at each other's work and compare ideas.

Go round the class, carefully checking that the questions have been written down accurately (without mistakes). If necessary, make a note of any incorrect questions and draw everyone's attention to these later. You may decide that your students need to do further work on this: if so, they can be referred to the Workbook exercise 1.1 or do work in class using *Use of English* Unit 1.

The examples of question tags are recorded. On the recording the speakers are using a **rising tone**, not the more casual falling tone, which foreigners find so difficult to master. Point out that the rising tone is used when you are not sure if you are right and are interested in hearing what the other person has to say. The falling tone, on the other hand, is used when you just want to check if you're right and only expect the other person to nod or just say Yes or No.

A more advanced class might be expected to master both tones, but an intermediate class need to understand both but will probably only need to use the more questioning **rising** tone.

C [cassette] Students should do the exercise in pairs. When they have written all their answers, play the tape which gives the correct answers. You may have to spend a little time on the 'rules' for forming question tags. Spend a little time getting students to read out the complete sentences and pay attention to their intonation. If they find this very hard, use the tape for repetition practice, pausing it after each sentence.

These are the correct answers, as recorded on the cassette:
1. You've met Mr Suzuki, haven't you?
2. It would be best to send them a reminder, wouldn't it?
3. They don't normally pay up immediately, do they?
4. You're waiting to see Miss Weber, aren't you?
5. Mrs de Souza isn't arriving till tomorrow, is she?
6. Your new receptionist doesn't speak English, does she?
7. It must be quite difficult to sound efficient and friendly towards the end of a long hard day, mustn't it?

[cassette] As we mentioned above, many students have considerable difficulties with question tags. Although they may be able to do exercises on them, actually using them automatically and fluently may be very hard. For this reason, we suggest some alternative expressions that are easier to use and which have the same function as question tags. Some examples are given in the Student's Book and recorded on the cassette. Further examples are given in exercise D.

D Students should work in pairs and complete the sentences, using the same information given in questions 1 to 7 above. After finishing, they should compare ideas with another pair.

Suggested answers (not recorded on the cassette):
8. I believe you've met Mr Suzuki.
9. Do you think you it would be best to send them a reminder?
10. I don't think they normally pay up on time. Is that right?
11. You're waiting to see Miss Weber – that's right, isn't it?
12. As far as I know, Mrs de Souza isn't arriving till tomorrow.
13. Am I right in saying that your new receptionist doesn't speak English?
14. It must be quite difficult to sound efficient and friendly towards the end of a long hard day, don't you think?

Extra activity

To give everyone further practice in asking questions, get the class to interview you. They should try to find out as much as possible about the place and country you come from. Encourage them to ask for factual information as well as opinions. This will be a good way for your students to get to know you better! (If you come from exactly the same region as your students, you may have to pretend to be a visitor from an English-speaking country you know well.)

Workbook

Workbook exercise 1.1 provides further work on forming questions.

1.3   Do you enjoy your work?

The speakers interviewed on the cassette are speaking naturally and at their normal speed. Your students will probably need to hear the tape two or three times.

1. ▭ The purpose of the first listening is to let students get used to the voices and get some basic information from the texts. It's a good idea to stop the tape after hearing each speaker.

   There may be a few tricky vocabulary items which, although not necessary for answering the questions and getting the gist of the passage, might just cause your students some trouble. Writing *some* of these up on the board and explaining them beforehand could speed up the listening process.

   The main points made by each speaker are <u>underlined</u> in the transcript. There may be other points they make that you or members of the class consider to be equally 'important'.

Interviewer: What do you do?
Peter: I'm described as <u>an area sales manager.</u> Um ... that would normally imply that one has somebody to manage. In my case, it's just a glorified sales rep. I go round <u>visiting shops,</u> maybe five or six per day when I'm travelling. The rest of the time I spend <u>in the office,</u> answering queries from customers about sales and planning the next trip. My trips usually last about two to three weeks and I go mostly to Germany, Austria and Switzerland.
Interviewer: What do you find rewarding about the work?
Peter: Well, <u>the travel</u> as much as anything else. Um ... the job is fairly badly paid, but the fact that I get free trips to the foreign countries more or less of my choice for most of the year does in some measure recompense for that.
Interviewer: What do you find frustrating or annoying about it?
Peter: Well, I've already mentioned <u>the pay.</u> Um ... obviously frustrating is also <u>customers that leave one waiting</u> ... um ... I have been known to get my own back on customers who leave me waiting for half an hour or so simply by selling them twice as much as I know they need. Um ... it's not a trick that I would recommend using all that often ... um ... but on the whole the frustrations of the job are minimal.

Sharon: I'm the <u>manager</u> of the department called <u>the Banking and Portfolio Department</u> for <u>a large multi-national corporation.</u> The

28

responsibility of that department is to handle all the banking matters ... er ... relationship, credit issues, opening and closing accounts. We also manage the ... er ... investment of the company's excess funds.

The best thing about working in the department th... that we have is that you get to take decisions at a relatively low management level in the company – you get to watch the decisions come, follow through and you get to see the effect on the bottom-line profit of the company. We are one of the few areas within a world ... er ... within a headquarters-type atmosphere where there is a profit centre, bottom line.

One of the things I find the most frustrating is that ... er ... the company is still very bureaucratic. We tend to produce a lot of paperwork and reports that don't seem to have any fit with the ... today's company business. And they've been generated for years and we continue to generate them ... er ... because management has asked for them. We are attempting to change that but it continues to be a source of frustration for myself and my staff.

Banker: I'm a commercial lender at the First National Bank of Lake Forest, which is a commercial bank in a suburb of Chicago with assets of about $400 million. It has recently been purchased by the ... er ... Northern Trust Bank in the city of Chicago, which has assets of about $7.7 billion. We are very much a community-oriented bank and my lending will be diverse ... er ... working with individuals, making mortgages and home construction loans as well as making personal loans and business and industrial loans. So very much of a general-purpose broad area of ... er ... lending.

What is enjoyable about what I do is the opportunity to work with the owners of companies in the area and with professional people that reside in the community. Er ... I'm working with owners of steel companies, with popcorn producers, with individuals that make washers for many purposes. And it allows me the variety of work that working at a large multi-billion bank does not have to offer as you'll be working in narrow job description handling one type of lending.

Some of the frustrations with the job are restrictions as to what you can do or not do for a customer, as many of the requests that we receive are either too small or too large for us to handle and at that point we don't really have the product to sell them, we have to defer them to our competition.

Receptionist: I'm Receptionist and I deal with incoming mail and people, which are the most important part of my job, dealing with people and I think possibly the most enjoyable part of it. I also send telexes and faxes.

Interviewer: And what is the most enjoyable part about your job?

Receptionist: I think meeting people ... um ... there are people from all over the country, all over the world, all walks of life, which is the most interesting part of my job. OK, people can be very irritating but they can be very nice as well, and I think the ... the nice ones outnumber the irritating ones really. It's a very people-orientated job, it's ... it's communication, whether it be with telex or fax and that can all be fun as well if you're having problems getting through and finding out why ... er ... the same way that sometimes you're trying to send a fax to someone and you get some poor soul in the Middle East speaking Arabic or something that ... um ... you unfortunately have got a wrong number but it's all part of the job and it ... it's fun. You don't very often get annoying people face to face. You get more annoying people over the telephone, because people feel that they can say things to you over the phone that they perhaps wouldn't say to you to your face. The same way that we perhaps say things to people over the phone that we wouldn't say to their face. So, no, I don't find people too frustrating face to face ... er ... because I think you can communicate far easier than over the phone.

[Time: 6 minutes]

2. As they hear the cassette again, get everyone to concentrate on the second half of each interview. There are no suggested 'correct' answers to this exercise – everyone should be encouraged to suggest what they personally think the main points were.
3. Form the class into pairs. Get everyone to compare what they have noted down with another student. It may be necessary to hear the recording a third time – students who have noted all the important points should just sit back and, with eyes closed, just imagine what kind of people the speakers are.
4. Now students should continue working in pairs and ask each other the questions in the Student's Book.
5. Now students interview each other. While they're doing this, go round offering advice and encouragement. Persuade students who are replying too laconically to expand on their answers.
6. Rearrange the class into groups of four (each pair with another pair). Each student should tell the new partners about his or her original partner – in other words, no one is talking about him or herself at this stage.

Before finishing, give everyone a chance to make comments and raise any queries they may have.

1.4 Have you met ... ?   *Functions*

This section introduces some expressions that are used when meeting someone for the first time, or meeting them again after an absence. Each conversation accompanies a different illustration in the Student's Book.

Procedure

🔊 First, play the recording through a couple of times. The purpose of the recording is to illustrate and present various exponents of the functions of meeting and greeting, used in context. There are no questions: students should listen to the recording a couple of times and notice how the expressions are used. After the first hearing of each conversation, ask the class to suggest who and where the speakers are. Allow time for everyone to ask any questions they would like to.

A *Alex White*: Oh good afternoon.
Chris Grey: Good afternoon.
Alex White: Er ... I'd just like to I introduce myself. Er ... the name's Alex White and I'm the new export sales co-ordinator.
Chris Grey: Oh, yes. I've heard of you. How do you do. I'm ... er ... Chris Grey. Pleased to meet you. Er ... have you just arrived?
Alex White: Er ... no, no, I got here ... er ... it was yesterday morning, but it ... it's the first time I've been up to this floor. So, Chris, what do you do?
Chris Grey: Well, I'm not very important really. I'm ... er ... Jenny Santini's assistant. She's head of personnel – have you met her?
Alex White: Oh yeah. I was introduced to her yesterday. Actually, I'm looking for Jim Price's office. Am I on the right floor for that?
Chris Grey: Er ... well, no actually, Mr Price is on the fifth floor. Er ... if you take the lift over in the corner you ...

B *Man*: Er ... Ms Smith ... er ... I'd like you to meet Mrs Jones. Mrs Jones is from our sales office in Toronto.
Liz Jones: Hi!
Claire Smith: How do you do, Mrs Jones. I've been looking forward to meeting you.
Liz Jones: Aha, please call me Liz.
Claire Smith: And I'm Claire.
Li Jones: Hi.
Claire: Well, Liz, did you have a good journey?

Liz Jones: Yeah, not too bad. God, there was all this fog at Heathrow, though.
Claire Smith: Oh no, what happened?
Liz Jones: Oh it was ... my flight was diverted to Bournemouth, ye ... and then we had to go by bus from there to London. So ... I didn't get to my hotel till lunch time, it was crazy ...

C *1st woman*: Mr Evans, um ... have you met Miss Lucas? She's from Argentina.
Mr Evans: Yes, I think we've met before. It's good to see you again!
Miss Lucas: That's right, hello again. How are you?
Mr Evans: Fine thanks. Er ... must be, what, a couple of years since we last met?
Miss Lucas: Oh, even longer – four years ago I think. In Miami, wasn't it?
Mr Evans: Yes! Yes, that was an interesting conference! Ha ... W ... would you both like some coffee?
Miss Lucas: Oh, yes, please. Black for me.
1st woman: Oh, thanks a lot, Mr Evans. Er ... white with sugar for me.
Mr Evans: Right.
1st woman: Er ... Miss Lucas, er ... whereabouts do you come from in Argentina?
Miss Lucas: Er ... well ... mm ... I live in Buenos Aires, but I was raised in Mendoza.
1st woman: Oh, was it ... that's in the north ...

[Time: 2 minutes]

When everyone has had a chance to ask any questions they like, ask them to 'study' the expressions in the speech balloons for a few moments and try to memorize the ones they think will be most useful or the ones they feel most comfortable with. Remind them that the only way to remember new expressions is by using them in class and revising them at home.

Now it's time for the role play activity. As this is the first use of Files in the book, you may need to explain the 'information gap' principle underlying this kind of exercise. The activity simulates what might happen when a visitor is passed from person to person within a company, being introduced to each other and taking part in a social conversation.

■ **Some sticky labels or pin-on badges are required for this activity.**

1. Divide the class into two teams:
   The A team look at File 1 on page 195 in the Student's Book, where they discover that they are to play the role of COLLEAGUES working in the same firm, ACME Industries. The B team look at File 7 on page 197 in the Student's Book, where they discover that they are to play the role of VISITORS to ACME Industries.
2. Make sure everyone understands more or less what they have to do, according to the instructions given in Files 1 and 7. If necessary, go through the instructions with the class. It all looks complicated but once they've done steps 1 and 2, step 2 keeps repeating itself.
3. To start off with, all the members of the A team ('colleagues') should choose a name and job title and write their own first name and title with their chosen family name on a label or badge. Meanwhile, the members of the B team ('visitors') will choose names and places of origin, but they don't need badges.
4. Start off the activity: the steps below are numbered in the same way as the steps in both Files in the Student's Book.

The steps in the Student's Book are as follows:

1. A 'visitor' finds a 'colleague' and introduces himself. They strike up a conversation until they receive a SIGNAL from you to stop and begin the next step.
   One way of doing this would be switching the classroom lights on and off or rapping sharply on the board, or even using a bell (a hotel reception bell is ideal and can be used regularly to interrupt pair and group work).
2. The 'colleague' then introduces his 'visitor' to another 'colleague'. They hand over their 'visitors' and the new pairs strike up a conversation until they receive a signal from you.
3. So it goes on with 'colleagues' handing over 'visitors' several times.
4. When everyone has met and talked to several other people, tell everyone to stop and go back to their seats.
5. Now, the roles are reversed and the 'colleagues' become 'visitors' and vice versa. First, they should choose names and the 'colleagues' should make badges. Then, exactly the same procedure is followed as in 1 to 4 above.

Discussion ideas

Ask the class to consider these questions:
What might happen if you don't introduce people to each other?

What might happen if you don't mention their position in the
   company?
Why is it important that women are introduced with the same 'weight'
   or emphasis as men?

Finally, allow time for questions and comments on this section.

Workbook

Workbook exercise 1.2 gives more work on this function, including a
recorded exercise.

1.5 Around the world   *Vocabulary*

This section involves some essential vocabulary and discussion. Steps A
and B could be prepared at home before the lesson. A large wall map
of the world would be useful in this lesson.

A   This step introduces some of the principles involved in forming
nationality words and introduces some of the one-off exceptions. It
should be done in writing, as spelling is important here. Students could
do this alone and then compare what they've written with a partner.

Answers
a Welshman or Welshwoman or Welsh person
an Australian
a Pakistani
a Frenchman or Frenchwoman or French person
a Canadian
a Swede
a New Zealander
an American
a Norwegian
a Japanese
an Indian
a Saudi Arabian
a Dutchman or Dutchwoman or Dutch person

Before going on to the next step, make sure students know the names
of all the countries that surround their own country and can spell the
name of each country, the name of a person from each and the
language(s) they speak there.

B   Students should work in pairs. They may need to consult a map of
the world to get ideas if their geography isn't very good!

Suggested, but not exhaustive, answers:
LATIN AMERICA: Brazil, Argentina, Venezuela, Chile, Peru,
 Uruguay, Guyana, Colombia, etc.
MIDDLE EAST: Syria, Saudi Arabia, Kuwait, Lebanon, Egypt, Abu
 Dhabi, Iraq, etc.
EEC: France, Italy, Luxembourg, the Netherlands (Holland),
 Germany, Spain, Portugal, Belgium, Greece, Ireland, Denmark,
 United Kingdom (UK)
EASTERN EUROPE: Poland, Czechoslovakia, USSR (Soviet Union),
 Yugoslavia, Bulgaria, Hungary, etc.
AFRICA: Nigeria, Kenya, South Africa, Egypt, Tunisia, Algeria,
 Morocco, Ghana, Gabon, Senegal, etc.
ASIA: Japan, Korea, China, Indonesia, Taiwan, Malaysia, Thailand,
 India, Pakistan, etc.

C Rearrange the class into groups of four (each pair with another
pair). As they are 'quizzing' each other, go round offering advice and
corrections.

Even you may need to consult a dictionary to determine whether a
person from Gabon, for example, is a Gabonean or a Gabonese! To
find out that the official language there is French and that the
Gabonese also speak Fang, you may have to consult a reference book,
such as *The Book of Answers* (Guinness Publishing).

If such information is of no interest to your students, you might like
to tell them not to worry about such details.

D Students remain in their groups for this discussion. The purpose
of this is to explore national stereotypes and re-examine them.
Hopefully, students will agree that it is not a good idea to presuppose
that everyone from a country is going to behave in the same way – but
let them decide this together.

If, after some discussion, everyone seems to think that there really is
such a thing as a typical Italian, German, American, Englishman or
African etc, then you may have to step in to insist that such stereotypes
are quite dangerous and not at all helpful.

Finally, ask if anyone has any questions or comments on what they
have done in this section.

1.6 Developing relationships

The four steps in this section concern the different ways of talking to
different kinds of people and with the way a relationship changes,
generally becoming more intimate and friendly, as time goes on.

One emphasis of steps C and D is 'small talk': talking about things that are not connected with business.

A   Students should work in groups of four to six as they discuss the questions. During the discussion, go round the class offering encouragement and advice.

When they're ready, ask each group to report to the rest of the class on the most interesting points that were made.

B   [cassette] Play the recording. Students will hear five extracts from some typical interactions that might be overheard in an international company.

Students should note down their answers to the questions in the Student's Book. Point out that they will have to guess some of the answers, basing their guesses on their own 'reading' of the situations. For example, no one in the first extract actually says 'I am a sales rep' – you have to work this out from what they say. There are no definitive right answers to this exercise: describing relationships can only be done in an impressionistic way – so students are asked here to form impressions as they make notes.

Pause the tape after each extract, so that students can compare their notes with a partner. At the end, replay the whole tape so that everyone can see who was right. If you think your students will find this difficult, pause the tape after each extract and ask everyone in the class to contribute their theories. Then replay the extract (having set the counter to 000 beforehand!) and see whose theory was right.

1

Sales Manager: Er ... Tony?

Tony: Yes?

Sales Manager: I'd like to see you for a minute, would you come into the office?

Tony: Oh, yeah, right.

Sales Manager: Good. Now, how did you get on in Copenhagen?

Tony: Ah, well, Carlsson had the flu, so I couldn't see him.

Sales Manager: Couldn't see him?

Tony: No, so I had to see his assistant. And, you know, we ... er ... we got on quite well, but ... um ... th ... er ... there are problems w ... er ... Crystals got in before us.

Sales Manager: Oh Lord!

Tony: Yeah, they were in last week. So ... er ... they ... you know, they ... they spend days there and ... er ... it was all wrapped up really by the time I got there.

Sales Manager: Is it ... is it a question of ... of ... of supply? Are we ... are we not producing enough for them?

Tony: Well, no, they didn't really look at the figures, quite frankly, and I showed them the figures and they ... they weren't interested.

Sales Manager: Yeah, well you see the trouble is that we've got a ... we've got an on-going problem ...

2

Boss: Now, Barry ... er ... and Susanna, have you got your worksheet in front of you – fact sheet here?

Barry & Susanna: Yes.

Boss: Now you can see here that Miss Henry is James Ferguson's personal assistant. That's pretty important to know. Ted Douglas is the chief export clerk.

35

Susanna: Mmm, right.

Boss: Er ... Barry, you're going to be working with Susanna very closely here ...

Barry: Good.

Boss: And ... er ... I think it's very important, Barry, that you ... er ... get together with Susanna over there and try to work out the ... the letter filing system here.

Barry: Uhuh.

Susanna: Mm.

Boss: Now, as you can see, we've ... er ... as you can see on your fact sheet here we've got it marked Urgent and Nonurgent.

Barry: Yeah.

Boss: Er ... anything Essential I'll take care of, OK? Haha.

Barry & Susanna: Haha.

3

Mr Green: OK ... er ... Martin, let's go through it again. You go to the airport.

Driver: Right.

Mr Green: Terminal 2.

Driver: Terminal 2.

Mr Green: Pick up Glenn Donaldson.

Driver: Glenn Donaldson.

Mr Green: Now I want you to write this down.

Driver: Yeah, I've got it down.

Mr Green: OK, he's arriving from Miami on the flight number LX432.

Driver: LX432.

Mr Green: Have you got that?

Driver: Yeah I've got it.

Mr Green: Right, off you go. Get back here as soon as you can.

Driver: Yes, sir, Mr Green.

Mr Green: Thank you.

4

Woman: Geoff, um ... could you just come over here a minute and look at this sketch?

Geoff: Yes, sure.

Woman: What do you think?

Geoff: Aha, yes, well you've put a lot of work into it, that's ... that's very good. I'm not too happy about this border round here ... um ...

Woman: No?

Geoff: Maybe you could try another go at that.

Woman: I will, I'll try again. OK.

5

Tony: Mrs Lang, could I have a word, please?

Mrs Lang: Oh, yes, Tony, of course.

Tony: I wondered if I might have next Friday off. My sister's arriving from Switzerland ... er ... I'd like to meet her at the airport.

Mrs Lang: Oh, Friday's rather difficult. What time does she arrive?

Tony: Well, the plane gets in at 4 pm.

Mrs Lang: Ohh ... I know, Tony! Why don't you go off just after lunch, then you'll manage to get to the airport on time to meet her at four.

Tony: Oh, thank you very much, Mrs Lang.

[Time: 2 minutes 55 seconds]

Suggested answers:

1. Tony and the other man have a cordial, informal relationship. Tony is an overseas sales rep and the other man is the Export Sales Manager. They're talking about problems Tony encountered on a visit to a client in Copenhagen.
2. The boss is very friendly and informal but is superior to Barry and Susanna. The boss is probably office manager and the other two are clerical staff. The boss is explaining who is who in the office.
3. Mr Green behaves very much as the driver's boss (he is quite authoritarian). Mr Green is probably the transport manager and

Martin is a driver. They are talking about a pickup Martin has to make at the airport.

4. The woman and Geoff are of equal status and they have an informal relationship, but she is perhaps younger or less experienced. They are probably commercial artists or designers. She's asking him to evaluate some work she has done.

5. Tony is junior to Mrs Lang, she is his boss and they have a fairly formal relationship. We can't tell what their jobs are. They are talking about Tony having time off on Friday.

C 🔣 The purpose of this activity is to simulate the way in which a relationship changes as you get to know someone better. Students will find that as the activity progresses, they will naturally become more intimate with each other, and the kind of conversation used with strangers (about the weather, for example) can be dispensed with. A different sort of small talk will develop.

The activity is in four steps. Set the scene before students look at the instructions in the Student's Book: it will be more effective coming from you than from the page.

To stop each phase of the activity, play the role of 'the tutor arriving' yourself. Your own relationship with the 'trainees' will change too:
Say 'Good morning, ladies and gentlemen' at the end of step 1; say 'Good morning, everybody' at the end of step 2; then 'Hello, everyone' at the end of step 3.

Each time, make sure you set the scene for the next step by discussing how the 'trainees' will have got to know each other better as time goes on. If everyone stands up before they start the next step it will be easier for them to assume their roles: they can imagine themselves 'arriving in class' and filling time till the 'tutor' arrives – or they should move to sit with a new partner for this activity. What they will talk about is likely to be 'small talk': note that 'Good weekend?' is a very useful gambit in parts 2 and 3, but try to make sure this idea comes from the class.

If you have a video camera and recorder available, all or part of the activity can be recorded on video for playback and analysis later. An audio recorder (with a good microphone) can be used in the same way.

D This activity continues the theme of changing relationships and using small talk. Perhaps point out that there are no easy formulae for small talk. You have to use your own ideas. But as you get to know someone better, you learn what subjects are suitable for small talk with that person.

1. Before they begin the role play in step 3, students should work in pairs and note down some suitable subjects that they like to talk about, according to the suggestions made in the Student's Book.

2. Rearrange the class into groups of four (each pair with another pair), so that students can compare ideas.

3. Split up the class into pairs (each student with a member of a different group from the one they were in in step 2).

   [recording icon] Ask everyone to look at the expressions in the Student's Book and play the recording.

   [role play icon] Now the role play can begin. Explain that the 'supplier' will arrive at the 'client's' office – so the 'supplier' should stand up and approach the client and wait to be offered a seat.

   Before they begin step 4 with a different partner, discuss what happened in this role play. What particular difficulties and awkwardness did they encounter? How could these problems be averted next time? Give students who have experience of talking to clients or sales people a chance to give the rest of the class the benefit of their experience.

4. Now, rearrange the pairs and let everyone have a second go. This time the interview should go much more smoothly. If possible, arrange the pairs so that everyone reverses roles and plays the other part.

Follow-up discussion

At the end ask the class what conclusions they have drawn from these activities.

- What aspects of small talk do they find difficult? What aspects do they find relatively easy?
- Does anyone in the class have any useful 'tricks' that they use when meeting someone for the first time, to break the ice and establish a friendly relationship?

1.7 It's not just what you say ...   *Discussion*

Social behaviour is an important aspect of dealing with people face to face. There may be national standards of appropriate behaviour, but many of these are by no means universal (see question 9 in the quiz, for example).

Appropriate behaviour partly depends on the various **signals** you give, mostly unconsciously, to the people you meet:

1. The style of language you use and the words you choose: it's important to give people the impression that they feel comfortable talking to you and that you're not in constant competition with them.

2. Your tone of voice ('Why?' or even 'Why is that?' can sound like a challenge or disagreement if spoken sharply).
3. Your expression: an unchanging silly smile looks insincere, but it's better than a frown (which looks like aggression even if to you it means puzzlement).
4. The noises you make: sighing, clicking your pen, tapping your foot all mean something – often much more than the words that are spoken. Imagine being told by a salesman: 'It's very good of you to see me ... *yawn* ... *sigh* ... Now, if I could just take up five minutes of your time...'!
5. Your body language and the way you stand or sit. If you have your arms crossed you may look defensive, if you slump in the chair you may look sleepy, if you sit upright with your shoulders back you may look eager and alert (maybe too much). Overdoing any of these signals may seem like play-acting and make you look insincere.
6. Your appearance: different business clothes are acceptable in different countries and in different businesses. What impression does a man in your business give if he doesn't wear a tie?
7. Even your smell! Millions of pounds are spent by men and women on perfume, after-shave and deodorants to combat body odour: different cultures have different comfortable smells.

Procedure

Step A should be done by students in pairs.
Step B is best done in larger groups of four or five.

To forestall any vocabulary problems, demonstrate the expressions and noises described in the quiz and discussion task, so that your students will understand them in the text:
    frown, grin, blink, sigh, yawn,
also: indigestion (hold your chest and show pain).

There are no correct answers to questions 1 to 8, but suggested answers to the last three questions are:
9 c, 10 c and 11 b.

While the discussions are going on, go round the class listening in and making notes on any language points you think students need to be made aware of. At the end of the discussion, mention these points to the whole class.

Follow-up discussion

As a way of debriefing students after this unit, ask the class these questions:

- Think of someone you know who is a bad speaker or conversationalist: what qualities make that person dull?
- Think of someone you know who is a good speaker or conversationalist: what qualities make that person admirable?
- What would you (realistically) like to be able to do in English by the end of this course?
- What aspects of your English do you think need to improve most of all?
- What have you learnt from this unit that you will be able to apply in future units and in your daily work?

Workbook

Contents for this unit:

1.1 Asking questions   Grammar
1.2 Have you met ... ?   Functions
1.3 Around the world   Vocabulary

Background information: Letters, telexes and memos

International business correspondence can take various forms: not only letters and telexes, but telefax (fax), electronic mail ('email') and teletex are being used more and more. Within a company, memos are commonly sent to convey information in writing.
The letter below includes information about the uses of these different forms of written communication.

   A typical 'standard' business letter in English consists of 9 parts – though many firms use a different 'house style' that their staff are expected to follow.

1. Sender's address (at the top or in the top right-hand corner)

                                        Cambridge University Press
                                        Shaftesbury Road
                                        Cambridge CB2 2RU

2. Date (on the right but could be after Receiver's address)

                                        7 May 19--

3. Receiver's name and address (on the left):

A. Reader
Unit 1
International Business English
Page 00

4. Attention line

For the attention of A. Reader

5. Salutation:

Dear Mr or Ms Reader,

6. Body of letter:

TELEX:
A telex is very quick, and readers often overlook some
errors of spelling and grammar. Abbreviations such as
TKS (Thanks) are common in telexes. The sender knows
when each telex has been transmitted and received. A
telex can be a legally binding document.

⟫→

41

LETTER:
In a letter, the emphasis is on a high quality
appearance. Letters have to be typed accurately with a
smart, clear layout. Letters are slow and, once posted,
dependent on each country's mail service. Important
documents or valuable items can be sent by registered
mail.

FAX:
A fax (telefax) is a facsimile copy of a document
transmitted by normal telephone lines to another fax
machine. Fax is becoming very common in business: in
Japan and the USA, there are more fax machines than
telex machines. A fax is not normally a legally binding
document.

COMPUTERS:
Email (and Teletex, mainly in Europe) is a way of
sending messages between computers. There are more
computers linked to Email in the UK than there are telex
machines.

MEMOS:
Internal mail within a company or between branches of
the same firm is usually in the form of memos: these may
be brief handwritten notes or longer, word-processed
letters. The style depends on the practice within the
company and on the relationship between the people
involved.

7. Complimentary close:

Yours sincerely,

8. Signature:

Leo Jones   Richard Alexander

9. Name and title of sender:

Leo Jones and Richard Alexander, Authors

© Cambridge University Press, 1989

2 Letters, telexes and memos

This unit introduces the skills required to deal with the writing tasks in Units 5 to 15. The emphasis you place on the different parts of this unit will depend on the needs of your students and what they are capable of doing already.

Written communication may take the form of letters, telexes, internal memos and, more and more these days, faxes and electronic mail – students need to be confident in using all these forms.

The various styles of writing that are used in formal business letters, memos and brief telexes are covered, though students who will have to write a lot of long, formal letters in their work will probably need to do further work on this.

We have taken account of the changes that have taken place in recent years in the style of business letters in English – your students may need to be made aware that the style that is now current is much less formal and old-fashioned than the style used in many other languages.

If any of your students lack experience of business correspondence, you may wish to photocopy the Background information (pp. 41–42) for them.

2.1 Speaking and writing   *Discussion*

By contrasting the recorded conversation and the written memo, we show how the different modes of communication are used and some of the shortcomings of both.

Procedure

A   Begin by getting everyone to read the memo. Get them to explain roughly what it's about.

B   ▱ Play the recording twice. Ask the class about the differences between the two texts: what information was missing in each and which seemed the more efficient way of conveying the information?
   (In the memo a lot more information is given and it is easier to

follow – and you have a permanent record. In the conversation there is an opportunity for discussion and for questions to be answered – but the details would only be given if they were demanded.)

Mr W: Ah, Maria, I wanted to see you, um ... did I tell you that we're starting up the English classes again?

Maria: Oh, are you? Great, good. Where?

Mr W: Er ... in the training centre, hopefully. We're getting Mr Roberts in again from ELS. So could you tell your people and let me have a list of names by ... um ... let's say Wednesday.

Maria: Yes, yes ... um ... Last time there was a bit of misunderstanding about the books they needed ... um ... who was going to pay for them.

Mr W: Oh really? Um ... no problem this time, we'll provide the books. But they will have to do some homework outside work, make sure they realize that. Um ... or else there'll probably be some prob-

lems. Er ... there'll be two classes, by the way: an intermediate class and an advanced one. But there will be a limit in each of the classes of ... mm ... probably about twelve.

Maria: Oh, really, a limit of twelve? Ah, what if there are more wanting to come? I mean, I can think of at least eight just in my department alone. Um ... how will you decide who can attend?

Mr W: Err ... mm, good point. Er ... I think we'll have to play that one by ear really.

Maria: OK, well how about running another class ...

[Time: 1 minute 5 seconds]

C   For the discussion, students should work in groups of three to five. Try to avoid making didactic statements yourself – business people have their own ideas and experience, and customs differ from country to country. You are probably less of an expert than many of your students, so let them give everyone the benefit of their experience.

The discussion may bring up some of the following points:

ADVANTAGES OF FACE TO FACE MEETINGS: more personal, more interaction and feedback possible, can make more impact, cheaper if no travel involved, you can smile ...

BUT you have to think as you speak, once you've said something it can't be rubbed out, saying something once may not sink in or be remembered.

ADVANTAGES OF WRITING: a record can be kept for the files, errors can be changed, you can write or read when you're in the right mood, you can take your time over planning and how you'll express complicated or delicate details ...

BUT writing takes longer, there is no feedback or the feedback is delayed, no 'personal touch', no smiles, no handshakes.

Do your students agree with this quote:

'Business does not need a special language of its own but it has added some technical terms to the English language, as practically every activity of civilised man has done.'

(BACIE Business letters guide).

2.2 The right address

In this section we look at the way addresses are laid out in the UK and
the USA, but the main emphasis is on SPELLING ALOUD: using the
alphabet fluently and understanding other people when they spell
words or names out loud to you.

If necessary, run through the alphabet with the class, reminding
them of the tricky letters (A and R, G and J, E and I, etc).

A Ask everyone to study the address labels in the Student's Book and
detect the differences between the layout of addresses in other countries (including the use of post codes or zip codes and street numbers).

Note that nowadays commas are not commonly used at the end of
each line, and it is now considered a little old-fashioned to write, for
example:

```
Cyril Old, Esq.,
34, Traditional Way,
Oldbury, OL6 1BC
```

Allow time for questions about the details shown on the labels,
including Esq. (short for Esquire: used only to address men in Britain
and slightly old-fashioned).

B ▭ Play the recording (at least twice) pausing as necessary for
students to take the dictation down. All of these addresses are read
aloud, which may provoke further discussion and questions.

```
Mr George James                  Ms Alison Freeman
Managing Director                Marketing Co-ordinator
Alan and James Ltd               United Packaging Inc.
Quality House                    11 East Shore Drive
77-81 London Road                Green Bay
Bristol                          Wisconsin
BL5 9AR                          WI 53405
Great Britain                    USA
```

```
Mr R.G. Flinders                 Miss J.V. Bernstein
Sales Manager                    Candex Convention Organizer
Independent Products Pty         Dominion Centre
18 Canberra Way                  80 Prince of Wales Drive
Liverpool                        Ottawa
NSW 2170                         Ontario
Australia                        KT5 1AQ
                                 Canada
```

Students can see the correct versions in File 77 in the Student's Book. Did your students make many mistakes writing down the addresses in this exercise? If so, tell them that the next section needs extra-special attention!

C   For this information gap activity students should work in pairs. Ask everyone to imagine that they are reading a list of addresses over the phone (maybe prospective customers that a salesman has to visit). They will each see four difficult addresses with hard-to-spell names, which they must dictate to their partner. One student looks at File 3, the other at 10. You may have to point out that these names and addresses are all genuine and typical of the kind that they might encounter in their work.

When they have finished, or had enough, play the model reading on the cassette. You'll need to stop the tape frequently. If you think this will be too difficult for your students, they could hear the recording first (to give them confidence) and then have a go themselves in pairs, before hearing the recording again at the end (see Files 3 and 10 in the Student's Book for the text of this recording).

Extra activities

D   To give further, probably easier, practice in spelling aloud, ask the class to imagine they are filling in a form. Give them these instructions:
1. Write down on a slip of paper:
     your own *full* name (with title: Mr, Dr, Miss, etc.)
     your home address
     your telephone number
     the name of your company
     your date of birth
2. Pass the slip to another student, who will dictate *your* personal details to the rest of the class.
3. Write down the information the other students dictate to you. When it's your turn, dictate the information on your sheet. Spell out any long or difficult names.
4. Check that your own personal details have been taken down accurately – with no spelling mistakes!

E   Here are some words in their British English spellings. Write them on the board and get the class to spell them out loud in their American English versions (here given in brackets):

centre ... (center)   labour ... (labor)
licence ... (license)   catalogue ... (catalog)
traveller's cheque ... (traveler's check)
instalment ... (installment)   programme ... (program)

Note that some alternative spellings, such as:

inquire/enquire, dispatch/despatch, realise/realize, utilise/utilize, etc are often a question of a company's 'house style', and there are no fixed rules. This book uses a variety of these in the letters and other texts but adheres to a house style in the rubrics and explanations.

You'll find more work on the differences between British and American English in *Ideas* by Leo Jones (CUP) Unit 19.

Workbook

There is more work on spelling in Workbook exercises 2.1 and 2.5.

2.3 Abbreviations   *Vocabulary*

The role of full stops (periods) in abbreviations is constantly changing. Many established abbreviations (eg, ie, Ltd, PLC, plc, etc) can be printed with or without periods these days. Less frequently used ones, especially ones that are just short forms of longer words (Dept., encl., Rd., Sq., and so on) tend to have full stops. Reassure your class on this score, as it's a thing some students do tend to get out of proportion. Your own preferences (or the firm's house style) should be made clear to the class. Point out that it hardly takes any longer to type, say, 'Department' than it does to type 'Dept.' or 'Dpt.', and to write 'paid' rather than abbreviate it to 'pd.'

If you anticipate that your students will find this very difficult, and that they won't know many of the abbreviations, get them to prepare this exercise at home (using a good dictionary – *LDOCE, OALDCE, Collins COBUILD Dictionary* or the fascinating *Penguin Wordmaster Dictionary*). If this isn't feasible, the following procedure will make the task easier:

1. Go right through the exercise *for* them in class, giving the corrected answers but not allowing anyone to make notes.
2. Get students in pairs to do it themselves trying to remember what you said.

Answers:
1. Road   Street   Square
2. Number
3. care of   for the attention of   Post Office Box
4. for example   that is   and so on / et cetera
   please turn over
5. Public Limited Company   Limited   Brothers   and Company
6. Corporation   Incorporated

7. at 3000 yen   copyright   registered   trade mark
8. postscript
9. carbon copy (normally a photocopy in fact!)   enclosure
10. this month   next month   (*ultimo, instant, proximo*)
    NOTE: students should not use these outdated terms in their correspondence.

Extra activity

Get everyone to jot down some common abbreviations of the same kind, that are used in their language (S.A., GmbH, etc). Then ask them to explain what each one stands for – as if telling an English-speaking colleague.

Finally, here are some other common abbreviations that your students may need to know:

a/c	account
admin.	administration
asap	as soon as possible
b/f	brought forward
c/f	carried forward
c.c.	cubic centimetres
cu.	cubic
do	ditto
doz. or dz.	dozen
ft.	foot/feet
in. or ins.	inches
m.	meters (US)/metres (GB) *or* miles
misc.	miscellaneous
lb. or lbs.	pounds (weight)
Jr	Junior
N/A	not applicable
oz	ounces
par. or § or ¶	paragraph
PC	personal computer
PDQ	pretty damn quick(ly)
pp	pages
p.p.	per pro. (on behalf of)
recd.	received
sq.	square (metres, feet, etc.)
Sr	Senior
Y	economy class
yd or yds	yards

2.4 The layout of letters

Even students who don't actually have to type or word-process letters themselves still usually need to check them through before signing them — and as layout is something that can create a good (or bad) impression, they should be aware of the conventions used in British and American correspondence.

A Encourage questions about the layout and stylistic conventions illustrated. Allow time for discussion of the conventions that apply in your students' country. Note that *Gentlemen,* is the American and *Dear Sirs,* is the British way of opening a letter to a company when you don't want to write to a particular person.

B Continue in the same way, encouraging questions from the class and comparisons with the conventions used in your students' country or countries. In this case, the typical American forms are:
    Sincerely and *Best regards*
whilst these are more typically British:
    Yours sincerely, Best wishes, Kind regards and *Yours faithfully*

C In this discussion, students with more experience of receiving letters from different firms are encouraged to tell the rest of the group about their impressions of other people's letters — possibly less embarrassing than criticizing one's own letters.
    The group discussion is to do with personal feelings, not any established 'rules'. Some of these points will probably be raised:
- The need for a certain amount of white space on a page (thus avoiding the so-called ZZZZ effect of long unbroken text)
- The way a document is divided up
- The use of headings and numbers
- The form and size of typefaces used
- It's better if letters are 'attractive and clear', and not dull or confusing!!

D This step is probably more suitable for upper intermediate and more advanced students. If you anticipate that your students will get quite involved in the activity and enjoy it, make sure you have enough time for them to do it adequately.

Extra activity

Ask the class to draft a letter to one of the people on the envelopes in 2.2, asking for their latest catalogue.

2.5 Joining sentences   *Grammar*

This section shows how conjunctions, adverbial connectors and prepositions can all be used to form complex sentences. As this is primarily a written skill, the examples are not recorded. If possible, students should read the examples and do some of the exercises at home before the lesson.

Presentation

Students should study the examples and be encouraged to ask questions. Point out that a long complex sentence is often much harder to understand, let alone write, than a series of short simple ones (as shown in exercise D below).

More advanced students can be reminded of (or asked to suggest) other adverbial connectors:
> *beforehand   afterwards   subsequently   meanwhile   simultaneously*
> *moreover   nonetheless*
and other connecting prepositions:
> *prior to*
> *owing to   in consequence of*
> *despite   regardless of*

Exercises

A   This easy exercise can be done by students working together in pairs. This is the **correct arrangement** of the sentences:

I never sign a letter before I have read it through.
I often prefer to write although a phone call is quicker.
I usually telephone in order to save time.
Please check my in-tray while I am away at the conference.
I shall be able to confirm this after I have checked our stock position.
I shall be able to confirm this when I have consulted our works manager.
We cannot confirm the order until we have checked our stock position.
Please reply at once so that we can order the supplies we need.
Please reply as soon as possible because we do not have sufficient stocks.

B   Again students can do this exercise in pairs or prepare it at home before the lesson. The answers should be written down. The exercise shows how prepositional connectors can be a very economical way of joining ideas in a sentence – encourage students to say which of the sentences they 'prefer': the original or the rewritten one. Are there any differences in emphasis or implication between the original and rewritten sentences?

Suggested answers:
1. *Example: make sure everyone knows what they're supposed to do*
2. I went to see the factory after looking round the offices.
3. I'll have to see the shipping manager before confirming the order.
4. There was a delay because of technical problems.
5. It was completed on time in spite of staff illness/absence/sickness.
6. The visitors arrived during your lunch break.
7. Due to a fall in the number of orders, the works closed down.
8. He will be in touch with you after his holiday.

C It may be necessary to point out some of the characteristics of headlines:
– simple present forms are used where normal writing uses past or present perfect verb forms
– to ... + infinitive is used to refer to future events
– articles are omitted.

Students should work in pairs to rewrite the headlines as complete sentences. While they are doing this, go round from pair to pair, checking their work, offering advice and answering questions. When everyone has finished, ask some members of the class to read out some of their sentences and discuss which of the suggestions are best.

Here are some **suggested answers** – many variations are possible:
   During the President's visit to Europe he addressed the European Parliament.
   As a result of the rise in imports from the Far East, the United States has introduced quotas.
   Acme Industries have suffered a fall in their profits. Consequently, their chairman has been asked to resign.
   Although the takeover bid was rejected, Mr Murdoch confirmed that his offer was still open.
   As a result of talks between trade ministers in Brussels, EC customs tariffs will change next January.

D This exercise shows how long sentences are not always easy to understand. It is more difficult than the previous exercises and may take some time to do – it could be set as homework and discussed in class later.

If the exercise is done in class, students should work in pairs. When the pairs have finished, ask them to read out some of their sentences to the rest of the class. Discuss any issues or points arising.

Suggested answers (many variations possible):
I am sending you our new catalogue. I feel sure that you will find many items of interest in it. You will find that our new range of colours will brighten up your office and improve its atmosphere.

If you work in an export department, you need a lot of specialized knowledge. You need to master the complex documentation and you need to know about the various methods of payment that are available. You also need to be able to write letters to overseas customers.

Writing to people you have not met face-to-face and establishing a personal relationship with them is difficult. But if you can do this, you can show them that you are a real person, not just a letter-writing machine.

Extra activity

Ask students in pairs to write down ten short sentences, one below the other. The sentences may be deliberately related to one another or unrelated. Then they should pass their list to another pair who must combine as many of the sentences as possible into up to five longer sentences, using the connecting devices presented in this unit. To make the task more difficult, the use of *and*, *but*, and *because* can be banned. The most ingenious combinations will give the greatest amusement.

Workbook

Exercise 2.6 in the Workbook contains further work on joining sentences.

2.6 It's in the mail   *Vocabulary*

This exercise can be done at any stage in the unit, where time is available. Students can do it in pairs, or it can be done at home and then discussed briefly in class.

If there seem to be too many new words here, go through the whole exercise supplying the missing words yourself. Make sure the class just listen and don't make notes at this stage. Then let them do it themselves in pairs, trying to remember what you said. (Often students do know such words and actually just need reminding – this technique helps them to do that.)

Answers:
 1. courier
 2. postage and packing   mail (US)/post (GB)
 3. registered
 4. return of post (GB)/return of mail (US)
 5. RSVP
 6. separate cover
 7. photocopy   carbon copy   duplicate
 8. printed matter
 9. stationery
10. general delivery (US)/poste restante (GB)

2.7 Better letters

This section looks at two aspects of letter writing: using the right style in your writing, and considering your reader at all times. It is only what the reader gets from your letter that is important. The ideas apply to other forms of writing too: memos, short reports and even, to some extent, telexes.

A   Students should work in groups of about four for this discussion. Hopefully, they will all consider the first letter to be old-fashioned, fuddy-duddy and dull.

Make sure they have time to find the actual turns of phrase that give the first letter its old-fashioned flavour and the second its more modern flavour. Many students may prefer something half-way between the two styles, particularly if they think the second one is too 'spicy' – but remember that it is a *sales* letter, designed to whet the reader's appetite!

B   The text is from a training course. Before or during the discussion, you may need to explain any words they might not understand.

Allow everyone to give their opinions about the 'Golden Rules' and find out to what extent they disagree with the rules. Find out what further rules they would suggest to a novice letter-writer.

2.8 To plan or not to plan?   *Discussion*

As this section is also discussion-based, it is best done on a different day from 2.7. It could be done after 2.9, if that is more convenient, or at the very end of the unit.

A [cassette icon] Students should work in groups of three or four. Start the discussion off by playing the tape:

'Well, I use the back of an envelope or a beer mat.'
'I write on a word processor and I don't make notes before starting.'
'I write an outline of the letter and then do a final draft.'
'Er ... I make notes on a large sheet of scrap paper.'
'Well, I just dictate it to my secretary and well, let her sort out the details.'
'Well, I ... I sit back and think for a few minutes before I start typing.'
'Well, I like to use the outlining program on my PC, just to organize my thoughts.'
'Mmm ... well, I use my own special method...'

[Time: 40 seconds]

B The '7 Steps' are from another piece of training material. Encourage students to give their views and to disagree with some of the points made if they wish. If, however, they agree that planning is of great importance, this text can be referred back to again and again when letter-writing tasks are done in later units. If you encourage students to alter the text to incorporate their own personalized amendments, it will be more memorable.

2.9 Writing memos

The style of memos can vary from scruffy handwritten notes to well-typed formal letters. Begin by finding out what kind of internal memos your students write and receive in their own work.

Procedure

A Encourage students to consider the kind of memo form that is used in their firm. Can it be improved on? How do the different parts of it translate into English? Could a bilingual memo pad be used?

B Students should continue to work in pairs for this activity. Perhaps remind them about the memo in 2.1 that they found fault with earlier.

1. Ask what the purpose of KLJ's memo is: what action are you supposed to take after reading it? What information is not given?
   The main trouble with it is that it is imprecise and consequently liable to be misunderstood or, more likely in most companies, disregarded.
2. The rewriting should be a team effort, with both partners contributing ideas. Perhaps point out that it should be made clear in the memo exactly what information KLJ wants from the staff and the

deadline for its submission. Numbered paragraphs and headings may help.

While they're doing this, go round the class offering advice and checking spelling, punctuation and so on.

3. Before everyone looks at File 97 to see the model version of KLJ's memo, get each pair to show another pair their work and ask for comments.

The model memo is better because it is more detailed, clear and precise. It is now absolutely clear what the reader is supposed to do as a result of reading it.

2.10 Writing telexes (and email)

The language of telexes and teletext is similar to that used in electronic mail and in short fax messages. Even though telex machines may one day be replaced by email and fax, the language required is likely to be quite similar. Students who don't use telex at all any more should imagine that they're writing fax or email (/iːmeɪl/) messages instead.

Procedure

First get the pairs to study the telex from Vancouver. Answer any queries they may have.

Point out that errors are common and tolerated in real telexes: the one from Vancouver is based on a genuine one but we've had to 'clean it up' to eliminate all the spelling errors, etc!

1. When they have read the first telex, the pairs should work together to draft a reply. Go round the class checking and helping. Once they've done this, get them to look at another pair's telex and make comments.
2. In File 108, there are two model telexes. The second one contains some common abbreviations. Which one do your students prefer?

Find out from the class which abbreviations your students use in their business telexes. Which ones are common? Make a list on the board, for the benefit of those with less business experience.

2.11 Sending messages

This integrated activity practises all the skills introduced in the first two units. To do it adequately will require a good half hour at the very least.

Procedure

Divide the class into an EVEN number of pairs so that each pair will be able to communicate with another one in step 3: this may entail having some groups of three.

Make sure each pair knows who their counterparts are.

As the Messages become progressively more complicated, students will build up confidence through experience. You will need to announce a deadline for the transitions between each of the steps, so that all four steps *plus* the follow-up discussion can be done in the time you have available.

1. Everyone discusses how to transmit the messages. Go round from pair to pair asking for their reasons – as if you are genuinely interested, not as a challenge.

    Students with more work experience should give advice to their less experienced class-mates at this stage, perhaps in a brief whole-class discussion.
2. While students are planning and drafting their letters or telexes, go round offering advice and checking spelling and vocabulary.
3. ▓ or ☎ Rearrange the class into groups of four (each pair with another pair). The students who have phone calls or visits planned should role play them, with one of each pair listening in and making notes, so that there can be feedback on the 'performance' afterwards. The partners should take it in turns here, and not let one do all the talking. (This activity could be recorded on video or cassette.)
4. Rearrange the class into pairs and get them to read their counterparts' draft letter, telexes and faxes. They should apply the criteria given in the 'Golden Rules' in 2.7 as they evaluate each other's work.

    Then the pairs should join up with their counterparts and discuss each other's drafts.

If the drafts need to be rewritten, students should do this as homework. If they are satisfied with their drafts, collect up all the written work and mark it.

Follow-up discussion

Find out what methods your students with business experience use to communicate in English.

What proportion of your communications do you **receive** and **send** in English:
*   by telex or teletex
*   by fax

- by airmail or surface mail
- by email (electronic mail)
- by internal memos
- by telephone
- by other methods (courier delivery, phone messages, etc)

Make a note of what you find out, so that you can take account of this in subsequent writing tasks and role plays.

What aspects of writing do the members of the class most need to improve, do they think? Should they return to any of the basic writing exercises in this unit at a later stage in the course, as revision or as remedial work?

Workbook

Contents for this unit:

2.1 Spelling and punctuation mistakes	
2.2 Take a letter ...	Vocabulary
2.3 Should we send them a fax or a telex?	Listening 🔲
2.4 Making a good impression	Writing
2.5 Can you tell me how to spell that?	🔲
2.6 Joining sentences	Grammar
2.7 Improve these letters	Writing

3 On the phone

This unit deals with basic telephoning skills as well as taking messages. These skills will be practised further in later units in telephone role plays. Students are also given a chance to discuss and develop their telephone techniques, and find out about each other's techniques and tricks of the trade. Present tenses and the functions of requesting, offering help and asking permission are also dealt with.

3.1   I'd like to speak to ...

This section introduces some of the difficulties that people encounter when trying to get in touch with someone on the phone and focuses attention on the need for a good 'telephone style'.

Procedure

A ▭ The first part of the recording shows some abortive phone calls. Play the complete recording through first so that students can get the general ideas, then play it again pausing every so often for students to discuss their answers together and then with you. This exercise is probably best done as a whole class.

Some of the places where problems and misunderstandings occurred are <u>underlined</u> in the transcript. Many of these problems were partly the caller's own fault.

Your students with experience of making business phone calls will probably be keen to suggest many other ways in which the calls could be improved.

PART ONE   **First attempt**

Telephonist: <u>... and Company</u>. Can I help you?

Caller: Er ... can I speak to Dr Henderson, please?

Telephonist: <u>Mr Anderson.</u> Just one moment, I'll put you through.

Anderson: Yes, Anderson, Accounts.

Caller: Oh, er ... hello, is ... is that Dr Bill Henderson?

Anderson: What? No, no, this is Peter Anderson. You've got the wrong extension. You probably want Dr Henderson in R & D that's ... um ... er ... 657. All right, 657.

Caller: Oh, um ... well, c ... can you connect me back through the switchboard please?

Anderson: Huh! Well, <u>I'll try ...</u>

Caller: Hello?

Second attempt

Telephonist: ... and Company. Can I help you?

Caller: Yes, I'd like to speak to Dr Bill Henderson, please.

Telephonist: Dr Henderson, putting you through.

Voice: 657.

Caller: Hello.

Voice: Oh, hello.

Caller: Um ... is ... is that Dr Henderson?

Voice: Er ... no.

Caller: Oh, er ... I'm trying to get hold of Dr Bill Henderson.

Voice: Oh, you want Bill. I ... I'll just see if I can find him. Um ... ju ... just a moment.

Caller: Thank you.

Henderson: Henderson.

Caller: Oh, good. Um ... good afternoon. This is Sylvia Perez. Er ... I'm calling you from France.

Henderson: Sylvia who?

Caller: Perez. P-E-R-E-Z. Um ... we met last month in ... in Berlin at the trade fair. You expressed an interest in our laboratory measuring equipment.

Henderson: Oh yes?

Caller: Well, the thing is I'm going to be in your area next month and I thought I might like to ... um ... call in and see you. I'd like to discuss the applications you might have for our equipment.

Henderson: Ah, I see. What's this about again?

Caller: Your enquiry about our laboratory measuring equipment. Didn't you get the literature I sent you?

Henderson: Yes, yes. Um ... that was very interesting. Um ...

Caller: Well, the thing is: is it OK if I come in and see you during my visit next month?

Henderson: I see. Yeah, all right.

Caller: Now, what about the morning of Tuesday 10th April, is that OK? Say at about ... er ... 11?

Henderson: I'll just see if I can find my diary ... Umm, yes, here we are. Er ... April 11th at 10 o'clock you said.

Caller: That's right. Now, um ... is that OK? Is that convenient for you?

Henderson: The next day might be better. Just after lunch for preference.

Caller: Right, so that's ... er ... the Wednesday. In fact, that'll suit me fine, that's great. Now, shall we say ... um ... 2.15?

Henderson: Er ... certainly, yes. 2.50, that's ... that's fine.

Caller: Oh and by the way, I'll be bringing our agent Don Rees with me i ... if that's OK with you.

Henderson: Oh, certainly. Er ... what was your name again?

Caller: Sylvia Perez, P E R E Z.

Henderson: Fine. I'll see you in April then. You know how to get to our lab, don't you? Goodbye, then, Miss Perex.

Caller: Goodbye, Dr Henderson – and ... er ... actually it's Mrs. Oh, and I'll ... um ... I'll write to you to confirm the arrangements just to make quite sure we've got everything ... absolutely right.

[Time: 3 minutes 20 seconds]

B In this step, students suggest how they might **reply** to the voices on the tape. Pause the tape after each bit, so that members of the class can make suggestions. This activity is best done by the whole class, so that all the suggestions can be discussed and evaluated.

PART TWO
1. ring ring '32543.'
2. ring ring '... and Co. Good morning.'
3. ring ring ... SILENCE ...
4. ring ring 'Hello.'

5. ring ring   '33543.'
6. ring ring   'Sales department.'
7. ring ring   'Lines from Birmingham are engaged, please try later'
8. ring ring   'Felco Industries, good afternoon.'
9. ring ring   'Dr Henderson's office.'
10. our phone rings   'Hello, this is Bill Henderson. You wanted me to get in touch...'

Suggested responses (many variations possible):

1. Is that Felco Industries? No? I'm sorry, I think I must have got the wrong number.
2. Hello, is that Felco Industries?
3. Hello? Hello?
4. Hello, is that 234 32453?
5. Oh, I'm sorry, I must have dialled the wrong number.
6. Oh, I wanted Dr Bill Henderson, can you put me through to him, please?
7. Oh bother, a recorded message!
8. Good afternoon, can I speak to Dr Bill Henderson, please?
9. Hello, this is ... (my name) ... Is Dr Henderson there, please? No? Could you ask him to call me, please?
10. Ah, Dr Henderson, thanks ever so much for calling back. I wanted to ask you...

C For this discussion students should work in groups of about four. If possible, make sure each group has someone with business experience in it.
  Among the points that are likely to be made are:

- A first time call to a stranger often involves mutual suspicion and uncertainty.
- You can make it easier if you speak slowly and carefully. The way that you say the very first thing (your voice quality) has a big effect on the rest of the call. Only the top man can just say brusquely 'Hello' on the phone.
- The caller must try to establish links, such as mutual concerns or acquaintances, and state his or her business clearly. Identify yourself or your department.
- It makes a big difference if the person you're talking to on the phone knows you – even if you've only corresponded.

Get each group to report to the class at the end on the points that were made.

Workbook

Listening exercise 3.1 deals with avoiding misunderstandings on the phone.

3.2 **Getting people to do things** *Functions*

Presentation

[cassette icon] The recorded conversations illustrate how the exponents are used in conversations – these are <u>underlined</u> in the transcript below.

Play the tape twice, once to give everyone time to get used to the voices and interpret the functions, the second time to focus attention on the use of the exponents in the speech bubbles. Pause the tape between the conversations for students to ask questions and to draw attention to the exponents that were used. Emphasize the distinctions between formal/informal situations and direct/indirect ways of talking to people. Point out that it helps to be polite and friendly when dealing with people, even if really you don't get on with them.

Note that if you are over-polite, this may well be interpreted as insincerity or sarcasm.

REQUESTING

Jane: Terry ... er ... <u>do you think you could help me</u> with a couple of things?

Terry: Er ... <u>sure</u>.

Jane: Um ... <u>do you think you could</u> send a copy of this report to Frankfurt for me?

Terry: Er ... yeah, do you want me to ... er ... fax it, or ... or send it by mail?

Jane: Oh, er ... fax, I think. Um ... now, let's see, then <u>would you mind</u> arranging accommodation for Mr Berglund, he needs it for Friday night.

Terry: Friday night, <u>sure</u>. Hotel Continental, as usual?

Jane: Mm, that's right. Now then, then <u>could you</u> get in touch with Sandy in New York after lunch and ... er ... ask her to call me tomorrow?

Terry: Um ... I'll be over at the factory this afternoon, <u>I won't be able to do that</u>.

Jane: Oh, er ... well, never mind. Well, <u>what I'd like you to do now is</u> to help me to translate this document into English.

Terry: Um ... Jane, <u>I'm sorry, but I ...</u> I can't. I've got this report to finish by 11 o'clock and it's just ...

Jane: Oh, Go ... mm ... well, look, at least <u>can you</u> just check my spelling and punctuation in this literature here?

Terry: Ha ... but my spelling is terrible. I ... I'll ask Annette to do it.

Jane: Oh, all right.

OFFERING TO HELP

Bill: Morning, Sally, how's it going?

Sally: Oh, hello, Bill. Look, I'm in a terrible rush, you know my plane leaves at three this afternoon.

Bill: Oh, yes, of course. Oh, well, <u>would you like a hand with</u> some things you've got to do?

Sally: Oh, <u>that would be great, i ... if you're sure it's no trouble</u>.

Bill: No, no trouble at all. Um ... <u>would you like me to</u> check today's correspondence?

Sally: Oh, yes, <u>that's very kind of you</u> ... um ... look if you do that, can you sign the letters for me as well, please?

Bill: Yes, of course, no problem. And then <u>shall I</u> call you a taxi to the airport?

Sally: Yes. <u>Yes, please</u>. Now, let me think, I'll need to leave straight after lunch so ... well, no, better make it 1.30, that'd be safe.

Bill: OK, 1.30. And <u>would you like me to</u> do anything about your hotel booking?

Sally: Ooh, heavens, yes, I'm glad you reminded me. Um ... I'm sure it's all might ... all right but would you mind phoning them to confirm the booking?

Bill: Of course. Of course, no problem. Er

... shall I deal with the weekly report?
Sally: No, thanks. I think I can manage to finish that now. It's nearly ready.
Bill: Sure?
Sally: Mm.
Bill: Um ... I know, would you like me to call Amsterdam for you?
Sally: Oh, that's very kind of you, n ... no. Let me think, no, I think I prefer to do that myself because there are some people I've really got to talk to.
Bill: OK, I understand. Well, if you need any more help, just let me know, huh?
Sally: Oh, terrific. Thanks, I will.

ASKING PERMISSION
Visitor: Um ... do you mind if I open the window? It's kind of stuffy in here.
Host: Well, er ... I'm afraid we can't open the window, because if we do open the window the air conditioning doesn't work!
Visitor: Haha, right, no. It's always that way. Er ... is it OK if I take off my jacket then?
Host: Oh, sure, yeah. Make yourself at home.
Visitor: Oh, right. That's better. Oh, um ... do you mind if I smoke? I notice nobody's smoking around here.
Host: Well, I'm sorry, but this is a non-smoking zone. We took a vote and then we came...
Visitor: Oh, I know. I've ... that's OK. I'm

trying to quit anyway, I figured it was something like that. Right OK. Um ... oh, by the way, may I use the phone to book a table ... er ... for lunch?
Host: Yeah, sure. Do you know somewhere good?
Visitor: Oh, oh yeah, absolutely.
Host: Great.
Visitor: No, I'll do that as soon as we've finished this. Um ... and ... er ... also ... er ... before we go, is it all right if I call my office, to see if there are any messages for me?
Host: Sure. Go ahead.
Visitor: OK, good, I'll do that as soon as ... just a few more lines here. Um ... OK, do you think I could get a photocopy of this leaflet done?
Host: Er ... oh, of course, yes. Well, I'll get Tim to do it for you. Tim!
Visitor: Great. Also can I send a fax of these proposals to our branch in Canada?
Host: Err ... I'm sorry, but the fax machine is broken down. We're waiting for somebody to fix it.
Visitor: Oh, that's OK. There's ... there's one next door, isn't there?
Host: Ah ... I don't know. I think so.
Visitor: Yeah, I saw one.
Host: OK.
Visitor: OK, fine.
Host: Right.

[Time: 3 minutes 20 seconds]

Activities

A In this information gap activity, students work in pairs, playing the roles of colleagues who work in the same office (like Sally and Bill in the recordings above). One should look at File 5, the other at 11. The File contains a list of things you want to do (and may need your partner's permission for), things you want your partner to do and things you'd like your partner to offer to do for you.

Encourage students to experiment with the exponents in the speech balloons as they talk to their 'colleague' and discourage them from using the simplest forms, like *May I*... and *Can you*...

B In this role play, students will be making and replying to requests in writing (by drafting telexes). One pair represents a firm marketing consumer goods, the other a firm of package designers and specialist printers and the exchange of messages concerns packaging and printing for the first firm's products.

Before dividing up the class, get everyone to study the examples of the telex requests. When any queries have been answered, form the class into an EVEN number of pairs. Make sure each pair of pairs is sitting near the other, as they will be 'sending telexes' (i.e. passing their written drafts) to each other. One of the pairs in the group looks at File 20 (customers), the other at 13 (printers).

C ☎ So that everyone has a change of partner, rearrange the class into different pairs. One of the pair should look at File 20 (customer) and the other at 13 (printer). They exchange the same information as in B, but this time speaking over the phone.

At the end, ask everyone what they found easy and what they found difficult in doing the activities in this section.

Extra activity

Ask everyone in the class to jot down some things they would like you or another member of the class to do, or which they would like permission to do. If appropriate, you can play the role of 'boss' while other members of the class are 'colleagues'. Then go round the class, asking each member to make his request or ask permission, by saying, 'Yes, Makoto?' or 'Kumiko, you wanted to see me?'

Workbook

There are several recorded exercises in the Workbook on the functions practised in this section: 3.3 to 3.6.

3.3 Using the phone   *Vocabulary*

This exercise on phrasal verbs can be done as homework or fitted in at any convenient time in class.

Allow time to discuss alternative 'normal' verbs that can be used instead of these idiomatic phrasal verbs.

Answers (alternative 'normal' verbs are given in italics):
1. pick up   *lift*
2. call/ring back   *return the call*
3. look up   *find*
4. put through   *connect with*
5. cut off   *disconnected*

6.	get through	*reach*
7.	hold on	*wait*
8.	put on	*ask him to come to the phone*
9.	hang up	*replace the receiver*
10.	give up	*stop trying*
11.	is over	*has finished*

Units 5 to 14 in the Workbook contain many more exercises on phrasal and prepositional verbs, as well as prepositional phrases and collocations.

3.4   Can I take a message?

Begin with a short class discussion on taking messages. Get the students who have experience of this to say what kind of information they always note down and why.

A   There are three phone calls to listen to. Students will probably need to hear each one at least twice. Call 1 goes with the example in the Student's Book, to show students how they can approach writing down the messages for calls 2 and 3.

In the transcripts of calls 2 and 3 the important points that should be noted down have been <u>underlined</u>.

1
Telephonist: REMACO, bonjour.
Mr Schulz: Hello, er ... it's Peter Schulz here. Could I speak to Monsieur Février, please?
Telephonist: Oh, just a moment, I'll see if he's in. I'll put you through.
Secretary: Hello, Monsieur Février's office.
Mr Schulz: Could I speak to Monsieur Février, please?
Secretary: Oh, I'm very sorry, he's ... er ... out at lunch. Can I help you at all?
Mr Schulz: Ah. Um ... could you ask him to call me today, please? Er ... preferably before 4 pm ... or ... um ... any time tomorrow. Er ... it's to do with the arrangements for the July ... f ... for the congress in July.
Secretary: Yes, who's calling, please?
Mr Schulz: This is Mr Schulz – Peter Schulz.
Secretary: Peter Schulz. And can I take your number, please?

Mr Schulz: Yes, er ... it's 01 456 9924.
Secretary: So that's 01 456 9924.
Mr Schulz: Yes.
Secretary: Peter Schulz. OK, Mr Schulz, I'll get Monsieur Février to call you as soon as he comes back to the office.
Mr Schulz: Thank you very much. Goodbye.
Secretary: Goodbye.

2
Telephonist: Green and Harding, good morning.
Paola: Oh, good morning. This is <u>Paola Andreotti</u> calling from Rome. I'd like to speak to Mr Guy Dobson, please.
Telephonist: Oh, certainly, ma'am, I'll connect you immediately.
Bob: Hello.
Paola: Oh, is that <u>Guy Dobson</u>?
Bob: Er ... no, it ... is that Paola?
Paola: Yes.
Bob: Oh, hi! This is Bob Swenson.

Paola: Oh, hi. Is Guy around?

Bob: Er ... just a minute, I'll check. ... Um ... no, he doesn't seem to be. He should be back ... er ... any minute. Er ... can I help you?

Paola: Um ... yeah. Look, can I leave a message with you?

Bob: Yes, sure.

Paola: It's urgent. There's been a mix-up about the labelling of product number 15437 B – that's the one for the Italian market.

Bob: Uhuh, I've got that.

Paola: And I'd like him to get in touch so that it can be cleared up.

Bob: OK.

Paola: Um ... he can reach me at this number till tomorrow evening, OK?

Bob: Mmm.

Paola: It's 002 558 9847.

Bob: OK. He can reach you at this number till tomorrow evening: 002 558 9847.

Paola: That's right, great. Thanks Bob.

Bob: OK, bye-bye.

3

Telephonist: Hello, Santos Trading.

Mr Wong: Oh, hello, this is Mr Wong here, calling from Singapore.

Telephonist: Yes, Mr Wong, who do you want to speak to?

Mr Wong: Um ... I'd like to speak to Mrs Cox, please.

Telephonist: Fine, putting you through.

Woman: Hello, can I help you?

Mr Wong: Oh, hello. This is Mr Wong calling from Singapore. Er ... may I speak to Mrs Cox, please?

Woman: Oh, I'm afraid Mrs Cox is away. She has the flu and she may not be back in the office till Monday. I expect her assistant, Mr Box, can help. I'll just see if he's in his office. Hold on a moment, please. ... Hello, Mr Wong?

Mr Wong: Yes.

Woman: I'm very sorry, he's out just now, can I take a message for him?

Mr Wong: Oh, yes, please. Will you tell him I won't be arriving in Melbourne until quite late this Saturday, at 1 am local time. And will Mrs Cox still be able to meet me?

Woman: Right.

Mr Wong: And also inform the Royal Hotel that I'll be arriving very very late.

Woman: Sure.

Mr Wong: Oh, wonderful, thanks. Could you please ... er ... telex or phone me to confirm that this is possible?

Woman: Right, I ... I'll take the message, I'll give it to Mr Box and I'm sure he'll be in touch with you. Thank you very much, Mr Wong.

Mr Wong: Thank you.

[Time 3 minutes 50 seconds]

B In this group discussion, students will be considering the qualities of both a good telephonist and a good receptionist. How important is it to 'smile when you're on the phone'? Are the required qualities different, and if so, should two different people fill such positions? How do the members of the class rate the telephonists who spoke in the three calls above?

Perhaps remind them that everyone who deals with people in person or on the phone may need similar qualities.

C This activity will require students to write down the ideas they have discussed in B above. It can be done by the same groups.

Extra activity

With students working in pairs, ask them to design a message form that will encourage their staff to take down all the necessary details when receiving messages on someone else's behalf. They might like to compare their final drafts with the one in 4.9.

There are more activities involving taking telephone messages in 4.9.

Workbook

There is a recorded exercise on taking messages in 3.8.

3.5 Present tenses   *Grammar*

Students often have difficulty remembering when to use the present simple and when to use the present progressive. Associating adverbs with each tense should help them to get this clear. Another problem is distinguishing stative verbs (like *belong*) from dynamic verbs (like *give*) in English, where a student's own language doesn't distinguish them grammatically.

Presentation

The example sentences (but not the lists of adverbs and verbs) are recorded so that students can hear them while they are studying the presentation section. You'll need to pause the tape between each group of example sentences.

The examples given in this section illustrate some convenient 'rules of thumb'. With a little thought most people can produce 'exceptions' like these:

Mr Brown always goes to the sauna after lunch today.
He's usually feeling sleepy at this time of day.

Perhaps introduce these more advanced points to the class:

- Some 'stative verbs' can also be used in a 'dynamic' way:
  I am measuring it, weighing it, etc.
- Four adverbs can be used with the present progressive to describe unexpected or annoying things that happen (too) often:
      always   constantly   forever   continually
  They're always ringing us by mistake. (i.e. They keep on ringing us.)
  He's continually trying to persuade us. (i.e. He keeps on trying to persuade us.)

Exercise and activities

A   This exercise can be done as homework, or by students working together in pairs. Note that in the last three sentences, where stative verbs are used, it is not really possible to use any of the adverbs presented above.

Suggested answers:
 1. *example: make sure everyone has got the idea of the exercise*
 2. normally require
 3. still prefers
 4. always blocks
 5. am still analyzing
 6. are now trying
 7. always speaks
 8. sometimes sounds
 9. usually pay
10. specializes
11. looks
12. depends

B   While students are preparing their questions, go round encouraging the less imaginative pairs. Check carefully that the questions have been written down accurately, bearing in mind the rules of thumb presented above.

C   When everyone is ready, rearrange the class so that everyone has a different partner to talk to. While they're interviewing each other, go round checking that the questions are being answered accurately.

Extra activity

The class could interview you and ask you the best (i.e. the most interesting) questions that they devised in B and asked in C above.

Workbook

Workbook exercise 3.7 contains more work on present tenses.

3.6   Talking on the phone

This sections allows students to discuss and compare experiences on telephone manners and the need to plan phone calls. Even students with no business experience will have personal experiences to contribute.

A   Students should work in groups of about four. If possible, make sure there is at least one student with business experience in each group.

Get each group to report to the rest of the class on its discussion.

B   [cassette] Here are more comments from business people for the groups to agree or disagree with. Play the tape while the groups are still together:

'Well, um ... a couple of lines on the back of an envelope are enough.'
'No, if I make notes before a call, I can't adapt to the other person's reactions.'
'Well, I get someone else to phone for me if I have to speak in a foreign language.'
'If I don't make notes beforehand, I'll forget what I need to say.'
'I try to "rehearse" an important call in my head before I make it.'
'I make much more careful notes before a phone call than I do before writing a letter.'
'I find a minute or two spent making notes before the call is better really than wasting time during it trying to think what to say.'
'I find it's a good idea to write down some of the phrases I want to use.'

Hopefully, students will agree that it is essential to plan phone calls they have to make in English, though they may not agree on the best method.

In later units in the course, make sure that students have time to do this before they do any of the telephone role plays: [telephone]

C   For this part of the discussion, students should refer back to 2.8, where the '7 Steps' for planning a business letter were discussed. Students, perhaps rearranged into different groups now, should amend these steps to make them suitable as guidelines for planning a business phone call.

3.7   Hello, my name's ...

[telephone] This role play works like a chain, with one part leading on to the next. It consists of four separate phone calls. While two of the group are talking, the other(s) act as 'observers' and listen and take notes, so that they can make comments afterwards.

In case this seems complicated, there is a flow chart below. Students have directions within their own books to follow the same sequence: once they have started the activity, their own instructions will keep them going in the right direction.

The ideal group size is three, so have as many groups of three as possible.

Make sure that the speakers are sitting BACK-TO-BACK – the observers could also have their backs to the speaker while they're listening in: there's nothing more off-putting than being watched while you're on the phone!

If students are working in groups of *three*:

1st call	A: 16	B: 67	C: 2*
2nd call	A: 91	B: 4*	C: 31
3rd call	A: 85*	B: 43	C: 50
4th call	A: 6	B: 64	C: 73*

If they're working in groups of *four*:

1st call	A: 16	B: 67	C: 2*	D: 2*
2nd call	A: 109*	B: 109*	C: 31	D: 36
3rd call	A: 85*	B: 43	C: 50	D: 85*
4th call	A: 73*	B: 64	C: 73*	D: 6

* The Files that contain instructions for the 'observers' are shown with an asterisk above.

After each call, make sure that the observer(s) give(s) the speakers feedback on how they got on and advice on how they might improve their telephone technique.

The 1st call is between Mr/Ms Tanaka, a supplier (16), and Mr/Ms Suarez, a customer (67), concerning a lunch date.

The 2nd call is between Mr/Ms LaRue, a customer (31), and Mr/Ms Peterson, in charge of shipping orders (91), concerning some delayed shipments.

The 3rd call is between a business person (43) and the Provence Restaurant (50), concerning the reservation of a private room and special menu.

The 4th call is between a business person (64) and the Hotel Cambridge (6), concerning the reservation of rooms and some special requirements.

At the very end allow time for students to ask you questions and give them feedback yourself on their performance.

■ P.S. Don't worry, this will work!

3.8 Give them a call! *Vocabulary*

A If there seem to be too many new words here, read the whole exercise aloud to the class, supplying the missing words yourself.
At this stage, make sure the class just listen and don't make notes.
Then let them do it themselves in pairs, trying to remember what you said.

(Often students do know such words and actually just need reminding – this technique helps them to do that.)

Answers:
1. switchboard operator (also in British English: telephonist) extension
2. wrong number
3. bad line
4. engaged/busy
5. off the hook
6. phone book   enquiries
7. receiver   insert   dialing/dialling   ringing   unobtainable out of order
8. IDD/international direct dialling   area code/dialling code
9. collect call/transferred charge call (also in British English: reverse charge call)
10. person to person call/personal call
11. outside line

Note that some British people refer to IDD as ISD (international subscriber dialling) and to the dialling code as the STD code (subscriber trunk dialling code).

B   To start everyone off, explain how you would use a public phone in your own country (UK, USA, Australia, etc).

Some facilities and services available in the UK are:

- Traveline 8021, Cricketline, Timeline 8081, What's on Line, Sportsline, etc.
- 0898 numbers: special information services, such as Stock Exchange prices and weather information
- Freefone numbers, 0800 numbers (toll-free)
- Phonecard (used in special phones), Telephone credit cards
- ADC calls: 'advise duration and charge' – the operator calls you back to tell you how much your call cost, which is useful if you're calling from someone else's house
- Some useful numbers:
    international operator for most countries 155
    for some far-flung countries 158
    emergency 999
    local operator 100
    international directory enquiries 153

What are the equivalents to these services and numbers in your students' country or countries and how would they explain to a foreign visitor how to use these services?

3.9 I've got some calls to make

☎ This is a much shorter 'chain', consisting of two phone calls. Students will be working in pairs without an 'observer' this time and should sit back-to-back for the calls:

Student A starts at File 18 and goes on to 66.
Student B starts at File 25 and goes on to 51.

The 1st call is between someone who works for a subsidiary of Medusa S.A. and someone at head office. They don't know each other. The caller requires information which the other person may be able to provide. Directions are given within each student's File on which one to look at next.
The 2nd call is between the same people, who now have spoken on the phone. The caller requires more information.

Allow enough time for each pair to have a reasonable conversation each time and to sort out all the sources of confusion in the information they are discussing (there are several potential problems built in to the role information).

After the calls, get some pairs to describe the calls they made to the rest of the class to see if there were any differences in the way the calls went.

Discussion ideas

What do you do if an answering machine answers? Do you ring back later when you've had time to compose and write out the message you'll leave?
Do you enjoy using the phone? Or do you put off making phone calls for as long as possible?
Is telephone selling common in your country – or is it illegal?
How would you react to a 'cold call' from a salesperson?

⋙→

Workbook

Contents for this unit:

3.1 Misunderstandings on the phone   Listening

3.2 Vocabulary

3.3 What would you write?   Functions

3.4 What would you like me to get you?   Functions

3.5 Can you help me?   Functions

3.6 Mr Brown, is it all right if I ... ?   Functions

3.7 Present tenses   Grammar

3.8 Three messages   Listening

Background information: Reports and summaries

In business, planning and writing reports, making summaries and taking notes are important skills which may be expected of everyone. We tend only to write reports when we are asked to, usually by our boss or superior. Many people are afraid of writing reports. There is no good reason for this. It's often simply a question of stopping and thinking about what it is you have to do and then doing it. And it is a question of practice.

It is important to remember that there are several types of report. Reports can be transmitted in the form of:
- conversations
- letters
- memos
- special forms
- separate documents of several pages.

They can be long, short, formal or informal.

Reports can serve various purposes. There are reports which inform, reports which provide background information to help someone make up their mind about something and there are reports which in themselves make recommendations or indicate a course of action.

There are many things you should do before you even think about 'writing' or drafting the report. You should first prepare or assemble your material and then plan how you are going to write the report. The preparation and writing of a report falls into four stages.
1. Assembling the material
2. Planning the report
3. Drafting the report
4. Editing the report

Any report – on the page – has three main 'parts' which must include four (sometimes five or even six) essential elements:

Parts	Elements
Parts	*Elements*
Introduction	{ Terms of reference or objective { Procedure
Body of the report	Findings
Terminal section	{ Conclusions { (Recommendations if asked for) { (Appendices)

⟫→

73

This structure should be evident in every report. In some cases you may need to have elements such as appendices at the end etc. For students of Business English it may be sufficient to speak of three main parts:

Introduction
Facts
Conclusions

4 Reports and summaries

This unit deals with how to plan and write reports. It is a unit which can be used either as an introduction for students with little experience in report and summary writing or else as revision for students who have dealt with report writing already and who need a quick review of the skills.

If any of your students are completely inexperienced in these skills, you may wish to photocopy the Background Information for them.

The focus is more on the interactive differences between writing and telling or talking rather than on the formal differences. The emphasis throughout is on sharpening and practising report, summary and note writing and on demonstrating that they can be viewed in a combined and integrated fashion. In particular the unit lays great weight on the preparatory and planning stages of all serious and professional writing activities. The emphasis is on encouraging organizational and management skills, as in Units 1–3.

INTRODUCTION BY TEACHER   In business we only write reports when we are asked to, normally by our boss or superior. Many people are afraid of writing reports. In this unit we want to show how report writing can be made easier. We shall be comparing it to other types of communication, such as speaking and personal letter writing. The unit takes up some of the elements of the unit on letters, telexes and memos. But it concentrates on the more specialized skill of writing reports and making summaries of conversations.

4.1   Writing v. telling

This section allows students the opportunity to think about and discuss the difference between telling someone something and writing it down. The importance of knowing and adjusting to the audience you are writing for is brought out in this section. (This has already been introduced in 2.1.)

Procedure

Students work in pairs. These are some prompts you can give depending on how you estimate the strength of the class: 'Maybe you wrote some letters, spoke to several important and not so important people on the telephone, had some visitors or decorators in the office, met a new member of staff, met customers, took an examination, took part in a training course, went to an interesting or boring lecture, read books, magazines, had an argument with your boss, went to an office or college party, etc.'

A   Ask each member of the class to write a short letter, on their own, to a friend or a member of their family who lives in America or another country, telling them what they did yesterday or last Friday.

Students work in pairs. After they have drafted their letters, ask them to look at each other's and discuss these questions:

What attitude or tone have you used?

What words or phrases have you used?

What words or phrases have you used which are friendly or personal?

Compare your two letters.

Have you both used the same kind of 'tone'?

What advantages do you find in writing down what happened to you?

What would have been the difference if you told your friends (on the phone or face to face) instead of writing down what happened?

B   Students work in pairs. They follow the instructions in the Student's Book for this step and look at the map of a factory site where a robbery took place. Some of the buildings are marked, others are not. Get them to ask their partner to guess the names of some of the buildings which are not marked.

C ⌷

1. Play the recording for the first time to enable everyone to listen to the interviews and write in the names of the buildings on the map which are still unmarked. They also have to mark in the place where the robbery took place and the place where the robber got into the factory.
2. Play the recording a second time, so that the students can also mark on the map where the people say they were. Pause briefly after each person has been interviewed.
3. Then play the recording a third time, if necessary, for students to verify their notes on who was where and doing what.

First interview

Reporter: Mr Johnson. I understand you were a security man at the factory on duty on the night of the robbery, is that correct?

Johnson: Ah.

Reporter: I wonder if you could tell us what actually happened?

Johnson: Well everything was quite normal. It must have been about 10 o'clock, I suppose. Well, I normally take about ten minutes to walk round the factory site, you know ...

Reporter: Mm.

Johnson: And I was just going past where the paint shop's quite close to the fence. Er ... well I was surprised to see that that part of the fence was hanging loose from a post, you know?

Reporter: Mmm mmm.

Johnson: I made a mental note to write about it in my nightly report when I got back to my office. The office is on the other side of the site from there, you know.

Reporter: I see.

Johnson: Near the ... near the main entrance. You see I still had to walk all round the main factory complex and through the machine shop area.

Reporter: Can you describe to us how you chased the thief?

Johnson: Er ... well. I'd done my round of that half of the site.

Reporter: Mm mm.

Johnson: And I'd just turned into the road between the assembly shops, when I saw a man in a black coat come out of the assembly shop on the left, well ... that's number two assembly shop. So I shouted to him to stop. He turned left and disappeared from view. And ... and when I reached the end of the road and looked round the corner I could see him running past the canteen quite fast.

Reporter: And did he stop?

Johnson: No, he just ... he just ran off between the machine shops and the paint-shop and ... and out of sight.

Reporter: Mm.

Johnson: So I naturally started to run after him. And when I got to the corner, I ... I could see he was running back to the ... er ... to the hole in the fence I'd seen, so I ... I ran after him. Well ... er ... just as he was getting through the hole in the fence I managed to catch hold of his leg. Er ... he was strong though. I'd say he was about, what, 25 years old. He kicked me. On the side of the head and I ... I fell down on the floor. I don't remember anything else.

Reporter: Did he knock you out, then?

Johnson: Uh ... I suppose he must have done, because when I woke up, Miss Jones was standing over me.

Reporter: And did the thief get away with anything of value?

Johnson: Uh ... I can't really say. There was a black bag next to the fence with some computer tapes in it. I ... I suppose that's what the thief must have been trying to steal.

[Time: 2 minutes]

Second interview

Reporter: Now Mr Bakewell, what exactly do you do in the factory?

Bakewell: Well, I'm a trainee production manager.

Reporter: I see. Now how did you come to be in the factory on that evening, the evening of the robbery?

Bakewell: Well ... ha ... it sounds a bit silly, but I'd just come back to get a ... get a report. Well I needed it for a conference the next day.

Reporter: What time would that be?

Bakewell: Ooh well, it must have been ... about ... um ... 8 o'clock.

Reporter: Good. Now, where do you work?

Bakewell: Well, I've got a small office in number two assembly shop. Just over there actually.

Reporter: So getting back to the time, you were in the building, when the robbery took place?

Bakewell: Oh, no, no. No, I'd left by then.

Reporter: I see. Well, what did you do?

Bakewell: Well, you see the lights were out in the assembly shop and so when I closed the door to my office I ... well ... I can't remember if it was locked or not. I mean, you see, normally the door closes automatically.

Reporter: Oh. Right, OK. Thank you very much Mr Bakewell.

Bakewell: Thank you.

[Time: 1 minute]

Third interview

Reporter: And your name's Joanna Ripley, that's ... er ... R-I-P-L-E-Y. Is that correct?

Joanna Ripley: Yes. That's right.

Reporter: Right. Now could you tell me what were you doing at the time of the robbery?

Ripley: Well, I was on night shift, you see. I'm a computer operator and we're on duty until 12 o'clock on the night shift.

Reporter: Mm mm.

Ripley: I always go down for a coffee with Miss Jones – we work together in the computer centre. We go down about 9.30 usually.

Reporter: Yeah. Mmm.

Ripley: And ... er ... well ... we go down and get our coffee from the coffee machine in the entrance hall to the canteen. To the left of that office block.

Reporter: Right. And did you see anything unusual?

Ripley: Well, we were on our way over to the canteen and ... well, there was a man near the paintshop.

Reporter: Did you know him? Er ... I mean did you recognize him?

Ripley: No, not really. You see it was raining quite a bit so we just hurried over to the canteen not to get wet.

Reporter: Mmm ... mmm, and what happened then?

Ripley: Well we were just coming out of the canteen. Oh, I suppose about ten minutes or so later and I heard somebody shout 'Stop!' And then I saw Mr Johnson from security running down the road between the paintshop and the machine shops, you see.

Reporter: Sure, yeah.

Ripley: And, well, I ... I think you know the rest. After a few minutes there was such a ... a loud shout from Mr Johnson that, well ... well Miss Jones and I obviously knew something had happened, so we went and looked.

Reporter: Ah, that was very brave of you.

Ripley: No, you don't think in situations, do you? I mean, we just found Mr Johnson lying on the ground.

Reporter: So did you see the thief, then?

Ripley: No. No sign of him at all.

Reporter: Ah, I see.

Ripley: I went to ring the ambulance, obviously, and the police, and Miss Jones went and gave Mr Johnson a bit of first aid.

Reporter: Fine, thank you, Miss Ripley, that's fine, thank you.

Ripley: That's all right.

[Time: 1 minute 40 seconds]

This is the completed factory map to show the class before the next activity is begun:

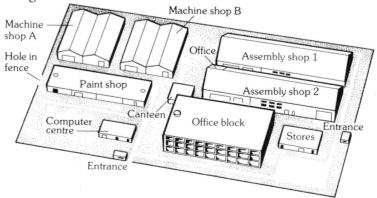

D Working on their own, students prepare and draft a report of what happened during the robbery, what the people were doing at the time and what they did after the robbery. Remind them that in their report they should try and decide how the robbery took place and what made it possible.

The report writing can be done as homework if convenient.

E Students work in pairs. They compare each other's drafts and follow the instructions in the Student's Book.

F Students work in pairs and discuss the advantages they see in writing over telling. Student A looks at File 21, student B at 92. The files contain a number of well-known claims about the efficacy of writing over telling, such as the advantage of having a permanent record and being able to plan what you want to write. Later, get them to discuss their findings in small groups of three or four.

(As is perhaps obvious, the two final pieces of information in each File are slightly less relevant than the others.)

4.2 Keeping it brief and to the point . . .

The purpose of this activity is to show that the specification of a report is very important if anything sensible or useful is to be produced.

There are several types of report. Reports can be transmitted in the form of:
— conversations
— letters
— memos
— special forms
— separate documents of several pages.

They can be long, short, formal or informal.

Reports can serve various purposes. There are reports which inform, reports which provide background information to help someone make up their mind about something and there are reports which in themselves make recommendations or indicate a course of action. What reports have the students dealt with so far? Which kinds of reports can they recognize among the ones in this unit?

Procedure

The activity for the students to follow is set out in the Student's Book.

A Students work in pairs. They read the memo and imagine that it is addressed to them. Remind them of the questions to be answered:

1. What do you think the managing director's aims were in writing the memo?
2. What – if anything – are you expected to do as a result of reading the memo?

B Students work in pairs and look at the report and answer the questions in the Student's Book.

C Students work in pairs. Draw attention to the fact that the intentions behind the managing director's memo are not explicit. They will probably have found it is difficult to decide what the managing director really wants to be done. Clearly the way you interpret the memo may have different consequences for the kind of memo you write. Students can be advised to consult File 78. The MD's wishes are somewhat clearer.

Students draft a report together. Then they compare their report with the MD's report in the Student's Book and the report of another group. After students have done the writing you can show them the 'model' report below and let them briefly discuss some of the things they find good about it. At this stage problems concerning planning and organization should simply be indicated but not discussed in full, as they will be dealt with in detail in 4.3.

Suggested points:
1. Numbering sections helps.
2. There is a clear introduction.
3. There is a conclusion.
4. In between there is the main body of the report.

Allow time for queries and problems to be raised.

[YOU MAY PHOTOCOPY THIS DOCUMENT]

From: Personnel Manager Division A
To: Managing Director

Date: 16 May 19—
Subject: Proposed Installation of automatic coffee machines

1. Following your memorandum of 27 April we carried out a
small study of staff views in 3 selected departments.

2. My personnel officer informally asked a representative
sample of office workers a number of questions. He asked
whether
   they drank coffee during their break
   they made it themselves or brought it with them from home
   they would be in favour of a shorter coffee-break
   they would use an automatic coffee-machine if
     available.

3. We can summarize the results as follows:

   65% said they enjoy a good cup of coffee
Only 5% brought their own coffee with them from home
25% would be in favour of a shorter coffee-break and
   finishing earlier
15% said they would use the automatic coffee-machine.
   But most added: if the coffee was <u>cheap</u>.

4. On 30 April, during a routine meeting with the chief
union representative, I mentioned that in some departments
the coffee-break was lasting a lot longer than is actually
allowed. The representative's answer was not very helpful.
She said the union would always insist on the coffee-break
being left as it is. There is a point beyond which no
negotiation would be possible without asking all the union
members in the company their opinion.

In conclusion, it seems important to draw the board's
attention to possible difficulties which the rapid
installation of coffee-machines could bring. We need to
discuss the problem a little longer and with more people
before taking any action, it would seem.

Ronald Greenfield

© Cambridge University Press 1989

4.3 First things first ...

The idea behind this activity is for the students to work through and 'think through' the preparation for report writing themselves.

Procedure

There are many things you should do before you even think about 'writing' or drafting the report. You should first prepare or assemble your material and then plan how you are going to write the report. The preparation and writing of a report falls into four stages. Some of the individual tasks involved are listed in the file for the students to look at in pairs in step A.

A Students work in pairs and follow the instructions in the Student's Book.

One reason for the lack of focus in the MD's message in 4.2A on page 32 was his failure to plan out what he wanted to achieve before actually sitting down and drafting it. In report writing preparation and planning are necessary preliminaries to any writing.

Students with less experience of writing reports might be referred back to 2.8 (planning a letter) to give them further ideas. Ask the class if there are any important steps missing from the list.

B Reassemble the students in groups of four (each pair with another pair) to consider answers to the questions in the Student's Book. Let the groups discuss what order they have arrived at, the reasons why and their partners' views.

After this step you may find it helpful to show students the recommended order and to let them respond to it. Remind them of the four broad stages of the process first and how each individual step fits in. Emphasize the fact that of the 16 separately distinguished steps 'only' 4 relate to the 'actual' writing of the report!

1. Assemble the material (item 1 below).
2. Plan the report (items 2 to 7 below).
3. Draft the report (items 8 to 11 below).
4. Edit the report (items 12 to 16 below).

This is the recommended order in which the planning and writing process can be best arranged:
1. Collect all relevant material – notes, documents, etc.
2. Consider the purpose of your report: who is it for, why does he or she want it, how will he or she use it?
3. Summarize the aim and emphasis of the report in one sentence.

4. Decide what information is important and what is irrelevant.
5. Arrange the points of information in a logical sequence and in order of importance. Make rough notes.
6. Draft a working plan on a separate sheet of paper.
7. Decide where you might need illustrations or diagrams.
8. Write the introduction: state the subject, state the purpose, summarize findings.
9. Write the body of the report.
10. Write the conclusion (and recommendations).
11. Summarize the report in a sentence.
12. Examine the draft. Does it do what the report is expected to do?
13. Check your grammar, spelling and punctuation and style.
14. Read the text aloud to yourself, or, better, to someone else.
15. Check your illustrations.
16. Ask someone else to look critically at your draft.

By way of summary and conclusion you may find the following notes helpful as prompts for the discussion:

Any report has three main 'parts' and must include four (sometimes five or even six) essential elements:

Parts	Elements
Introduction	{ Terms of reference or objective { Procedure
Body of the report	Findings
Terminal section	{ Conclusions { (Recommendations if asked for) { (Appendices)

This structure should be evident in every report. In some cases you may need to have elements such as appendices at the end, etc. For students of Business English it may be sufficient to speak of three main parts:

Introduction
Facts
Conclusions.

Allow time for queries and questions to be raised.

4.4 A company report   *Reading aloud*

This activity is divided into two steps. The first gives practice in
listening for detail. The second provides practice in pronouncing
stressed syllables when reading aloud.

Procedure

A ⬛ Students work in pairs for this part of the activity. The
instructions are clearly laid out in the Student's Book. Before you play
the recording, remind everyone to read through the report beforehand
and to attempt to work out from the context what words have been
deleted. Allow time for queries and questions. Play the recording at
least twice. You may employ the procedure of 'shadowing' the second
time (see Introduction). After the students have discussed their answers
in pairs, discuss the answers in the class as a whole. In what ways does
an article such as this differ from the kind of report dealt with in
earlier sections?

This is the complete text:
Glauri, the West German engineering and process plant group, is beginning to
benefit from its slimming down and cost saving measures, but is still cautious
about future prospects for orders.
   Mr Erich Dietrich, chief executive, said that earnings should recover slightly
this financial year, despite the cost of the early retirement scheme aimed at
reducing the workforce.
   Glauri, a subsidiary of Metallco the metals, chemicals and trading concern,
does not publish its exact earnings, but has said they dropped last financial
year as it went ahead with costly rationalization measures.
   Glauri executives said that orders were now particularly difficult to predict
because of the payments problems of developing countries, the uncertainty in
the fall of the dollar and the drop in the oil price.
   Mr Dietrich said that the industrialized countries, including West Germany
and the US, were becoming more important sources of orders for Glauri.
Domestic orders accounted for 25 per cent of Glauri's total orders in the last
financial year and as much as 36 per cent so far this year.
   There was a strong trend towards projects involving environmental protec-
tion, such as desulphurization plants for power stations.

[Time: 1 minute 30 seconds]

B Students work in pairs. Student A looks at File 41, student B at
File 32, where they will have two halves of a similar report to read aloud
to each other. This is part of a company report for KfW (= Kredit-
anstalt für Wiederaufbau).

4.5 Using the passive   *Grammar*

Using the passive continues to present difficulties to intermediate and even more advanced students. In particular, deciding *when* to use the passive will still require practice.

This section merely gives brief treatment of the major points to be considered. The examples concentrate on the broad outlines. Further work may be necessary using the Workbook or exercises from other sources (*Use of English* Unit 29 is recommended).

Presentation

If possible, students should read step A through before the lesson.

Otherwise, exercises A to E should be done by students in pairs, with time after each exercise for discussion and questions.

If time is short, exercise C could be set as homework, but it still needs to be discussed in class to clear up possible misunderstandings. Suggested answers are given below.

A   Students work in pairs and read through the examples. Make sure any queries are cleared up before students start exercise B in pairs — though it is to be expected that doing the exercise will give rise to further questions.

The difference in focus between each of the pairs of sentences is fairly straightforward.

We use the passive in English if we do not wish to draw attention to the person who is engaged in a particular action or process. Indeed the passive is very useful when you want to emphasize the *object* to which the action or process is happening rather than the *actor* carrying out the action. So we can say

the passive is used in English

when it is the use of the passive we are interested in and not *who* is using it (speakers of English). Consider some further examples:

Company targets are set every year.

The factory was set up in 1985.

In both cases, we are concentrating on the company targets or the factory and we are perhaps more interested in when the actions happened than in who carried them out.

Exercises and activity

B   Students work in pairs. Student A looks at File 12, student B at File 106, where they will have two price lists to discuss, on which the prices of different items have been changed. They have to find out from each other what has been changed, reduced, etc and by how much. Perhaps ask sample questions for the class to get started:

What about the cassette recorders? Have/has the price been changed in your revised price list?

Has the XLI cassette recorder been reduced in price?

How much does it cost now?

Has the price of the headphones been changed?

What else has been reduced?

Which prices have been increased?

Which have not been affected?

C Students work in pairs to transform the sentences into the passive. Draw attention to the use of *get* in passive constructions, cf. example 6 ('the staff got paid').

Suggested answers:
1. IBM computers are used by six out of seven of the world's largest corporations.
2. Payment is enclosed with our order.
3. The report will be sent as soon as it has been completed.
4. The delivery should be received by Friday.
5. He may have been notified before the invoice arrived.
6. The staff was/got paid every Friday evening.
7. FCS's new computer was marketed in Europe only.
8. When he came back from lunch, the report had been corrected and re-typed.
9. The premises have been enlarged since my last visit.
10. Similar investments are being made in other parts of the world according to a newly published report.

D Students work in pairs.

Additional questions which might be raised are:

Who do you think is doing the suggesting, regretting and feeling in each case? How would you re-write the sentences?

Suggested answers:
1. I suggest that the company should install coffee machines, so that the workforce can use the maximum time for more productive work.
2. The management/we feel(s) that Mr Brown is too old to continue in his present position.
3. We/the company/the board of directors regret that we/they failed to inform the shareholders of the risks they were taking by investing in South Africa.

E Students look at the text in the Student's Book. Ask why they think the passive is used here.

The style of writing in Business has undergone some changes in recent years. Mention some of these points to the class now that they have done the exercises in this section:

> Traditionally there has been a tendency to over-use the passive in business writing, particularly in reports. The habit was probably connected with the mistaken idea that reports need to be 'objective' and hence one needed to remove 'people' with their subjective opinions from factual reporting. This led to a style of writing which was cold, lifeless and lacking in vitality. If the impersonal passive is used a lot, it makes it difficult to read letters or reports. There is a trend now towards using the active form. Of course the passive does have important uses as we have seen.

A further use for it is when you are describing an automated process where no people are directly involved.

Extra activity

Further practice can be given by listing a number of well-known products. Ask students to give you the names of some, together with a number of well-known companies.

companies	*products*
Mercedes-Benz	soft drinks
Exxon	chemicals
ICI	electrical goods
Nestlé	furniture
...	...

Then ask questions such as: 'What do Thomson/Grundig/Philips manufacture?' Students will answer 'They manufacture computers, etc'. Answer will include an active construction. Then ask 'who are electrical goods manufactured by in your country?' etc. Student answer expected: 'Electrical goods are produced by X here.'

Now go round the class or alternatively ask the first student to ask his or her neighbour a similar question and so on around the class as a whole.

What about chemicals? Who are they produced by in your country? Answer must include a passive construction.

Finally, allow time for the class to raise any questions concerning problems or difficulties they may have had doing the activities and exercises.

Workbook

Workbook exercise 4.3 provides further work on using the passive in English.

4.6 Punctuation

This activity is straightforward. Follow the procedure in the Student's Book.

A Suggested answers:

1 ,   8 !   5 " "   2 /   3 ()   11 ?   13 '
12 ' '   4 ;   10 :   9 .   6 –   7 —

B Suggested answers:
1. *full stop* (British English) / *period* (American English)
2. *comma*
3. *question mark*
4. *hyphen*
5. *dash*
6. *exclamation mark*
7. *double quotation marks / double quotes / double inverted commas*
8. *semi-colon*
9. *colon*
10. *stroke/oblique/slash*
11. *brackets/parentheses*
12. *apostrophe*

C Students work in pairs and decide where to add punctuation. Remind them that they will also need to add some Capital Letters.

This is a possible appropriate version. Notice that in a number of places a semi-colon might have been used instead of a full stop:

Suggested answer:
From: The Managing Director
To: All Office Staff
Date: 25th November 19––

As a result of the productivity survey carried out in the factory, more rapid and more efficient ways of operating are now being applied. In the factory, productivity has been increased by over 50 per cent. The management intends to apply these same methods to office staff in order to reduce costs. Our company must adapt in a competitive world. We aim to find ways of avoiding unnecessary actions by all staff. We therefore propose to pay a month's extra salary to any person who in the management's opinion has put forward the most practical suggestion to improve a particular office routine. All suggestions should be sent to the MD's office before the end of next month.

Workbook

Workbook exercise 4.4 gives further practice in 'correct' punctuation.

4.7 Summaries and note taking

For this activity, students work in pairs.

Procedure

A   Encourage everyone to read through the notes and raise questions concerning vocabulary *before* you first play the recording.

[cassette icon]   Play the recording twice, pausing after each extract to allow everyone time to decide which of the notes goes with which conversation.

1
It's about that order for Billingham's, John. Yeah. Er ... their buyer rang to say, they were willing to take 10 more sets of the 532, because, well, it's really been so effective in their new processing system. Mm, yes, that's right. Yes, they've been able to cut their production time by nearly a third. Haha, yes, it's good news, isn't it? Well, if you can get the stuff out and delivered by the end of the month, it could well mean that the division will get an increase in the monthly bonus. Yeah, well I'm sure they'd all be glad to hear that!

2
Hello there. This is Bob Billingham speaking. Ha, yeah, yeah, I'm just calling to let you know about my time of arrival. Er ... let's see, I'm coming in on flight CK532 next Thursday. Yeah, yeah it gets in at ... er ... 17.10. Oh, yeah, yeah, yeah that's good news isn't it? Yeah, I was ... er ... hoping to come on the third of the month but ... er ... I had to postpone my trip for nearly a month. We've had so many prob-

lems with that new processing system. You know what I mean. Um ... yeah anyway, um ... anyway ... I ... I can tell you all about that next week, OK. Um ... no, your division is going to have to help us out there. Ha, yeah, I'm afraid that's the case. Right so ... er ... if you can be thinking about that ...

3
Um ... but what we've got to do is find out what went wrong with the last payment. Er ... now ... er ... I've been looking at the file for CKs and it seems as though we were billing them for two batches of T140s last month instead of one. Well this may be how the misunderstanding arose. Well, yes exactly. That could be how the ... er ... 532 figure came up. Now ... now look, what I suggest is that we send them a new invoice with the batch next month and simply deduct the extra amount from the total ...

[Time: 2 minutes 5 seconds]

Students put the notes in the order they think the best. This is the correct order of the notes. As you can see, 3 (in the Student's Book) doesn't have a 'correct' order. Using such methods as pattern notes, but also the other methods, e.g. flow charts and numbered sections can be helpful when making notes for letters and reports. They represent some of the different ways of helping to prepare and plan what you wish to write. (See Tony Buzan, *Use Your Head*, BBC Publications, 1974, for further ideas along similar lines.)

1.

2.

3.   1. CKs last payment faulty
      2. Reason for 532 figure
      3. ... wrongly billed ...
      4. for two lots of T140s instead
         of one
      5. suggest sending new invoice ...
      6. deduct extra from total

B [cassette] After listening to the recording, in which a media buyer
describes his work, students work in pairs and draft a summary of the
fourth conversation using one of the methods for writing personal
notes they have encountered in this section. Then they show their notes
to another pair and look at the other pair's notes.

4
... Er, well I work in advertising and in this
town where I live, New York, that is one of
the major industries. Um ... and I am ... I
am what is called a media buyer ... er ... I
work for ... I personally I am ... I work
freelance, although I have worked in permanent positions in agencies here in town.
But for the last few years I have worked
freelance, which means I go from one
agency to another and sign on for a ... a
period of time to help them purchase the
television time in various cities across the
country and sometimes radio to run the
commercials which the client has produced.
So I'm like a broker in a way. Yeah. And

... and I ... not only products but I have worked on political campaigns as a media buyer, where the candidate is the product and you really approach it in very much the same way. Very much the same way. The candidate is a product, just as a dog food is a product or ah ... er ... detergent, dish-wash ...... liquid and ... and just anything really. I mean, they advertise everything now – you name it and it's on television. There is nothing for sale that they don't advertise on television. And it didn't use to be that way. So it's ... of course, that means there's more business, you know. There is always more and more business all the time.

[Time: 1 minute 20 seconds]

Allow time for feedback and queries at the end.

4.8 Summarizing a conversation

Taking notes of conversations one has had or telephone calls one has made involves summarizing what you have heard. This section provides practice in the skill. It is important to stress that one needs to make sure that the main points are clearly recorded so that another person can make sense of them (a record for the files).

Procedure

A Students should work in pairs. Before they hear the conversations, students should look at the extracts from the three summaries of a conversation.

Play the recording. It will be necessary to play the conversation a second time.

Norman: How do you do. My name is Bob Norman. I'm with Rotaflex. Can I help you in any way?

Brown: Oh. Hi. My name's Tim Brown. How're you doing? Pleased to meet you.

Norman: I'm fine ... fine thanks and how about yourself?

Brown: Fine thanks. I wanted to ask you about your rotary printer you have here.

Norman: Ah, yes, now you mean our R75.

Brown: Yes, that's right the R75. Now, what I'd like to know is can it deal with high quality embossed greeting cards? That's the sort of thing we're involved with.

Norman: Certainly. That's no problem at all.

Brown: Fine. Now, you see, we're looking for replacements for our twenty-year-old machines.

Norman: Mm mm.

Brown: So we need the latest technology.

Norman: Right.

Brown: Now, if we were interested in making a firm order, how quickly could you deliver the machines?

Norman: Well I can't give you a firm delivery date myself at this moment. But we can deliver pretty quickly.

Brown: My firm would be interested in ten machines.

Norman: Yes. Oh that's very good.

Brown: So I was wondering, could we get a 15% discount on an order that size?

Norman: Well ... er ... as you can see from our catalogue here, we normally offer 12% on orders of that kind.

Brown: Yeah ... yeah, I read that. But your neighbours down the hall there, they're willing to give me 15%.

91

Norman: Well, ha, of course, we'd ... er ... be delighted to do business with you, Mr Brown. And so I'd like to draw your attention to the latest laser-driven technology which the R75 contains.

Brown: Yes very interesting, but the discount *is* important.

Norman: Look, if you'd like to wait just for a few moments ... er ... I can get through to my head office and I'll inquire about any special arrangements which we might be able to make.

Brown: No, no, please don't bother about that just now. There's not that much of a hurry. I still have to report back to my board.

Norman: Ah yes, I understand that.

Brown: Look here's my card. It'll be quite enough if you just drop me a line about things like the discount in the course of the next two weeks.

Norman: Yes, of course. Yes, er ... very well Mr Brown. I'd be only too pleased to do all that for you. It's been ... er ... very pleasant talking to you.

Brown: Mmm mmm.

Norman: Oh, and here's my card as well.

[Time: 2 minutes]

B [cassette icon] Students listen to the recording again. They should then continue the summary which they find the most appropriate.

Reassemble the students in groups of four (each pair with another pair) to compare their summary and to discuss the reasons why they prefer one to another.

Allow time for feedback and queries.

4.9 Summarizing a message orally

This activity is concerned with the skill of taking an oral message and relaying it orally. Practice is given in taking notes on the telephone and summarizing them orally to another person.

Procedure

The instructions in the Student's Book are to be followed. The listening exercises are *divided up into two main parts* – B involves matching up sets of notes with particular recordings, while in D students are expected to take notes themselves.

A Students work in pairs and first look at the advice. Which do they find most useful? Which piece of advice do they find the *most* helpful? Why? Get them to compare their opinions with another pair. Draw attention to the fact that most companies have their own phone notepads such as are contained in the book. This simplifies the taking of telephone messages.

B Students work in pairs. They look at the notes *before* they hear the recording.

🔲 Play the recording, pausing briefly after each message. Students decide which message goes with which set of notes.

FIRST PART **Message 1**
Yes that's fine. Thank you very much. Goodbye ... That was the receptionist from the Station Hotel. She was just confirming the booking we made for the French visitor, M Piccoli, for tomorrow night and Thursday. Um ... a single room, with bath and WC for two nights, it was.

Message 2
Er ... there's a Mr Johansson, from Uppsala calling at the office tomorrow. He's really here to see the research people. But he wonders whether he can bring round some samples of the home interior paints his firm, Bicolor, are manufacturing. I told him you were free at about 11 o'clock, if that's all right. Um ... I'm supposed to ring back and say it's okay.

Message 3
A Mr Akombo called on long-distance from Lagos. They've still not received those components we sent. They weren't on the overnight flight from Stansted and he's getting a bit impatient. He said he's sending a telex with longer instructions. He wants you to contact him when it arrives.

Message 4
Oh, and Miss Courtney rang to say she'd arrived at Lisbon airport and had been met by the PA of Mario Doares of Industrias Conservas. They're going directly to the factory for a quick tour of the plant and then there'll be a talk with their managing director later on. She'll get straight through tomorrow on the preliminary results of the meeting. Oh, and she'd like someone to be available to advise in case there are any changes in the costings.

[Time: 1 minute 30 seconds]

C Students work in pairs and take it in turns using their notes to tell each other what the telephone messages were about. Be prepared to circulate around the room helping with queries and problems during this step.

D 🔲 Students listen to the second part of the recording. Play the second part of the recording, pausing briefly after each message. This time they take notes themselves and then compare their notes with a partner.

SECOND PART **Message 5**
Hello. This is Jeremy Tan. Er ... yes, that's spelled T-A-N. Yes, I'm from Oriental Graphics. Mmm. Yes, I'd like to leave a message for Mr Lacey. It's about your offset printers. Could he let me know the present price of the PL 590 lithographic press? No. No it's not priced in your latest catalogue. Yes. Perhaps he could call me back today, please. My number is 093 562 7035. That's right. Thank you very much. Bye.

Message 6
Good morning. Er ... my name's Mary Whitaker from Whitaker and Company. I'd like to leave a message for Mr Krefeld about his letter of the 5th of June. Um ... please will you tell him, we need further information before we can make a firm proposal. And would you ask him to call me back this afternoon at about four. Er ... as I have an appointment in town till about then. Thank you.

Message 7
Hallo! Er ... this is Jonathan Shelley calling from Offshore Products. Hallo. Yes, I'd like to leave a message for Jeremy Spencer. Yes, it's about the meeting tomorrow at 10 am. I'm afraid I won't be able to make it until later, now ... er. I suggest 12 noon instead. Yes, if it's possible could you ask him to call me later today before 5 pm. Yeah. And my number is 021 563 2427. That's right. Bye.

Message 8
Hallo. Er ... this is Mr Santini from Milan. I want to leave a message for Mrs Mac-

Pherson about her visit next week. We ... we couldn't get a room for her this time at the Hotel Excelsior. So we've booked a room for her at the Rafael. Um ... yes. She's stayed there before. But if it's inconvenient, would she mind ringing me as soon as possible? Oh, yes, she should have my number. Thank you. Goodbye.

[Time: 2 minutes 10 seconds]

Model notes

1

TELEPHONE NOTES

DATE .... TIME ....
MESSAGE FOR *Mr. Lacey* ....
....
FROM *Jeremy Tan from Oriental Graphics*
MESSAGE *about our offset printers*
Can you give present price PL 590
lithographic press not in latest
catalogue. Can you call back
today on 093 562 7035?
TAKEN BY ....

2

TELEPHONE NOTES

DATE .... TIME ....
MESSAGE FOR *Mr. Krefeld* ....
....
FROM *Mary Whitaker from Whitaker and Co.*
MESSAGE *re letter 5th of June - needs*
more information before making firm
proposal. Please call her back this
p.m. about 4. Not before, as out
of office
TAKEN BY ....

3

TELEPHONE NOTES

DATE .... TIME ....
MESSAGE FOR *Jeremy Spencer* ....
....
FROM *Jonathan Shelley from Offshore products*
MESSAGE *re 10 am meeting tomorrow -*
unable to be there at 10 - suggests 12
noon instead. Please call him later
today before 5p.m. Tel. No.
021 563 2427
TAKEN BY ....

4

TELEPHONE NOTES

DATE .... TIME ....
MESSAGE FOR *Mrs. MacPherson* ....
....
FROM *Mr. Santini from Milan* ....
MESSAGE *about her visit next week*
couldn't get a room at Hotel Excelsior.
Have booked at the Rafael - if
inconvenient please ring asap
Usual number
TAKEN BY ....

Allow time for feedback and queries.

4.10   Writing reports and summaries   *Vocabulary*

This exercise can be done by students working in pairs. It can be done at any stage during the unit if you have time available, or done as homework.

Answers:

1. transmit	6. topic
2. clarify	7. essentials
3. observe	8. submit
4. classify	9. cover
5. recipient	10. circular

Workbook

Other important vocabulary is introduced throughout this unit and in Workbook exercise 4.7.

4.11   Communication in business   *Discussion*

This section provides the opportunity to summarize many of the basic business skills which have been dealt with in the first four introductory units. Students work in groups of 4 or 5 for the two parts of the discussion.

The main purpose of this discussion from your point of view is to discover and agree on the emphasis you'll be placing in subsequent units. A class who agree, say, that letter writing is of little relevance to them will be asked to write telexes when there is an activity involving writing. A class who agree that making telephone calls is an essential skill they must develop will spend longer on the phone call role plays

(☎).

A   This follows up the point raised earlier in the unit about the difference between writing and telling (4.1), among other things.

B   When the groups have agreed on what are the most important things to remember, the discussion may be opened up for the class as a whole to pool its ideas on which forms of communication they ought to or would like to be able to perform in English.

Workbook

Contents for this unit:

4.1	A company report	Reading aloud 📼
4.2	A report	Writing
4.3	Passive	Grammar
4.4	Punctuation	
4.5	Summaries and note taking	Listening 📼
4.6	Summarizing telephone messages	Listening 📼
4.7	Vocabulary	

Background information: The place of work

There are many occasions on which you can be expected to talk about your firm. This may include actually showing someone physically around the place of work or premises. But it may more generally involve referring to the way in which the company is organized and run.

Firms are a very important part of the economy. They are responsible for producing goods and services. Businesses use materials and change them in some way to produce goods or a service. Businesses come in every shape and size. While the vast majority of the world's businesses are small, large firms often dominate the economy in some countries. Indeed, the income of the world's largest fifty industrial companies added together represents more than half the total output of the United States.

Large businesses differ very much from small ones in a wide variety of ways. In many countries there are both private firms and nationalized firms belonging to the government. A small private firm may have just one owner but a very large firm has thousands of shareholders.

In very large firms the owners have very little to do with the day-to-day running of the firm. This is left to the management. Very large companies may be organized into several large departments, or sometimes even divisions. The organizational structure of some companies is very hierarchical with the board of directors at the top and the various departmental heads reporting to them. Often the only time shareholders can influence the board is at yearly shareholders' meetings

Some firms may only produce one product or service. Others may produce many different products: in fact they may seem to be like a collection of 'businesses' inside one company. The bigger a business becomes the further it may expand geographically. Many large firms have manufacturing plants and trading locations in several different countries spread around the world. The physical surroundings of most modern places of work, especially offices, are becoming more and more similar. Although there may be differences from country to country, offices do not vary very widely. Office furniture tends to be similar – desks, chairs, filing cabinets, office equipment such as typewriters and, increasingly perhaps, personal computers or computer terminals on many desks.

Recently, firms have become more aware of how greatly the 'atmosphere' of the workplace can influence the effectiveness of their employees. Modern business offices may be more spacious and better lit and heated than in the

>>>→

past. But of course this is a feature that will vary from firm to firm and may be dependent on the size of the company and its corporate 'philosophy'. Some large businesses may have their employees working in large open-planned offices with air-conditioning and no walls between the departments. Others may emphasize the usefulness of letting their staff work in individual offices.

5 The place of work

In business there are many occasions on which you can be expected to talk about your place of work. This may include actually showing someone physically around the office or premises. But it may, more generally, involve referring to the way in which the company is organized. Furthermore, people in business may often be called upon to describe to outsiders or friends what their company actually does; they may even be expected to talk about what their company has done in the past and about the contemporary developments of a firm.

This unit also provides students with practice in acting within the company and work environment – in this connexion the increasing trend towards computerization in office work is also dealt with. At the same time the unit also presents opportunities to use the relevant language for talking about the place of work in general. A later unit (14) will concentrate more specifically on the relations between *people at work*.

5.1 Getting to know the place ...

The activity is straightforward.

A   This is a preparatory step before doing the listening activity. Students work in pairs and decide which points they hold to be important. If you have students both with and without work experience make sure, wherever possible, that pairs are formed in which there is one student with experience and one without. Then the inexperienced student can ask which points the experienced agrees with or not. After the pairs have decided which are the most important items to bear in mind, let them compare their list with another pair's. You may then ask the class as a whole to discuss which they consider the most important items to be.

B   Before you play the recording, students work in pairs and study the floor plan and also the items in the box. Any vocabulary items should be dealt with. Get the students to say where they think particular items are likely to go. You will probably need to play the recording a second time.

Mr Bronson: ... ah, well, that just about covers everything for the moment.

Margaret: Mr Bronson, you wanted to see me?

Mr Bronson: Oh ... Margaret, yeah, thanks for coming down. This is Michelle Duhamel ... er ... Margaret Brown.

Margaret: Hello Michelle.

Michelle: Pleased to meet you.

Mr Bronson: You'll be working with her.

Margaret: Ah.

Mr Bronson: Margaret, ah ... what I'd like you to do is to show Michelle around the offices, just so that she can get an idea where everything is. Is that OK?

Margaret: Of course. Er ... yes, I'll take her on a little tour, shall I?

Mr Bronson: Yeah, good idea, I'll see you later this afternoon, Michelle. Let's say ... 3 o'clock. OK? Bye bye now.

Margaret: All right Michelle, let's go out into the corridor.

Michelle: The trouble is I've noticed not all the doors have got names on them, so it's all a bit confusing.

Margaret: Well, I think the best thing is if we go back to Reception and then I'll take you round the offices on this floor.

Michelle: OK, that's a good idea ...

Margaret: ... well here we are ... er ... back at the main entrance. So let's go through Reception into the main corridor. OK?

Michelle: Hm hm.

Margaret: Right opposite us is the Post Room, you see?

Michelle: Yes.

Margaret: Then if we go up the corridor ... haha ... we come to Mr Gruber's office.

Michelle: Aha.

Margaret: He's the General Manager. His secretary is Mrs Santini and if you go through this door here on the left you have to go through her office before you get to Mr Gruber's. A ... and we just passed the Personnel Manager's office

on the right, that's where we started from.

Michelle: What was all that noise coming from the room between Reception and the Personnel Manager's secretary's office?

Margaret: Aha, yes. That's the Photocopying Room.

Michelle: Ah.

Margaret: It's not always as noisy as that – I think they must be using both of the big machines or something! Er ... and if we carry on a bit further ... er ... we pass the lifts. That's the way you'll get up to the top floor, where you'll be working. We'll go up there later, though ... um ... and the next door on the right is where the Systems Analysts are. And right ahead at the end of the corridor is where the data processing takes place.

Michelle: Aha.

Margaret: I don't think we have to go right to the end, but if you just look up the corridor you'll see two doors on the right and two on the left.

Michelle: Yes.

Margaret: OK? At the far end on the right is the Accounts Manager's office – you have to go through his secretary's office to find him. And the other door on the right is Book-keeping. And then on the far end on the left is the Stationery Store and that just leaves the Typing Pool here on our left – as you can hear!

Michelle: Er ... what's through the glass doors at the end?

Margaret: Ah, that's the Canteen. It's only open at lunchtime and in the evenings. We get our tea and coffee from machines – there's one in Reception and another one inside Data Processing on this floor. Well, I think that's about it on this floor, ha ... so ... um ... shall we go up in the lift?

Michelle: Er ... just one more thing, if we've got a moment.

Margaret: Yes, sure.

Michelle: Um ... where's the ladies?

Margaret: Oh, I'm sorry, yes of course. The toilets are right opposite the Photocopying Room. The ladies is right next to the Post Room, OK?

Michelle: Aha, fine.

Margaret: OK, here's the lift. Shall we go up to our floor?

[Time: 3 minutes]

This is the completed floor plan.

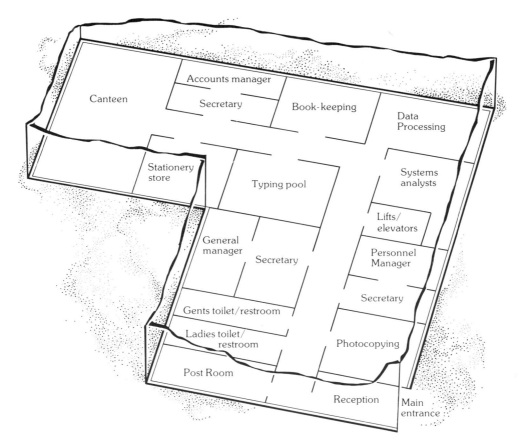

Extra activity

These are additional questions you can ask the students to answer. Write them up on the board perhaps before a third playing of the recording:

1. What is the name of the new employee? (Michelle Duhamel)
2. What is the name of the Personnel Manager? (Mr Bronson)
3. What time does the Personnel Manager say he'll see the new employee at? (3 o'clock)
4. Who is the General Manager? (Mr Gruber)
5. What is the name of his secretary? (Mrs Santini)
6. Where will the new employee be working? (on the top floor)

7. When is the canteen open? (at lunchtime and in the evenings)
8. Where are the coffee machines? (in Reception and inside Data Processing)

Extra discussion ideas

Students with work experience can be asked by the others in the class about their first day at work. What is the most pleasant memory they have? What unpleasant memories do they have? What sort of office did they work in? A small or big one? What advice would they give to people on their first day in the firm?

Allow time for feedback and queries.

5.2 Agreeing and disagreeing   *Functions*

This exercise is fairly straightforward. The instructions in the Student's Book can be followed.

Presentation

If possible get the students to look at the presentation section *before* they come to class. This will give them a better chance of remembering the expressions and will lead to a more informed and interesting discussion of the topic in class.

The examples ('That's exactly what I think', etc) are recorded, so that students can hear as well as see the sentences that are used.

Exercises and activities

Begin by getting the class to look at the examples in speech balloons. Discuss the points made in the text. Do a quick repetition exercise. Ask the class to suggest how the incomplete sentences might continue. Draw attention to the fact that some of the sentences given are more formal than others. Some will be used between friends and acquaintances, while others are typical for people you know less well or strangers.

A   Play the recording. Pause the recording after the first conversation to give students time to think and write down their answers together. Play each conversation twice. Students work in pairs and decide what the topic of the conversation is. They also mark the expressions which are used.

First conversation

First man: It's quite clear that our office is much too overcrowded, here in the city centre. We ought to move some of the departments out of town.

First woman: You know, that's exactly what I think. What's more, why don't we move the whole office and save rent at the same time?

Second man: I can see what you mean, but think of the problem of transport. How would our staff get to work?

Second woman: Now, that's just what I was thinking. Not everyone has a car you know.

Third woman: Well, I don't think it's a good idea either. Our customers have got used to us being here. If we move we'll lose business.

Third man: Well, my opinion, for what it's worth, is that moving some of our staff out of the city would mean more space for the others.

Fourth woman: Mm, that's a good point and we would also keep our office in the city for our customers.

Fourth man: I agree entirely. Why don't we stay where we are?

[Time: 45 seconds]

Second conversation

First man: I believe we should have a firm in to do the office cleaning, it would be much cheaper than paying our own staff.

First woman: Yes, I'm all in favour of that. What's more we could get a firm in to do the gardening as well. We could save a lot of money that way.

Second man: Perhaps, but don't you think the work would get done better by our own staff?

Second woman: That's quite right, I couldn't agree more with that. Outside workers never have the same contact with the company and don't care as much.

Third man: I see things rather differently myself. Our own cleaners and gardeners simply don't work hard enough because they know they can't be sacked.

Fourth man: I can't say I share your view on that. People who work for sub-contractors are surely the last people you can expect to do a good job.

Third woman: I couldn't agree more. Sub-contracting such work is no cheaper in the long run than paying our own workers to do a good job in the first place.

[Time: 50 seconds]

Make sure any queries are cleared up before students begin exercise B – though it is to be expected that doing the exercise will give rise to further questions.

B Students work in pairs and follow the instructions in the Student's Book. Let each pair present one of the dialogues they have written if there is enough time. Alternatively, this step can be given as homework.

C In this activity students work in groups of three or four. The instructions in the Student's Book are to be followed. Then the groups should split up and ask the members of another group what they can agree on or have agreed on. Selected groups can be asked to say if they have agreed on how management should act. Let the class as a whole comment and say whether they agree.

Workbook

Exercise 5.2 in the Workbook provides further practice on this function.

5.3 Computers   *Vocabulary*

This exercise can be done by students working in pairs. It can be done at any stage during the unit if you have time available, or done as homework.

Answers:

1. keyboard
2. disk drive
3. monitor
4. display
5. menu
6. printer
7. disk
8. mouse
9. microprocessor
10. software
11. modem
12. hard disk
13. ROM (Read Only Memory)
14. operating system
15. RAM (Random Access Memory)

Workbook

Other important vocabulary is introduced throughout this unit and in Workbook exercise 5.4.

5.4 Explaining the company organization

This activity focuses on how the divisions and departments of a company are related to one another, and the use of job titles within the company.

Procedure

A Students work in pairs and look at the 'organogram' of Biopaints plc. Encourage them to try and guess what the missing work titles might be.

B [cassette] Play the recording the first time. This listening exercise involves listening for detail. Give everyone time to compare their answers and then play the recording a second time. Students then change partners and compare their answers.

Presenter: Today we are talking to John Knox about the structure of Biopaints plc. John's the General Manager of the Bath factory. John. Do you think you could tell us something about the way Biopaints is actually organized?

John Knox: Er ... yes, certainly. Um ... we employ about two thousand people in all in two different locations. Most people work here at our headquarters plant. And this is where we have the administrative departments, of course.

Presenter: Perhaps you could say something about the departmental structure?

John Knox: Yes, certainly. Um ... now ... er ... first of all we've got four main divisions. There's the production division which, as the name suggests, is responsible for production operations. And as you know we've got two factories, er ... one here in Bath, UK, and the other in Lille, France. Er ... Philippe Rochard is the other General Manager, there in Lille.

Presenter: And you're completely independent of each other, is that right?

John Knox: Oh, yes, yes. Our ... our two plants are fairly independent. I mean, I ... I am responsible to Bill Williamson, the Production Manager, and we have to cooperate closely with ... with Helga Meier, the Marketing Manager.

Presenter: Mm.

John Knox: But otherwise, as far as day to day running is concerned, we're pretty much left alone to get on with the job. Haha. Oh, and I forgot to mention the most important division of all, some people say. That's finance. Er ... the Financial Director is Fred Rasmussen. He's a very important man. And his task is to make sure the money-side of things is OK. The accountant and such people, they report to him directly.

Presenter: Is that all? Um.

John Knox: Oh no, no, no, no. There's personnel.

Presenter: Yes.

John Knox: That's quite separate. David Hopper is Personnel Manager. And the Training Manager reports to him of course.

Presenter: But I imagine that a firm such as your own has smaller departments within the divisions?

John Knox: Oh yes, that's the case, yes. I mentioned that we are fairly independent.

Presenter: What about Research and Development? Isn't that a separate department?

John Knox: Well, in terms of the laboratories, there are ... there are two er ... one at each production plant. But it's a department in the production division and it has a single head. And that's Piet van De Geer.

Presenter: Are there any other features worth mentioning?

John Knox: Well, if we take our division, which of course I know best, we've got several other departments, which all report, as I said, to Bill Williamson and which I am responsible for on this site. Er ... now there's the ... er ... planning department. Ray Wood is in charge of that. And a purchasing department er ... they buy in the materials for production.

Presenter: Yes, and what about the board of directors and the chairman?

John Knox: Yes, well they're at the top, aren't they, of course? I ... I mean, a couple of the executives are directors themselves. The Managing Director, of course, that's Ernest Roberts and then there's ...

[Time: 2 minutes 30 seconds]

This is the completed chart.

WHO'S WHO AND WHAT'S WHAT AT BIOPAINTS plc

BIOPAINTS plc

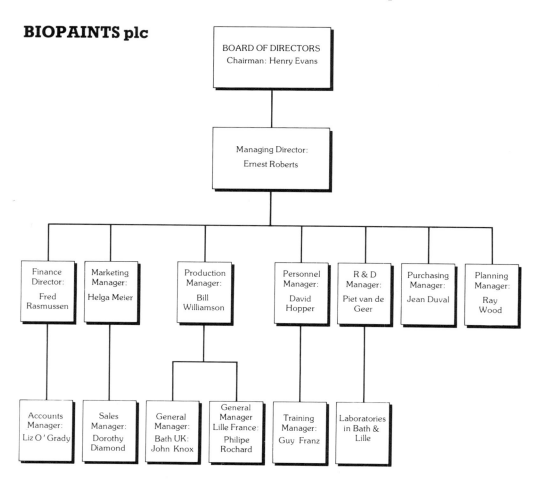

C Students work in pairs and follow the instructions in the Student's Book. Encourage the students to give reasons for their answers.

Suggested answers:
The Public Relations Manager reports to the Marketing Manager; the Advertising Manager too. The Accounts Manager reports to the Financial Director, while the Works Manager probably reports to the Production Manager.

Draw attention to the fact that American job titles differ from British ones. These are rough equivalents:

$	£
President	Chairman
Chief Executive Officer*	Managing Director
Vice President	Director
Financial Controller*	Accountant
Director*	Manager
(e.g. Personnel Director*	Personnel Manager)

* Many British firms now use these titles

D   Students should work in pairs. Student A looks at File 19, student B at File 26. They are expected to ask each other questions and complete an information gap exercise based on the organisational diagram of a fictitious company. This is the complete diagram for the activity.

EUROCHEMCO ORGANOGRAM

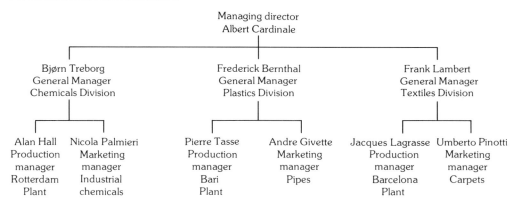

5.5   What the company does . . .

Follow the instructions in the Student's Book for this exercise.

Procedure

A   Students work in pairs. Let students compare their answers in the class as a whole.

Answers:
Top line: vehicle manufacturing, catering, engineering, transport,

Second line: banking, microelectronics, insurance, chemicals.
Bottom line: retailing, aerospace, shipping.

B   Students work in pairs. Despite the fact that there is a lot of
vocabulary which may be unfamiliar, impress upon everyone that it is
not needed in order to do the exercise. The task is reading for *gist*.

C   Students work in pairs. This exercise practises reading for information or scanning.

Suggested answers:
last five years we have invested in research and development, property
   and plant
13 percent of sales income
13.8 percent *of sales*
Return on total assets was 14.5 percent
30 *other countries*
solvency (equity/asset ratio) was 50 percent
SF340 *airliner*
SAAB began manufacturing vehicles in the 1890's and aircraft in the
   1930's
1985 is the year to which the results refer
47 000 *people*
profits 2.8 billions
capital expenditure amounted to 4.4 billions
the Group sales were SEK 32 billions

D   Students work in pairs for this writing activity. When they have
finished, they compare their letter with another pair's and exchange
suggestions for improvements.

[YOU MAY PHOTOCOPY THIS DOCUMENT]

TIMSON TRANSPORTATION SERVICES
P.O. Box 5321, Milton Keynes MK5 7OP United Kingdom

                                                    10 December 19xx

        Saab-Scania AB
        Corporate Communications
        and Public Affairs
        S-581 88 Linköping
        Sweden

        Dear Sir or Madam
            Our company is currently investigating the possibility of
        seeking a partner in the area of transportation research.

Your advertisement in the Economist recently was brought to
our attention by a customer. Accordingly we are writing to ask
if you could send us further information of your company's
activities.
      We thank you in advance for your trouble.

Yours faithfully,

Les Dewson

Les Dewson
(HGV Traffic Manager)

© Cambridge University Press 1989

E   Students work in small groups. They list at least three advantages
and three disadvantages they can see in working for a company like the
one described in the advertisement. After they have completed their
lists they compare them with another group's.

Allow time for queries and problems to be raised if there are any.

5.6   Company news

This is a listening for gist and detail exercise. The headline serves as an
'advance organizer'.

Procedure

A   Students should work together in pairs and follow the instructions
in the Student's Book. The object of this step is to prepare the ground
for the listening exercise.

B   [cassette icon] Play the recording once. Students should work in pairs and
compare their responses to the way the press conference turns out.

C   Play the recording once more. But remind students to look at the
extracts in the Student's Book, before you do so. Students should work
in pairs. You will need to play the recording at least twice. It may also
help to stop the recording about half way through to allow the
students to match up the written statements with what they hear. It is
important that the students read through the statements *before* beginning this part of the exercise. Note that the printed statements are
typically 'written' English.

Male journalist: Is it true Mr Northfield that Flaxco intends to close down even more of its European plants?

Northfield: I'm not sure what you are getting at. How do you come to ask such a question? Who's mentioned any closures of plants in the first place?

Male journalist: Well, put it another way then: Are European operations going to be reduced along the lines of recent years? I ... I mean, it is true that Flaxco has taken over several companies abroad, particularly in the USA and ... and has even expanded its workforce there.

Northfield: There are a number of developments which you appear to be confusing, if I may say so.

Journalist: A large number of jobs have been lost, though, at your European plants?

Northfield: Look let me try and put things into perspective for you. I'll give you some facts first of all. Our production resources have been concentrated steadily over the past few years. So, now we have focused our manufacturing facilities in Europe, but not only here.

Journalist: After closing down two plants in Antwerp and Leeds.

Northfield: Please, let me continue. We have limited our production to certain medicines which are prescribed in large quantities. At the same time, and this appears to be something you've neglected to mention, we have been expanding our marketing activities abroad.

Female journalist: Have you any plans to increase the workforce here in Europe, Mr Northfield? I'm sure many people would be keen to hear what you have to say on the subject.

Northfield: I ... I really must insist once more that it's impossible to view the performance of the company, and I'd like to stress the very successful performance of the group over the past few years, solely from the point of view of Europe. Indeed it would be stupid to do so. I mean, we have nearly two thirds of our workforce in subsidiaries and associated companies overseas.

Female journalist: Is it true that it wasn't always like that?

Northfield: As I was saying. We have 60% of our employees involved outside of Europe. Now that in itself gives you an indication of how international we have become.

Female journalist: Could I ask you another question concerning the R & D expenditure of the group? Is this going to be made in Europe or around the world?

Northfield: Again, I can only repeat what I've been saying: we are an international operation and we have a research facility in Italy, which as you know, is very important. Furthermore we have just started a new research unit in the USA, which is inevitable given the large size of our operations in that country and the expansion of our market share there in the past 6 or 7 years.

[Time: 2 minutes 50 seconds]

D Students do this step in pairs.

Suggested answers:

Some of the points are perhaps uncertain, but arguably the extracts marked 'Yes' are mentioned, if indirectly:

... This year's results are the latest in an unbroken sequence of rapid growth over the last six years. (NO)

... The successful penetration of major international markets has been the driving force behind the recent growth of the group. (YES?)

... The group has concentrated its resources and effort on medicines of the highest quality. (NO)

... Our concentration on prescription medicines has enabled us to devote resources and management effort to the development of our main business. It has led to very large increases in profits and earnings. (YES?)
... our biggest research effort, by far, is in the UK ... (NO)
... but we are also expanding our basic research activity in Italy as well as in the USA. (YES)
... our group sells its products in one hundred and fifty countries through a network of seventy subsidiary and associated companies. (NO)

Allow time at the end for queries and problems to be raised. Ask the students what they have learned from this activity.

5.7 Referring to the past   *Grammar*

Most students have difficulties in using the various tenses which can refer to past time in English. In particular, knowing when to use different tense forms is something that requires practice.

This section gives a concise treatment of the major points to be considered. The examples concentrate on the broad outlines. Further work may be necessary using the Workbook and exercises from other sources (*Use of English* Units 3, 4 and 5 are recommended).

Presentation

If possible students should read the presentation step through before the lesson. Otherwise, this can be done in pairs.

The examples ('How long have you been working for the company?' etc) are recorded, so that students can hear as well as see the sentences that are used.

These are some of the further points you may wish to raise or emphasize concerning the various tenses used to refer to the past in English.

The present perfect simple and progressive are used typically with adverbs such as: *just, yet, already, for many weeks, since last year, all this month, so far, lately, recently.*
Further examples:
   British Rolling Mills have been producing bright steel bars for
      Britain's engineering industries for over 50 years.
   My colleague has been working in the office since 1978.
   I've used/I've been using a computer for a long time.
   She's been trying to get through to head office all morning.
   You have been on that phone since 10.15....

The past simple is used to refer to actions and events happening in the

111

past. Typical adverbs which accompany the past, by contrast with the present perfect are:

last night, yesterday, last week, in 1967.

The past progressive refers to an action or event that was already happening at a point or moment in the past, or to temporary actions and situations.

I was talking to Mr Green when the phone rang.
I was working for Acme Corp. in 1980.

Note also the possible confusion which can arise with the present perfect. You may need to draw attention to the difference between different pairs of tenses. Firstly, present perfect v past simple, e.g.

Our firm *has supplied* this kind of transformer before. We *supplied* one to Elba Electrics last year.

And present v. present perfect, e.g.

They're *now working* on the new contract. In fact, they*'ve been* busy for several months.

Exercises and activity

Leave time after each exercise for discussion and questions. If time is short exercise A could be set as homework, but it still needs to be discussed in class to clear up possible misunderstandings. Make sure any queries are cleared up before students start exercise B and C in pairs – though it is to be expected that doing the exercises will give rise to further questions.

A Students work in pairs and fill in the gaps with a suitable verb form.

Suggested answers:
1. Our company has been using/has used/has had computers in its offices now for a long time.
2. We're very busy today. The phone has hardly stopped ringing since I arrived in the office this morning.
3. Have you visited Madrid before? Yes, I went there last year on business.
4. In 1986 our enterprise opened a factory in South America.
5. I started working here when I left school.
6. 'Is your secretary still looking for the file?' 'Yes, she has been searching for it for the past twenty minutes.'
7. I'm sorry to keep you waiting. I was making a phone call to Paris.
8. While you were having lunch, Mr Casagrande phoned.
9. We sent/posted the letter to them a week ago, but we haven't received a reply yet.
10. His firm sent him to their New York office and he's been working there ever since.

B   Students work in groups of three or four and follow the instructions in the Student's Book.

C   Students first work in pairs with someone from a different group. Then encourage them to circulate around the class as outlined in the Student's Book.

Allow time for the class to raise any questions concerning problems or difficulties they may have had doing the activities and exercises.

Workbook

Workbook exercise 5.5 provides further work on using the past forms in English.

5.8   A firm's history

Procedure

Students work in pairs for steps A to E. It may be helpful to vary the pairs; E in particular needs to be done with a fresh partner to provide variety.

A   After students have agreed on a list in pairs, they compare another pair's list. The class as a whole can also compare their lists.

B   Students work in pairs. This is a reading for gist exercise.

C   Students work in pairs to complete the information missing on the table.

Suggested answers:

Dates	What happened?	Who did what?
1847	Siemens was founded	Werner Siemens & Johann Georg Halske
1849	Company was established near Sprendlingen	Johann Philipp Holzmann
1866	Invention of dynamo machine	Werner Siemens
1882	First large foreign order completed	Holzmann Co
1917	Philipp Holzmann Aktien-Gesellschaft founded	does not say
1950	Foreign business restarted	Holzmann Co
1983/4	Recorded annual sales of DM 46 billion	Siemens Co

113

D   Students again work in pairs and complete the second table.

Suggested answers:

Company	Siemens	Philipp Holzmann
Locations of company activities	in 25 countries	Middle East, Africa, USA
Activities of both companies up to 1940s	power engineering	built railways, power stations, large buildings, bridges
Recent activities of the companies	an innovative leader in electrical and electronic market	one of largest concerns, has an associated American company

E   Students work in pairs. Student A looks at File 23, student B at 40. Between them they complete the information describing the Lucky–Goldstar company (a huge Korean conglomerate).

5.9   Company world   *Vocabulary*

This exercise can be done by students working in pairs. It can be done at any stage during the unit if you have time available, or done as homework.

Answers:

1. involved
2. launched
3. corporate
4. administrate
5. prosper
6. commerce
7. merged
8. phases
9. taken over
10. white-collar

Workbook

Other important vocabulary is introduced throughout this unit and in Workbook exercise 5.4.

5.10 The new office

This discussion allows the class the opportunity to consider the advantages and disadvantages of computers at work.

Procedure

A Students follow the instructions in the Student's Book. Working in pairs they list what they see as the advantages and disadvantages of using computers in offices. Let them compare their list with another pair. The class as a whole can be asked to compare their lists, if there is time.

B This is a listening for gist and matching exercise. Before they hear the recording students look at the summaries in the Student's Book.

Students work in pairs. Play the recording through twice pausing between each extract to give students time to find their answers.

Presenter: We asked a number of people who work in offices to tell us what they thought about the introduction of new technology into office life: computer terminals, visual display units and so on. First, Anita, a secretary.

Secretary: You're being pushed into a different world – a keyboard world. It takes away the role of secretary. It makes your role very, very different. Um ... you ... you find yourself thinking – what are these machines doing to me? At the end of the day you feel, well ... when you've switched off the machine, that you've unplugged yourself...

Presenter: And now Peter, an office administrator.

Office administrator: Well all our bosses have terminals on their desks, but they don't use them. I'm not sure why. Perhaps it's just as well because the system's overloaded enough as it is. If ... if too many try to use it, it just breaks down.

Presenter: Next we hear from Roberta, an office design consultant.

Office design consultant: We interviewed more than 300 people from different organizations attempting to automate their offices. There were few. I mean, less than 5%, success stories. Senior management tend to think that if they install a computer system in their offices and give the staff a couple of days' training, amazing new levels of efficiency will be attained. Well, of course they're wrong. New technology means that jobs have to be rethought, redesigned ... and unless they're redesigned properly, then things will get worse, not better.

Presenter: On now to Andrew. He is a bank clerk.

Bank clerk: My old job was ordering up bits of stationery, such as money bags, you know. I used to write the orders on special order forms by hand and ... and specify the number of items required. But now I do this at the computer terminal. I have to keyboard in numbers for ... for everything. Every individual item has a code and also a figure for the number of items I order. You can imagine the kinds of mistakes that you can make if you are on the terminal all day. You can order 4000 packets of item 2, instead of 2 packets of item 4000! And it's so boring, typing in numbers all day long.

Presenter: Our next interviewee is Edward,

115

who works as a personal assistant for a large international company.

Personal assistant: Computerization is very much the unknown. Er ... we've got these computer experts and ... er ... system analysts who are setting up the computer and linking it to all our work stations. But ... er ... oh, a lot of the work they do, nobody knows about. I've no idea what they are doing a lot of it for. I don't know where it's all leading to.

Presenter: And now we hear from a typist. This is Monica.

Typist: Um ... as for word processing. Well all the adverts say how much easier it makes your life and everything. But it has made my life much more difficult. When they're dictating, they can say any-thing they didn't like. It doesn't matter if they don't like it because they can just knock it out later. I'm the one who's left with twice as much work. If they've got something urgent they need doing, and you've been on the machine for three hours, they don't say: 'Well, can you do it?' or 'Do you want a rest?' They say 'Do it'.

Presenter: And finally we hear from William a clerk with a well-known London shipping company.

Clerk: It's an awful thought. But if VDUs carry on growing as quickly as they are, then office life as I knew it when I left school, won't exist. Everyone'll be a VDU operator.

[Time: 3 minutes 40 seconds]

Answers:
1. Without organizing office jobs differently, introducing computers does not help much.   **Roberta**
2. Computers create more work.   **Monica**
3. Computers reduce everything to numbers.   **Andrew**
4. People begin to feel like machines.   **Anita**
5. Future office work will be unrecognizable.   **William**
6. Computer systems do not always function.   **Peter**
7. The purpose of computers is not always clear.   **Edward**

C   Students work in pairs.

D   Groups of three or four are formed for this step. Ask the groups to compare their results.

E   Students work in groups of three or four for this activity. Let them show their 'perfect office' to another group for their comments.

Extra discussion ideas

Which things would you change in your office if you had the choice and the personnel manager asked you?

Which jobs would you prefer to do yourself without any help from machines?

Which jobs would you be glad to leave to a machine to do?

How do you think working life will be different in, say, ten years' time?

Workbook

Contents for this unit:

5.1 Prepositions – 1
5.2 Agreeing and disagreeing   Functions listening
5.3 Prefixes   Word-building
5.4 Vocabulary
5.5 Referring to the past   Grammar
5.6 Asking for information on a company Letter writing
5.7 Telework   Listening

Background information: Import and export

An import/export transaction usually requires a lot of complicated documentation. Many different arrangements have to be made and this can be difficult when one firm is dealing with another on the other side of the world.
Between countries within the European Community, trade is simpler and many firms pay for goods by cheque and use their own transport to deliver goods across frontiers. From 1992, no special customs documentation will be required for trade between firms in different parts of the EEC.

Many **specialists** may be involved, including:

1. A shipping agent and/or freight forwarder (forwarding agent) will take responsibility for the documentation and arrange for the goods to be shipped by air, sea, rail or road. These services may be carried out by the supplier's own export department, if they have the expertise.
2. Airlines, shipping lines, railway companies or haulage contractors will actually transport the goods.
3. Both the importer's and exporter's banks will be involved in arranging payments if a letter of credit or bill of exchange is used.
4. Customs and Excise officers may need to examine the goods, check import or export licences and charge duty and/or VAT.
5. A Chamber of Commerce may need to issue a Certificate of Origin, if this is required by the importer's country.
6. An insurance company to insure goods in transit.
7. A lawyer if a special contract has to be drawn up.

Many different **documents** may be needed, including:
- Bill of lading
- Sea Waybill
- Shipping Note
- Dangerous Goods Note
- Air Waybill
- Certificate of Insurance
- Single Administrative Document (SAD), used within the EEC
- CMR International Road Consignment Note
- EUR Movement Certificate, used within the EEC.

Many of these documents can be replaced with computerized procedures. Standard 'aligned' export documentation is often used, where the required information is entered on a master document and then photocopied to produce all the required documents.

Many import or export deals are arranged through an exporter's **agent** or

118

distributor abroad – in this case the importer buys from a company in his own country and this company imports the goods. Alternatively, the deal may be arranged through an importer's **buying agents** or a **buying house** acting for the importer, or through an **export house** based in the exporter's country. In these cases the exporter sells directly to a company in his own country, who will then export the goods.

Prices for exports may be quoted in the buyer's currency, the seller's currency or in a third 'hard' currency (e.g. US dollars, sterling or Swiss francs). The price quoted always indicates the **terms of delivery**, for example:

- 'ex-works' – the buyer pays for and arranges all transportation and insurance
- CIF: 'cost, insurance and freight' – the price includes all transportation to a named port or airport in the buyer's country
- DDP, 'delivered duty-paid' – the price includes all the transportation and insurance in transit right up to the buyer's premises

The terms of delivery that are most common depend on the kinds of goods being traded and the countries between which the trade is taking place.

Vocabulary exercise 6.3 deals with these abbreviations, known as Incoterms.

Methods of payment may be on a 'cash with order' basis (or cash deposit with order), on open account (as in most domestic trade, where the buyer pays the supplier soon after receiving the goods), by irrevocable letter of credit or by bill of exchange. Exporters and importers often prefer the security of payment by confirmed irrevocable letter of credit when dealing with unknown firms in distant countries. (Unit 7 provides more information about methods of payment.)

In choosing a firm to **supply** you with materials for your production process, various criteria are applied – and the lowest price is not necessarily the most important one of these. For more information about this, look at Unit 8.

For further background information, we recommend the illustrated booklets issued free of charge by international banks for the benefit of exporters and importers. For example, *Services for Exporters* and *Services for Importers* published by Midland Bank International, are particularly useful and attractive.

6 Import and export

This unit deals with some standard situations connected with importing and exporting goods: 'making and answering enquiries', 'making and accepting offers' and 'placing, acknowledging and filling orders'.

The functions of getting and giving information and grammatical rules involved in referring to future time are also covered.

In real life there would sometimes be complications and face-to-face negotiation might take place on prices, terms of delivery, etc. In this unit we just deal with the basics and with dealing with overseas customers on the phone and by telex or letter. More advanced or experienced students might like to spend longer on the finer points.

Solving problems connected with payment for goods is dealt with in Unit 7, solving problems connected with delivery and after-sales will be dealt with in Unit 8.

6.1 Getting and giving information   *Functions*

A This step looks at the importance of creating a good impression.

1. Begin by playing the first version of the conversation. Ask students to comment on the impression both speakers give. Hopefully, members of the class will identify the speakers' tone as hostile, aggressive and impatient – they're hating every minute of the conversation.
2. Play the second version of the conversation. This time the speakers are friendly and helpful to each other – they're enjoying talking to each other.
3. Now play the second version again and ask the class to identify how each speaker makes himself sound 'nice'. It's a combination of their tone of voice, the way they hesitate (putting *Er . . .* before a request for information) and the polite forms they use (saying *Could you tell me when . . . ?* instead of just *When . . . ?*). These polite forms are <u>underlined</u> in the transcript below, and will be focused on in B.

First Version:
Rusconi: Rusconi.
Garcia: Hello, this is Al Garcia.
Rusconi: At last! When can we expect the next consignment in our warehouse?
Garcia: Late Thursday or early Friday, depends on the traffic and the

weather. When will you accept deliveries?

Rusconi: Up to 4 pm and from 7.30 am. Er ... whose trucks are delivering the goods?

Garcia: Two of ours, and the others are on hire from Alpha Transport.

Rusconi: How do you spell Alpha?

Garcia: A-L-P-H-A

Rusconi: How many trucks will be coming?

Garcia: Five.

Rusconi: Will they arrive all on the same day?

Garcia: Two will set off half a day early, so they should arrive Thursday. The other three will arrive towards midday Friday. How long will it take to unload each truck?

Rusconi: About an hour. We can't unload more than two at a time, you know.

Garcia: I want to know what happens if one truck arrives late. Can you unload it on Saturday?

Rusconi: I don't know. Our warehouse manager would know.

Garcia: What's his name?

Rusconi: Mr Ferrari.

Garcia: What's his number?

Rusconi: 345 9800 extension 71.

Second Version:

Rusconi: Jupiter Products. Tony Rusconi speaking.

Garcia: Hello, this is Al Garcia.

Rusconi: Hello, Mr Garcia. How are you?

Garcia: Fine, thanks, I'm phoning about our delivery next week.

Rusconi: Ah yes, good. I was just about to call you. Er ... could you tell me when can we expect the consignment to arrive in our warehouse?

Garcia: Yes, as far as I know, the trucks should arrive late Thursday or early Friday, it depends on traffic and weather. Er ... what time will you accept deliveries?

Rusconi: The latest time we can start unloading is 4 pm, but ... but we can start as early as 7.30 am. Er ... could you tell me whose trucks are delivering the goods?

Garcia: Yes, certainly. Two of them will be ours, and the others are on hire from Alpha Transport.

Rusconi: Let me just make a note of that. Er ... can you tell me how you spell Alpha?

Garcia: Yes, of course. It's A-L-P-H-A.

Rusconi: Fine. A ... and I'd also like to know how many trucks will be coming.

Garcia: Ah ... there will be five altogether.

Rusconi: Can you tell me if they will arrive on the same day?

Garcia: I'm not entirely sure, but ... er ... as two will be setting off half a day early, they should arrive Thursday. Er ... the other three will arrive towards midday Friday. Could you let me know how long it will take to unload each truck?

Rusconi: Yes, er ... each truck will take about an hour. Er ... I think you should know that we can't unload more than two trucks at a time.

Garcia: I see, well, thanks for letting me know that. Er ... I wonder if you can tell me what'll happen if one of the trucks arrives later and can't be unloaded on Friday? Do you know if it can be unloaded on Saturday?

Rusconi: I'm afraid I don't know, it might have to wait till Monday. Er ... you'd have to ask our warehouse manager about that.

Garcia: Could you just remind me what his name is again?

Rusconi: Yes, of course. He's ... er ... Mr Ferrari.

Garcia: Ah, and ... er ... can y ... can you tell me his number?

Garcia: Yes, it's 345 9800 extension 71.

Garcia: Good. Thank you very much. It's ... it's nice to talk to you. Goodbye.

Rusconi: Bye now, Mr Garcia.

[Time: 2 minutes 45 seconds]

B   The examples in speech balloons aren't recorded. The second version of the conversation above can be played again to illustrate how the exponents can be used in context. Students should study the useful expressions, preferably at home before the lesson. Answer any queries that may be raised.

Perhaps explain the purpose of 'probing questions', which are used to find out more detailed information and explain how questions can be fielded and how we can hedge.

C   You may need to circulate round the class, helping less imaginative students to think of more information to note down. When everyone has done this, remind them that they should make an effort to avoid the easiest question forms and maybe ban the use of direct Wh– questions altogether for the duration of this activity.

D   Student A looks at File 17, B looks at 42. Each has a partially illegible price list. Between them they can work out all the missing information, by asking each other questions.

Extra activity

Students ask you for the same information they got from their partners in C above. While answering you could demonstrate some hedging and delaying techniques (repeating the question, complimenting the questioner, only partly answering, etc) so that other members of the class feel constrained to ask you supplementary probing questions.

Workbook

There is further work, including recorded exercises, on these functions in 6.1 and 6.2.

6.2   Making enquiries

This is an integrated activity, where students have a series of interconnected tasks to perform. As they follow the steps in the activity, students develop their knowledge of the company and product. They'll be using a wide range of language skills.

Procedure

Begin by making sure everyone has read the company description and is aware of the role they'll be playing. Each step is clearly explained in the Student's Book, so you should refer everyone to the instructions

when making sure they all know what to do at each stage in the
activity. You may need to guide them through the steps and perhaps
make sure they don't spend too long on each step.

Throughout the integrated activity, students will be working in pairs
(with one group of three, if you have an odd number in the class).
Larger groups can be formed for the discussion in step H.

A [cassette] Once everyone has read the description of the firm, play the
recording of the phone call. Ask everyone to imagine they've just come
into Mr North's office and he's on the phone – they are 'Mr North's
assistants'. Students may need to hear the recording twice. Perhaps ask
them to guess what 'Fritz' is saying to Mr North during the call.

Mr North: ... Oh, yeah, we had a really
good time up the mountain. Yeah, nice of
you to take us up, nice of you. Er ... I
know what I wanted to ask you: have
you had any dealings with Arcolite? ...
Uhuh, oh, that can't be true. Arcolite
Batteries? ... Yeah, but they've been
doing real well ... Well, if you got this
from him, I guess ... er ... I guess there
must be some truth in it ... Yeah, we ...

we kind of depend on them, they've been
supplying us for ... for quite a long time
now ... No, they're our ... er ... sole
suppliers. Hmm. Well, thanks for the tip.
I'll ... I'll get my new assistants to
investigate ... Sure. Nice talking to you.
Goodbye, Fritz.

[Time: 40 seconds]

Then everyone reads the newspaper article before deciding what to tell
Mr North when he returns to the office.

B The letter is very friendly and informal, as befits a letter from one
chum to another. A letter to other companies would need to be more
serious and formal, though it would contain exactly the same information.

C While everyone is drafting their letter, go round offering advice
and suggesting corrections or improvements. Check spelling and punctuation.

D Now the completed drafts are passed to the pair on the left, and
comments are made. There is a model version of the letter on page 125,
which you may photocopy for your students if you think this will be
helpful.

E [phone] In this role play, Student A has to change role and become
Jim Dale. The role information is in File 96. During the course of the
conversation, we discover that Ramco can supply Broadway with
Hercules batteries in 4 weeks at 10% less than Arcolite's price.

At the end of the role play, both students step back into their
original roles.

F The letter from Artemis describes another suitable battery.

G Now the pairs should discuss the offers of Rex, Ramco and Artemis and decide what action to take. Should Mr North's old chum be favoured with sole supplier status? If so, what advantages and disadvantages might there be?

H For this discussion the pairs can be arranged as groups of four or five – or this can be done a little later, after the pairs have spent some minutes considering the question.

Here are some points that may be made in the discussion. If possible, make sure each group has one member with business experience. With a less knowledgeable class, these points could be written on the board or OHP and then arranged in order of importance by each group in the discussion:

CONSIDERATIONS IN CHOOSING A SUPPLIER:
  price
  need to import?
  ability to deliver on time
  after-sales service
  technical support services
  credit (how long before he wants to be paid)
  quality of goods
  financial health
  ability to meet urgent orders
  friendship

Extra discussion ideas

What are the advantages of having a sole supplier?
What are the advantages of having many suppliers?

ONE SUPPLIER: better service (price, credit, etc); maybe better price, good relationship → help in crisis; easier for production to assemble identical components
SEVERAL SUPPLIERS: deliveries more secure from strikes or bankruptcy; may get better price by shopping around, more competitive, less complacent

See also the Background Information for Unit 8 on page 160.

[YOU MAY PHOTOCOPY THIS DOCUMENT]

BROADWAY Autos

XXX Xxxxxxx Xxxxx, 62008 Xxxxxxxx, Xxxxxx

TELEX 889765   **TELEPHONE 0473 88999 (8 lines)**

(name and address of supplier)

3 November 19—

Dear Sirs,

Lightweight Polymeric batteries

We are the manufacturers of BROADWAY delivery vehicles and electric vehicles for disabled people. Our company is a subsidiary of BroadWay International Inc. of Portland, Oregon.

We are seeking an alternative supplier of lightweight batteries to power our vehicles. As far as we are aware you do not have a local distributor of your products in this country. I enclose copies of our technical brochures for your information. An exact description of the goods we require is given below.

Polymeric Batteries (These will be connected in groups of two or four in our factory)

Maximum Size: Height: 200mm Depth: 200mm Width: 300mm
Maximum Weight: 5kg
Output: 1000 watts @ 12 volts
Rechargeable life at full power: 8 hours
Labels: Each unit should bear a label giving:
    the output of the battery,
    its month and year of manufacture,
    your own company's name and country,
    a product code number and a unique unit number
Quantity: 4,800 units
Delivery: by 15 January 19—

Please quote us your best CIF price, giving a full specification of your product and shipping date.

We would need to have samples of the batteries to test in our laboratories before placing a firm order.

We usually deal with new suppliers on the basis of payment in our currency by irrevocable Letter or Credit.

If our laboratory tests are satisfactory, and you can provide us with a good price and service, we will be happy to place more substantial orders on a regular basis.

We look forward to receiving an early reply to this enquiry,

Yours faithfully,

F. A. North
Buying manager

© Cambridge University Press, 1989

125

6.3 Sales and delivery   *Vocabulary*

A If there seem to be too many new words here, read the whole
exercise aloud to the class, supplying the missing words yourself. Then
let them do it themselves in pairs, trying to remember what you said.
Alternatively, both parts can be prepared at home and then discussed
in class.

Answers:
1. volume   margin
2. retail   point of sale   value added tax   wholesale
3. inventory control / stock control   backlog   hold-up
4. special delivery   crates
5. grade   premium   bulky   surcharge
6. tender   triplicate   deadline
7. cash with order   cash on delivery
8. bill of lading   bill of exchange

B Much of this information may seem arcane and confusing to
students without business experience. In this case, this section could be
omitted, or returned to later in the course. With a group who are
involved in importing and exporting, find out which Incoterms they
customarily use in their trade. Perhaps the most common ones are
FOB, C&F, CIF and DDP.

Note that the terms *freight*, *freight carriage* and *carriage* all mean the
same thing.

Answers:
1. buyer/importer
2. supplier/exporter
3. free alongside ship
4. free on board
5. cost and freight
6. cost, insurance and freight
7. carriage   insurance paid
8. delivered carriage paid
9. delivered duty paid

6.4 Answering enquiries

This integrated activity simulates making and answering enquiries
about products. Although probably none of your students are involved
in industrial counter-espionage, the language used when answering
enquiries is similar whatever the product!

Procedure

Steps A and B are preparatory to the integrated activity, they could be done at home before the lesson. Make sure there is enough time for everyone to do all the steps – and that there is sufficient time for giving feedback and discussing each step. You may well need to give some help in the early stages.

Students will be working in pairs during this activity.

A First of all, make sure everyone is clear about the products described in the advertisement. Answer questions about vocabulary, especially: *bug, eavesdropping,* and *scrambler*. These products are similar to products that really are on the market, by the way.

B Students look at the OUTLINE for a letter answering an enquiry. As the details will vary enormously according to the product and trade practice, there are no universals here. Allow students with business experience to say what they would add or not include in the model letter. If possible, ask anyone involved in importing or exporting to bring to class an example of their own correspondence.

C This step involves answering Enquiries #1 and #2 by TELEX. To answer the enquiries, students will need to look at their inventory level, easily found in File 115 at the very end of the Student's Book.

If the class needs help with the first task, the first telex could be composed on the board or OHP with the whole class chipping in with suggestions.

When they have finished, each pair should pass their completed draft telexes to the pair on the left and ask them to comment. Have they conveyed the right information in an attractive way?

D 🎞️ This step involves answering Enquiries #3 and #4 by LETTER. The recorded call provides a model of how to answer enquiries on the phone (in step F – though the tone may be rather too effusive for some students' tastes!) and requires students to alter the stock position printout in File 115.

FIRST CALL

AntiSpy Products, good afternoon ...
Hello, yes. Oho, Mr Saito, hi, hi, how are you? ... Good, good ... OK, the LR 44, yes, we've had quite a rush on those and ... er ... there's been a delay on supplies, I'm afraid. ... We only have nine in stock ... Mm ... Oh sure, eight's ... eight's no problem at all. I can get them to you by the end of the week. ... Er ... will you be able to pick them up at Narita, as usual? ... Fine, fine. OK, that's eight items of product LR forty n ... four. OK, can you send us a telex to confirm this please, Mr Saito? ... Thanks very much ... You're very welcome. Bye now, Mr Saito.

[Time: 1 minute]

When they have finished, each pair should pass their completed draft letters to the pair on the left and ask them to comment. See the questions for evaluating letters in step C in the Student's Book.

E ▱ This step involves answering enquiry #5 by either telex or letter – as students think fit. Again there is a phone call to listen to beforehand.

SECOND CALL

AntiSpy Products, good afternoon ... Hello Mr Brewster, nice to hear you ... Sure, how many would you like? ... Well, I'll just have to check the stock position ... Oh, I'm sorry we only have 75 presently. Er ... more available at the end of May.

... All right, I can let you have all 75 right now ... Absolutely. Can you just confirm this by telex please? Well, thanks very much. And you have a nice day, Mr Brewster. Bye-bye.

[Time: 30 seconds]

When they have finished, each pair should pass their completed draft telex or letter to the pair on the left and ask them to comment. Have they conveyed the right information in an attractive way?

A final draft could be set as homework.

F ☎ This step involves answering Enquiries #6 and #7 on the TELEPHONE. The pairs could be rearranged at this point to give students practice in talking to someone different. There are two calls, so that each partner has a chance to speak on behalf of AntiSpy Products.

In the first call, student A (Agencia Léon) looks at File 59 and B (AntiSpy Products) looks at 105. This call concerns certain details mentioned in the telex in the Student's Book. Student B calls Student A with answers to the queries.

In the second call, Student A looks at File 69 and B looks at 45. Here Student B calls AntiSpy Products with an enquiry about the advertisement.

At the end, allow time for students to comment on each other's telephone performance.

Follow-up discussion

Which of the tasks were most difficult? (If it was a written task, students could do a final draft as homework.)

How is your students' own experience different from the idealized world presented in this scenario?

What can go wrong when answering enquiries – and how can such problems be avoided?

6.5   Importing and exporting *Discussion*

Try to make sure that at least one member of each group is working or has worked in a firm that imports or exports. If you have just one or two people in the class who have practical knowledge of foreign trade, the rest of the class can 'interview' them.

Note that some students may be cagey about revealing trade secrets – a golden opportunity to use some of the 'hedging' phrases introduced in 6.1!

If you have a class entirely without work experience, they cannot do this activity, and it should be omitted.

6.6   Looking into the future *Grammar*

The main problems that students have when referring to the future are covered in this section: it may be necessary to remind them that there is no 'future tense' in English.

Presentation

⬜ The examples in the speech balloons are recorded. Answer any queries your students may have before starting the exercises.

Here are some more points that are not made in the Student's Book, but which you may like to remind your students about:

- Use of present simple in SUBORDINATE CLAUSES:
  I'll let you know when he *arrives*.
  I won't let the production people know until the order *has been confirmed*.

- After a verb like *hope* or *think*, *will* is used more than *going to*:
  I hope / am sure / expect / assume that we will have the consignment ready for dispatch on Monday.
  I hope that the flight isn't / won't be delayed.

- Talking about a process which will be going on (i.e. which will have started but not finished) at a particular time:
  We'll still be unloading the goods at 3pm.
  When I'm 30, I'll be looking for a better job.
  Please don't call after 12.30, Mr Carter will be having lunch then.

- *Will* tends to be used more in writing, *going to* is more common in speech.

- Here are some common expressions that are used when referring to the future:

   We're talking about next week.
   We're looking at next week.
   Soon   without delay   before too long   in due course
   as soon as possible   at your earliest convenience
   by return of post   in three weeks' time

Exercise and activities

A   The exercise can be done as homework, or by students working in pairs – or alone and then comparing answers in pairs.

Suggested answers – some of these may be open to discussion:
1. *example: make sure everyone knows what to do*
2. What time does the train from Birmingham arrive?
3. Where are you meeting Ms Carpenter before the conference?
4. Are you going to book a table for lunch?
5. If I call you before 5pm, will you still be in your office?
6. Will you let me know when the goods arrive in your warehouse?
7. When will you have finished typing the report?
8. What will you be doing after the meeting this afternoon?
9. When are you going to write/send a telex to ACME Industries...?

B and **C**   These activities are interdependent, as the group in step B needs to be dispersed into different pairs in step C. The easiest way to organize this is to have an even number of groups. Then the members of one group can quickly pair up with the members of another.

Extra activities

The members of the class can interrogate you on your own plans for the future.

Further discussion can be initiated as whole-class activity:
- What do the members of the class think will happen in their own firms in the next few years?
- What do they think they will be doing in, say, five years' time?
- Imagine that today is 1900. What will happen in the world / your country this century?
- Now imagine that it is 1999. What will happen in the world / your country in the next century?

Workbook exercise 6.7 contains more work on this topic. Unit 17 in *Use of English* may also be useful for remedial work in class.

Note that this theme is expanded in 10.10 Possibility, probability and certainty and that the work on conditionals in 8.4 is also related.

6.7 Placing and filling orders

This integrated activity covers the stages of dealing with an export order, with each step corresponding to a different date in the process. Additional information for each step is provided in the Files at the appropriate time. Each step involves deciding what to do and then writing a telex or letter.

Procedure

Students work in pairs, though a less experienced class should perhaps do it in groups of three. The completed telexes and letters can be 'delivered' to you, so that you can check them and later provide feedback on the quality of the English. If this would take too long (in a large class), students can show their work to another pair and ask them to comment. Final drafts of some of the telexes or letters could be done as homework.

Begin by making sure everyone understands what they have to do. It is not practicable to contact Naves Limón by phone. Be prepared to interrupt the activity from time to time to offer advice to the whole class.

Make sure there is enough time to do justice to the activity – if necessary the action can be resumed in a later lesson, thus adding to the reality of time passing!

A   The draft telex on page 68 contains some errors. First students should spot the errors and correct them. Here are extracts from the telex with the errors underlined:

```
..179,800 (IN WORDS: ONE SEVEN NINE THOUSAND
EIGHT HUNDRED)..
```

```
..PACK EACH PB 5000 FOR EXPORT IN A 40-FOOT
OPEN TOP CONTAINER..
```

```
..AND VALID FOR 90 (NINETY) DAYS FROM THE DATE
OF YOUR ORDER..
```

```
..MR RICHARDSON SENDS HIS BEST REGARDS..
```

Students may find other points they wish to change, to make the telex clearer and more friendly or polite. For example, maybe 'Good afternoon' isn't an appropriate greeting in a telex to a different time zone. And maybe *all* the figures should be given both in words and numbers.

In steps B to G below, students are referred to as 'we'.

B File 86 contains an order from Costa Rica, which has to be checked. Then we have to send a telex to Alpha Marine, the anchor suppliers.

C File 103 contains a telex from Alpha Marine, answering our own telex from step B, and a telex from our freight forwarders. Now we have all the information we need to be able to acknowledge the Costa Rica order. We send a confirmation by telex and also a covering letter to accompany the pro-forma invoice which will be sent by airmail.

D Shipwreck? Disaster? File 55 contains reassuring news in a telex from Costa Rica, which must be replied to – probably again with both an immediate telex and a covering letter.

E File 48 contains a directive from Mr Richardson, instructing us to send a follow-up letter.

F As it's nearly Christmas and we want to maintain a good relationship with Naves Limón, we send a seasonal telex.

G File 33 contains a reply to the telex we sent in step F. Naves Limón want to be our agents in Central America – is this a good idea? Before replying to it, we will need to discuss what action we will take. Even if this only involves writing a note to Mr Richardson, asking for a ruling, perhaps we should tell him what we think about the idea.
    At this stage, the EXTRA ACTIVITY below can be introduced, which deals with the problems of choosing an agent.

Extra activity

Tell the class that Mr Richardson thinks that it might well be worthwhile appointing an agent or distributor in Central America.
    Explain the situation:

Mr Richardson wants us to draft a report on the kind of firm that would be suitable.
The first thing we should do is arrange these points (on the board or OHP) in order of importance:

> We're looking for a company ...
> ... who can act as our selling agent (they are paid commission).
> ... who can act as our distributor, selling at a marked-up price.
> ... who can hold good quantities of our stock.
> ... who can provide after-sales service on our behalf.
> ... whose staff and management we get on well with.
> ... who have a large, active sales force.

... whose financial standing and growth record are good.
... who are centrally placed within the territory.
... who are a large, efficient firm with a big turnover.
... who are a small firm who can provide the personal touch.
... who have a modern showroom and good technical facilities.
... whose other products don't compete with ours.

If we do decide to go ahead and appoint Naves Limón as our
agent/distributor, what points have to be made clear in the agreement
or contract?

Follow-up discussion

How do the idealized events in the Sunworld scenario relate to your
  own real-life experience?
What other procedures need to be carried out, that were assumed to
  have been done in the Sunworld scenario?
Out of all the tasks you performed in this unit, which were the most
  difficult? Do you need more work on these?

Workbook

Contents for this unit:

6.1 Making enquiries on the phone   Functions 📼
6.2 What do they want to know?   Listening and reading 📼
6.3 Vocabulary
6.4 'J.I.T.'   Listening 📼
6.5 Prepositions – 2
6.6 Airfreight or road transport?   Reading
6.7 The future   Grammar
6.8 Measurements   Vocabulary
6.9 Thank you for your order ...   Writing

133

Background information: Money matters

Very often in business situations people have to talk about money with clients and customers and either physically handle money or perhaps deal with figures and money on paper. Particularly if you work in the accounts department of a large firm you may have to send a customer a reminder because they have not paid an invoice. Or you may have to fill in invoices for customers' orders. You may even have to decide whether customers can have further credit and delay paying their outstanding bills: this is called 'credit assessment'. If you are working in international trade you may need to be familiar with the different types of payment that exist.

In most middle-sized and large firms there is an Accounts department which deals with the money paid out to clients for goods delivered and the money received from customers for goods supplied.

The following table gives you a very general idea of the different activities

Accounts

Dealing with money coming in and going out from a firm.

Purchasing:	delivery notes[1] invoices }	IN	←	from customer
	cheques etc payments – (you pay the invoice)	OUT	→	to customer
Sales:	delivery note – internal		←	IN
	invoice credit note[2] }	OUT	→	to customer
	payments – cheques etc (you invoice the customer)	IN	←	from customer

Notes: [1] document indicating goods have been delivered to the firm from a supplier
[2] document sent to a customer who has paid more than was required

which involve money in an accounts department. Two of the most important processes are paying customers and billing or controlling credit of customers. It is normal to send a *pro-forma* invoice in advance when supplying goods to a customer. In a situation in which the customer is known and reliable, firms may send an invoice *after* the delivery.

7 Money matters

In business there are many occasions on which people have to deal with money and talk about money. Within a company there are business situations in which receipt of money and the payment of money is the central occupation. This unit gives students the opportunity to use and practise English in some of the most relevant settings. These include 'reminding a customer of non-payment', 'invoicing customers' and dealing with 'credit assessment' of customers. Various types of payment may be encountered in international trade. Some of the more common ones are discussed below under 'Methods of Payment in Foreign Trade'.

One of the more common methods of payment is 'payment by letter of credit'. This is dealt with explicitly in 7.3. Particular practice is given in this unit on 'reminding a customer of non-payment' and 'dealing with cash-flow problems' as these are areas in which communication in English is most likely to be required.

But more general situations and settings in which people talk **about** money and related matters, such as foreign currency, shares and business ownership, and the financial performance of a company are also treated in this unit.

Methods of Payment in Foreign Trade

1. **CWO – Cash with order:** This is uncommon since you are in effect extending credit to your supplier: in addition you run the risk that the goods will not be despatched in accordance with the contract terms. Nevertheless, provision for partial advance payments in the form of deposits (normally between 10 per cent and 20 per cent of the contract price), or progress payments at various stages of manufacture (particularly for capital goods), is often included in the contract terms. The remainder of the payment will usually be made by one of the methods described in the following section headed 'Open Account'.

2. **Open account:** This is a simple agreement whereby you agree to pay for the goods after you have received them, usually on a monthly basis. There are various ways in which you can send money to your supplier under open account and he may wish to stipulate the method to be used, for example:

Cheque: This is usually the slowest method of payment and may result in your supplier having to bear charges from his own bank and also from UK banks since a cheque has to be cleared through the international banking system before he receives credit. Different banks have different methods and this could take as long as a month.

For these reasons your supplier may not consider payment by cheque acceptable.

Banker's Draft: You can arrange for your bank to issue a draft drawn on an overseas bank in either sterling or foreign currency. You send this direct to your supplier who pays it into his bank account, at which time he will usually be given immediate credit.

Telegraphic Transfer: This is the fastest method of sending money abroad but costs a little more than most other methods of transferring funds. Your UK bank instructs an overseas bank, by cable or telex, to pay a stated amount of money to your supplier. Foreign currency or sterling may be sent in this way. If you wish, the overseas bank can be instructed to advise your supplier immediately funds arrive.

International Payment Order: You can arrange for your bank to instruct an overseas bank, by airmail, to make payment to your supplier. International Payment Orders may be slower than Telegraphic Transfers, but are slightly cheaper because there are no cable costs.

International Money Order: These can be purchased from your bank. You post the money order to your supplier and he receives immediate credit from his bank in the same way as with a draft. This is a very cheap and simple way to make payment of relatively small amounts.

3. **Documentary Bill of Exchange:** This is a popular way of arranging payment and offers benefits for both you and your supplier. The main advantage is that you are not required to make payment until your supplier has despatched the goods. Your supplier has the advantage of knowing that legal procedures exist for recovering money owing against bills of exchange and, if the goods are sent by sea, is able to maintain control of the goods through the document of title until you have agreed to make payment. It is in effect a demand for payment from your supplier. He will draw it up on a specially printed form or on his own headed notepaper and forward it to his bank, together with the documents relating to the transaction. These may include a transport document evidencing that the goods have been despatched.

The overseas bank will send the bill and documents to a bank in the UK for 'collection'. The UK bank will notify you of the arrival of the documents and will release them to you provided that:

- if the bill is drawn at 'sight' you pay he amount of the bill in full when it is presented to you.
- if the bill is drawn payable after a certain number of days you 'accept' the bill, i.e. sign across the bill your agreement to pay the amount in full on the due date.

7.1 ... what did he want to know? *Grammar*

Reported speech continues to pose problems for intermediate and advanced students. Choosing the correct verb forms and making the corresponding adjustments elsewhere are areas which still need practising.

This section merely gives brief explanations of the major points to be considered. The table only concentrates on the bare bones of the changes made when statements, requests and questions are reported. Further work may be necessary using the Workbook and exercises from other sources (*Use of English* Units 19 and 20 are recommended).

Presentation

If possible get the students to read this through before the lesson.

Exercises and activity

Exercises A to C are to be done in pairs, with time after each exercise for discussion and questions.

If time is short, exercise A could be set as homework, but it still needs to be discussed in class to clear up possible misunderstandings. Suggested answers are given below.

Make sure any queries are cleared up before students start exercise A – though it is to be expected that doing the exercise will give rise to further questions.

A Students work in pairs to transform the sentences into indirect speech.

Suggested answers:
3. When did it arrive?
   He asked when it had arrived.
4. Are all the things you ordered included?
   And whether all the things which we had ordered were included.
5. Did you get the invoice too?
   He asked whether we had got the invoice too.
6. Have you paid the invoice for the last shipment yet?
   (He also asked) whether we had paid for the last shipment yet.
7. Because I haven't got a record of the payment.
   ... Because he hadn't got a record of the payment.
8. Does the amount on the invoice correspond with what you ordered?
   He asked whether the amount on the invoice corresponded with what we had ordered.
9. If it doesn't, we can give you a credit note to cover the difference.
   He said that if it didn't they could give us a credit note to cover the difference.
10. Will you be paying the new invoice immediately?
    He asked whether we would be paying the new invoice immediately.
11. Please try and send the cheque before the end of the month because our accounts department is considering changing the conditions of payment for future orders otherwise.
    He asked us to try and send the cheque before the end of the

138

*month because their accounts department was considering chang-
ing the conditions of payment for future orders otherwise.*

12. I hope we can continue working together.
    He hoped we could continue working together.
13. And we hope to keep you as a regular customer despite any
    troubles you may be having.
    *And they hoped they would keep/to keep us as regular customers
    despite any troubles we might have been having.*

B Before playing the recording, make clear to the students that the
focus of the exercise is on 'reporting the gist of what has been said in
their own words' – not every single word of what they have heard.

Play the recording to the whole class:

Um ... well, you see, money's very tight at the moment.

Um. Well, I'd like to ask for an extension of credit.

Yes, you see, we have a considerable overdraft already.

And our overheads have to be thought about.

Mm. Well, a major problem is that our own customers are going through a difficult period too.

Oh, we've a number of outstanding accounts ourselves, so we know exactly how you feel.

Yes ... yes, well we hope that our bank will show us some generosity and allow us to overdraw our account.

Mmm mmm. Oh yes and what's more we have just granted one of our major clients an extra two weeks' credit. They've accepted our offer.

As if that isn't enough. We've a large crisis on our hands with another customer who owes us a lot of money.

Yeah, he's just gone bankrupt.

Look, what do you suggest we do about the money we owe you?

[Time: 55 seconds]

Suggested answers:
Money *was* very tight at the moment.
And *he'd* like to ask for an extension of credit.
They had a considerable overdraft.
And *their* overheads *had* to be thought about.
A major problem *was that their own customers were going* through a
  difficult period too.
*They had a number of outstanding accounts themselves, so they knew
  exactly how we felt.*
He hoped that their bank would show them some generosity and allow
  them to overdraw their account.
And what *was* more *they had* just granted one of their major clients an
  extra two weeks' credit and they had accepted their offer.
And as if that *wasn't* enough, they *had* a large crisis on their hands
  with another customer who *owed them* a lot of money.
He *had just gone* bankrupt.
He *asked what should be done* about the money they owed us.

C 🎭 This is done in pairs. Student A looks at File 38, student B at 57.

Each student reports a conversation he or she has had with a colleague in the context of paying and dealing with bills. They have been talking about a person they deal with in the course of their work. It turns out that the two people have completely opposite perceptions, opinions, impressions and views of the transactions! The payer sees herself as a very punctual, efficient and regular payer of her debts and sees the supplier as slow and unhelpful; the supplier sees herself as understanding, helpful and friendly and sees the customer as being very irregular, slow and unpunctual. At the end, allow time for everyone to comment on the activity and to ask questions, if they wish to.

Allow time for the class to raise any questions concerning problems or difficulties they may have had doing the activities and exercises.

Workbook

Workbook exercise 7.1 provides further work on using reported speech.

7.2 Billing, invoicing

NOTE: If you don't know much about dealing with accounts, the summary table in the Background Information on page 134 gives some idea of the multitude of dealings with money which go on in an accounts department. Naturally enough, not every eventuality can be dealt with here. Instead, this unit concentrates on the basic process of paying, billing and controlling credit from customers (see 7.2, 7.3 and 7.4).

In this section, we have a special case which necessitates a change of price since the order was taken. Even assuming a *pro-forma* invoice had already been sent, a new one indicating the change of price would still have to be sent. This is essentially the nub of the exercise: negotiating the notification of a new price and entering it into the invoice.

Procedure

A 🎭 Remind everyone to look first at the various documents before they begin to fill in the invoice. Be prepared to explain any vocabulary items which students may have problems with as they read through the documents.

Encourage them to use 'local information' and details that are personally relevant, such as addresses and names they are familiar with. They should perhaps decide where their company is situated and where the client is located. For students who find this difficult, you can suggest their company is in Rotterdam and the customer in Corby, England – the model invoice below is filled in accordingly.

After everyone has completed the invoices, they should compare what they have done with another pair, or this can be discussed as a class.

Suggested answer:
[YOU MAY PHOTOCOPY THIS DOCUMENT]

INVOICE FACTURE FACTURA	RECHNUNG FACTUUR	
Seller (Name, Address, VAT Reg. No.) *Universal Utensils, Rotterdam*		C.C.C.N No.
	Invoice No. and Date (Tax Point)	Seller's Reference *LS 43352/91*
	Buyer's Reference	
Consignee *N/A*	Buyer (If not Consignee) *Vesta Vehicles Earlstree Industrial Estate Corby, Northants UNITED KINGDOM*	
	Country of Origin of Goods *HOLLAND*	Country of Destination
	Terms of Delivery and Payment *FOB Rotterdam Payment against sight draft accompanied by documents through Rabobank*	
Vessel/Aircraft etc. *MS Jupiter* — Port of Loading *Rotterdam*		
Port of Discharge *Felixstowe*		
Marks and Numbers: Number and Kind of Packages: Description of Goods *UU LS 433*	Gross Weight (Kg)	Cube (M³)
Specification of Commodities *Sensor switches Type A6D*	Quantity *35 gross*	● Amount (State Currency)
	TOTAL	
	Name of Signatory *Ms Sanchez*	
It is hereby certified that this invoice shows the actual price of the goods described, that no other invoice has been or will be issued, and that all particulars are true and correct.	Place and Date of Issue	
	Signature	

© SITPRO 1987 V5

© Cambridge University Press 1989

B ☎ Student A looks at File 80, student B at File 74. Remind the students that Student A has to call Student B of *another* pair, while B calls A of another pair. In this way everyone is 'active'.

C After step B, students go back to their original pairs, read the letter together and draft an appropriate answer. After they have drafted their letters, students look in pairs at another pair's letter, acting the part of John Granger and commenting on tone and form.

Suggested answer:
[YOU MAY PHOTOCOPY THIS DOCUMENT]

VESTA VEHICLES

Earlstree Industrial Estate   Corby   Northants   United Kingdom

20 February 19xx

Universal Utensils,
Rotterdam

Dear Mr Granger

Account No. 645/Hrs-0098/Invoice No. 04276

We refer to your letter of 14 February 19xx, concerning the payment of Invoice No. 04276.

As you state in your letter, the sum of £98,000 was incorrectly entered into the invoice.

Since our accounts department has recently received new computing equipment we can only conclude that the error occurred before the program had been fully tested.

We apologize for any inconvenience we may have caused you and look forward to doing further business with you in the future.

Yours sincerely,

M. Sanchez

M Sanchez

© Cambridge University Press 1989

D A similar procedure can be adopted with the acknowledgement. Students look at File 56 for the telex from Mr Granger, which provides the starting point for the activity.

7.3 Payment by Documentary Letter of Credit

This is a role play exercise done as pairwork.

It is fairly straightforward and the procedure is described in the Student's Book. There may be a number of items of terminology which you can go through with the whole class before letting them loose on the pairwork phase. It may help to introduce briefly the method of payment dealt with here. See the following:

Letters of Credit

The **Irrevocable Letter of Credit** is the most commonly used method of payment for imports. The exporter can be sure that he will be paid when he dispatches the goods and the importer has proof that the goods have been dispatched according to his instructions.

The 'letter' is an inter-bank communication. The two banks take full responsibility that both shipment and payments are in order.
1. The importer and exporter agree a sales contract and the terms of the Documentary Credit.
2. The importer asks his bank to open a Documentary Credit in the exporter's favour.
3. The importer's bank (the issuing bank) sends a Letter of Credit to a bank in the exporter's country (the advising bank).
4. The exporter presents the shipping documents to the advising bank as proof that the shipment has been dispatched. If everything is in order, he is paid.
5. The advising bank sends the documents to the issuing bank.
6. The advising bank sends the documents to the importer, who uses them to obtain delivery of the goods.

Perhaps start with the pairwork and deal with the vocabulary questions on an individual basis.

This exercise gives the opportunity to revise abbreviations such as FOB, CIF, etc which were used in Unit 6 Imports and exports.

A partial glossary of some of the technical terms:
revocable = a letter of credit etc which is able to be cancelled
bills of exchange = documents containing an instruction usually to a bank to pay a stated sum of money at a specified future date or on demand
drawn at sight = a bill of exchange which is payable when the beneficiary presents it at the bank is said to be *drawn at sight*
of a particular tenor = according to stated terms or in a specified manner or at a specified time
port of discharge = the port at which the cargo is unloaded etc

A   This is the correct numbered order. It is also given in File 98 in the Student's Book.

Most Credits are fairly similar in appearance and contain the following details (numbers correspond to those in the example):
1. The type of Credit (Revocable or Irrevocable).
2. The name and address of the exporter (beneficiary).
3. The name and address of the importer (accreditor).
4. The amount of the Credit, in sterling or a foreign currency.
5. The name of the party on whom the bills of exchange are to be drawn, and whether they are to be at sight or of a particular tenor.
6. The terms of contract and shipment (i.e. whether 'ex-works', 'FOB', 'CIF', etc.).
7. Precise instructions as to the documents against which payment is to be made.
8. A brief description of the goods covered by the Credit (too much detail should be avoided as it may give rise to errors, which can cause delay).
9. Shipping details, including whether transhipments are allowed. Also recorded should be the latest date for shipment and the names of the ports of shipment and discharge. (It may be in the best interest of the exporter for shipment to be allowed 'from any UK port' so that he has a choice if, for example, some ports are affected by strikes. The same applies for the port of discharge.)
10. Whether the Credit is available for one or several shipments.
11. The expiry date.

B   This is an exercise in listening for detail. First, let the students have time to read through the passage before hearing the recording. Then play the recording in which a bank expert discusses problems encountered in using letter of credit documentation. Play the recording at least twice with sufficient time in between for students to think about what they are reading.

um ... now you'd be surprised at the kinds of mistakes people make when using letter of credit documentation. Um ... well these errors can often lead to rejection on ... on the very first presentation. Er ... the research department of our bank found that ... er ... 25% of the documents were rejected. Now there were different reasons. Um ... the main ones were things like the fact that the letter of credit had expired, or the documents were presented after the period stated by the letter of credit. Or, of course, the shipment was late.

If you think about it, it's ... it's quite amazing really. Er ... but I ... I can't stress enough the need for consistency between different documents. I ... I mean, for instance ... um ... our bank study found out that spelling inconsistencies or mistakes are part of the problem. Well ... that is ... um ... the description or spelling of goods on invoices was different from that in the letter of credit. Or, the weights were different on the export documents. Er ... then the amounts of money value shown on the invoice and ... and the bill of exchange differed too. Even the marks and numbers were found to be different. Er ... then another thing we found was that the amount of money mentioned on the letter of credit was smaller than the value of the order. Or, the shipment was short. Then you ... you might even find that some documents were missing which were called for in the documentary letter of credit. We even had cases where signatures had not been witnessed as required for certain documents presented. Or else facsimile signatures were used where they're just not allowed. And this is by no means the end of the list, which goes on and on; but ... haha ... I won't bore you any more, ha. All in all almost 50% of the documents presented along with the letters of credit were rejected on their first presentation and this meant sometimes long delays in payment with all the complications that can involve. And I don't need to tell you ...

[Time: 2 minutes]

Suggested answers:

1. expired	7. marks and numbers
2. after	8. for less
3. late	9. exceeded by
4. spelling	10. shipment
5. weights	11. signatures of witnessings
6. amounts of value	12. facsimile signatures

C   Before the more general discussion, let everyone go through and compare their answers to B in pairs.

Follow-up discussion

At least one member of each group should be working or have had work experience for this discussion to work most effectively. Rearrange the groups if necessary to take this factor into account. If there are just a couple of people in the class who have encountered problems with such documents, the rest of the class can 'interview' them. A class entirely without work experience (or commercial training) cannot do this activity.

   If your students have had work experience the following set of questions might be posed:

What are your own experiences of making foreign payments?
What method(s) do you use in your firm?
What method do you never use and why?
What method would you advise small companies in your country to use? Why?
Are there any standard practices which are different from the methods of payment mentioned? What are they? Are they preferable? Why?

Finally, as this step deals with quite a lot of 'difficult' vocabulary, give the students a chance to go back over the activities they have been engaged in and to raise any queries they may have.

7.4   Reminding a buyer of an unpaid invoice

The main skill practised in this section is that of writing. As in the rest of the course, students are encouraged to work in pairs. The activities involve three firms: Stateco, the firm the students work for, Lateco, a firm the students remind of outstanding payments and Waitco, a company they wish to delay payment to, themselves. The activity is specially laid out in the Student's Book. The configuration allows 'models' for students' own drafts of letters etc to be presented. Hence there is a first reminder and a second reminder for the students to refer to in drafting their own. A request for deferred payment serves as a model for the next writing task. Lateco's accession to the deferred payment request then serves as a model and the accompanying or covering letter from Waitco can also serve as a model. Remind the students that 'alternative' wordings are possible and desirable. They ought not to just copy the model.

Summary of firms and people involved, together with how documents are linked:

Ms Benedetto   Stateco
Pierre Lacoste   (Credit controller) Waitco
John Brown   (Chief clerk, Accounts) Lateco

Summary of tasks:
Monday, 12 June:
Listen to the conversation and read the first reminder from Waitco to Stateco dated 15 June 19xx
Tuesday, 20 June:
Draft a first reminder to Lateco
Thursday, 22 June:
Read the second reminder from Waitco to Stateco dated 21 June 19xx
Friday, 23 June:
Draft a second reminder to Lateco
Monday, 3 July:
Read the request for deferred payment from Lateco to Stateco dated 28 June 19xx
Tuesday, 4 July:
Draft a request for deferred payment to Waitco
Monday, 10 July:
Read the letter from Waitco to Stateco dated 7 July 19xx and draft a reply to Lateco's letter of 28 June above
19 July:
Read Thank You letter from Lateco dated 17 July 19xx
Cheque arrives with letter from Lateco and now you can...
Send cheque with letter to Waitco.

Procedure

The series of linked activities – reading and writing – are laid out in the Student's Book. Students should be discouraged from simply 'copying' the exact wording of the model letters. Students should work in pairs for this activity. Allow time for students to compare their drafts after each step.

A 📼 Monday 12 June begins with an exercise in listening for gist. Students should compare their answers in pairs. They should listen and make a note of some of the reasons given for the late payment. The recording also provides a number of arguments and ideas for the subsequent writing tasks. Play the recording at least twice and allow time for queries concerning vocabulary items.

Ms Benedetto: Good morning! I'm sorry to ring you like this.
John Brown: That's all right.
Ms Benedetto: But did you receive our January shipment?
John Brown: Yes ... yes we have.
Ms Benedetto: When did it arrive?
John Brown: Um ... it arrived on the 25th January.
Ms Benedetto: And are all the things you ordered included?
John Brown: Er ... yes, thank you, yes.
Ms Benedetto: Did you get the invoice as well?
John Brown: Er ... yes, yes.
Ms Benedetto: And have you paid the invoice for the last shipment yet?
John Brown: Um ... I'm afraid we haven't managed ....
Ms Benedetto: Because I haven't a record of the payment and our department was just getting a bit worried about it.
John Brown: Yes ... um ... money is very tight at the moment, you see.
Ms Benedetto: Ah.
John Brown: I'd ... er ... like to ask for an extension of credit.
Ms Benedetto: Mm.
John Brown: You see, we have a ... a considerable overdraft.
Ms Benedetto: Ah.
John Brown: And ... um ... our overheads have to be thought about.
Ms Benedetto: Mm.

John Brown: A major problem is that our own customers are going through a difficult period too.
Ms Benedetto: Ah ... yes I know how that is.
John Brown: We have a number of outstanding accounts ourselves, so we know exactly how you feel.
Ms Benedetto: Yes.
John Brown: Um ... we're hoping that our bank will show us some generosity and allow us to overdraw our account.
Ms Benedetto: Er ... well I hope so as well, ahah.
John Brown: And ... er ... what's more we have just granted one of our major clients an extra two weeks' credit and ... um ... they've accepted our offer.
Ms Benedetto: Mm ... mm.
John Brown: And as if that isn't enough. We have a large crisis on our hands with another customer who owes us a lot of money.
Ms Benedetto: Yes, I think I know what you mean. We have a similar problem.
John Brown: They've just gone bankrupt.
Ms Benedetto: Oh dear.
John Brown: Yes. So ... er ... what do you suggest we do about the money we owe you?
Ms Benedetto: Well, please try and send the cheque before the end of the month. Because our accounts department is con-

sidering changing the conditions of payment for future orders otherwise.

John Brown: Yes ... er ... well, we will do our best.

Ms Benedetto: I hope we can continue to cooperate together.

John Brown: I hope so too.

Ms Benedetto: And we hope to keep you as a regular customer despite any troubles you may be having.

[Time: 2 minutes]

From now on, students work in pairs for the series of linked reading and writing tasks.

Monday, 12 June Students read the first reminder from Waitco to Stateco.

B *Tuesday, 20 June* Students decide what to do and what to write. Remind them to date their drafts. Then they show their drafts to another pair to comment on the form and tone.

Students can be referred to Unit 2 (Letters, telexes and memos) for information on how to lay out and draft letters etc, if necessary.

C *Thursday, 22 June* Students read the second reminder from Waitco to Stateco.

D *Friday, 23 June* Students draft a second reminder to Lateco using the model reminder from Waitco, and then show it to another pair for comment. They look at the other pair's draft.

E *Monday, 3 July* Students read the letter from Lateco to Stateco

F *Tuesday, 4 July* Students draft a request for deferred payment to Waitco and show it to another pair. They look at the other pair's draft.

G *Monday, 10 July* Students read the letter from Lateco to Stateco. Then they draft a reply to Lateco's letter of 28 June above, show it to another pair and look at the latter's draft.

H *19 July* Students read the letter from Lateco. Then they draft a letter to Waitco, show it to another pair and look at the latter's draft.

Follow-up discussion

Allow time for the class to raise any questions concerning problems or difficulties they may have had doing the activities which have not been dealt with while you have been circulating around the class and which are perhaps of a more general nature and hence of relevance to most of the class.

7.5 Dealing with cash-flow problems

The purpose of this activity is to give students the opportunity to practise some of the language and situations encountered in the previous sections in a more communicative activity. Students deal with the problems of cash-flow from both sides of the equation: as people who have to make apologies for non-payment and as people who are insistent on receiving their rightful payments.

Procedure

Arrange the class into groups of six consisting of three pairs. This will work all right of course with 6, 12 or 18 students. Here are some suggestions as to how to arrange the groups with 7 to 11 students for step C – the phone call.
Each step can be arranged as follows:

B *Adonis:* A1 A2
   Brimo: B1 B2
   Chimera: C1 C2

C A1 phones B2.
   A2 phones C1.
   B1 phones C2.

D A1 A2 draft
   B1 B2 letters
   C1 C2 and send

E *Adonis*   read letter from *Brimo*
   Brimo   read letter from *Chimera*
   Chimera read letter from *Adonis*

Where your class consists of 7 to 11 students, you should have the students do the activity of steps A, C and D in groups of three. This will lead to a duplication of phone-calls in step C. But this way everyone will be active.

with 7 students:
  A1 → B2
  B1 → C2
  C1 → A2 + A3
    (share a role)

with 8 students:
  A1 → B2 A3 → B3
  A2 → C1
  B1 → C2 (duplicate a phone call)

with 9 students:
  A1 → B2
  B1 → C2
  C1 → A2 + A3
  B3 → C3

with 10 students:
  A1 → B2 C3 → A4
  B1 → C2
  C1 → A2
  A3 → B3

with 11 students:
  A1 → B2 A3 → B3 + B4
  B1 → C2 C3 → A4
  C1 → A2

with 13 students:
  A1 → B2 A3 → B4 + B5
  B1 → C2 B3 → C4
  C1 → A2 C3 → A4

with 14:   with 15:   with 16:
  as with 8 + 6   as with 9 + 6   as with two groups of 8

with 17 students:
  either the teacher participates in a group of 6 or the procedure for an extended group of 8 and 9 is followed.

■ An alternative to the role-sharing suggested above might be to have the third person acting as an observer and then commenting on the performance of the other people in the follow-up.

A Students first look at the records of the firm Intertex. As a class they should try to work out whether Intertex have paid regularly in the past and should answer the questions in the Student's Book.

B 🖳 Pair A look at File 113, pair B at 15 and pair C at 52, where they will find information about the company they work for. Encourage them to study this information before moving on to step C.
  Allow time for questions concerning vocabulary and pronunciation.

Descriptions of the three companies:
  Adonis SA produce yarn to sell to fabric manufacturers and sell a big quantity of a special type to Brimo SpA (and don't get paid).
  And Brimo SpA sell their fabric to garment manufacturers and sell a big quantity of a very special type to Chimera GmbH (and don't get paid).
  And Chimera GmbH sell their garments to wholesalers and companies and sell a large quantity of overalls to Adonis SA (and don't get paid).

C 🕿 In the case of odd numbers of students, refer to the instructions for arranging the class above.
Student A1 should telephone student B2
Student A2 should telephone student C1
Student B1 should telephone student C2
One of each pair plays the role of Credit Controller for their company.
The other member of the pair plays the role of Accounts Manager of their company.
The Credit Controller rings up. The Accounts Manager answers.
Students should follow the instructions in the Student's Book. Remind everyone to make notes before beginning the phone calls.

D Have the original pairs draft the letter or telex together, explaining why they require more time in order to pay the outstanding bill.
  The model version of the telex on the next page may give some ideas to less imaginative or less experienced groups. POINT OUT THAT THIS MODEL MAY NOT REPRESENT THE WISEST OF CHOICES!

[YOU MAY PHOTOCOPY THIS DOCUMENT]

```
15TH DECEMBER
INVOICE LN 985

KINDLY REQUEST FURTHER DELAY OF 30
(THIRTY) DAYS TO PAY INVOICE NO. LN 985
ARE EXPERIENCING GREAT PROBLEMS WITH LARGE
CUSTOMER.
PROMISE TO PAY PUNCTUALLY ON 15TH NEXT MONTH.
PLS NOTIFY RECEIPT OF THIS TELEX.

SINCERELY

CHIMERA GMBH
```

© Cambridge University Press 1989

E   Collect the completed drafts and deliver the letter to another group for comments.

After step E reassemble the class and ask each group to report on what their decisions were. Encourage the others to ask questions, particularly about their reasons for their decisions and the action they will undertake.

Follow-up discussion

Ask students what they have learned from this activity. If there are students with work experience, they should be interviewed by the others about any occasions they know of on which similar problems of non-payment occurred.

7.6   How much did you say that was?   *Reading aloud*

A   Students work in pairs for this part of the activity. The instructions are clearly laid out in the Student's Book.

Suggested answers:
1 k   2 b   3 h   4 d   5 e   6 c   7 j   8 i   9 g
These are items remaining:
  a   three pounds sixty-six
  f   seventeen hundred and ninety-five
  l   one and a quarter per cent

Allow time for queries and questions after the exercise.

B   ▭ Before you play the recording, remind students to read through the report beforehand. Play the recording at least twice. The second time you may find it helpful to employ the technique of

151

'shadowing' (see Introduction). After the students have discussed their answers in pairs, discuss the answers in the class as a whole.

Volvo earnings rise by eleven percent in first quarter

Volvo, the Swedish automotive, energy and food group, increased its profits by ten point nine per cent in the first quarter of this year despite a fall of five per cent in group turnover.

Profits after financial items rose to two point four five billion Swedish kronor (three hundred and forty-five million dollars) compared with two point two one billion Swedish kronor in the first quarter of last year. The group was helped by a two hundred and fifteen million Swedish kronor foreign-exchange gain on loans – compared with a gain of thirty million Swedish kronor a year earlier – as well as by interest earnings of a hundred and nine million Swedish kronor – compared with seventy-seven million Swedish kronor in the first quarter of last year.

Operating profits were virtually unchanged at two point one three billion Swedish kronor compared with two point one billion Swedish kronor in the first quarter of last year. Volvo expects to make a productivity gain this year of at least five per cent.

The group's liquid funds, inflated by the record profits of the past two years, climbed to eighteen point two five billion Swedish kronor by the end of the first quarter from fourteen point four billion Swedish kronor a year earlier.

Volvo profits, at least in the short term, have been hedged against the impact of the falling dollar, but the lower dollar exchange rate shows clearly in the group's sales figures. Volvo turnover fell five per cent to twenty point six billion Swedish kronor from twenty-one point eight billion Swedish kronor in the first three months of last year despite a substantial rise in the volume of car sales.

You will need to check through the correct figures with the students before they move on to activity C.

Suggested answers:
1. eleven per cent
2. first
3. ten point nine per cent
4. this year
5. two point four five billion Swedish kronor
6. two hundred and fifteen million Swedish kronor
7. seventy-seven million Swedish kronor
8. two point one three billion Swedish kronor
9. last year
10. eighteen point two five billion Swedish kronor

C This activity gives more practice in using figures and numbers in English. It is not important to get the arithmetic right but these are the answers to the subtraction sums:

1. the difference in profits between this year and last
   = point two four billion Swedish kronor (= .24bn)
2. the increase in the foreign-exchange gain on loans
   = one hundred and eighty-five billion Swedish kronor (185bn)
3. the change in operating profits
   = point O three billion Swedish kronor (0.03bn)
4. the rise in liquid funds
   = three point eight five billion Swedish kronor (3.85bn)

5. the amount their turnover fell by
   = one point fourteen/one four billion Swedish kronor (1.14bn)

D ⬛ Student A looks at File 104, student B at 79. Each student has a copy of an air waybill in which the figures are badly blurred. This is an information gap activity in which they have to help each other complete the correct figures.

7.7   The results were good … *Read and discuss*

This is an exercise in reading for detail and scanning. It entails scanning both text and diagram-type material, i.e. extracts from the Managing Director's report and the charts and notes about GKN, for specific information.

Make sure everyone reads the questions before they look at the texts.

■   As preparation for this exercise you can ask students to collect information on the financial performance of a similar company in their own country in anticipation of the discussion. See below for the kind of company they should be on the look-out for.

Students should work in pairs for this first activity.

Suggested answers:

1. Depreciation of plant buildings and equipment (NB a second sum of £68 million is also mentioned; but see question 11 below).
2. £132 million pre-tax profits; the amount is mentioned in the extract from the report and also in the table under the trading surplus chart.
3. Continental Europe (£77 million, 53% of the total).
4. They were lower than the previous year.
5. The reason given in the text: 'largely because of the transfer of our special steels and forgings operations to be part of United Engineering Steels.'
6. £31 million.
7. £68 million.
8. £599 million for wages, salaries and related costs.
9. 60% in all.
10. £43 million. Interest on bank borrowing and other loans to finance the business.
11. These are the earnings of the year after taxes of £51 million and £13 million as payments to minority shareholders (= £64 million together) had been deducted from the £132 million profit before tax.
12. In all, £22 million – two stages are mentioned in the extract from the report: the first, £9 million and the second, £13 million.

Further information

GKN used to be called Guest Keen & Nettlefolds plc and were a Redditch-based company (near Birmingham, England). As part of a corporate 'facelift' they were transformed into GKN plc some years ago.

GKN's activities include production of special steels and forgings (metal components produced by the process of hammering), the production of commercial vehicles (lorries, etc) and agricultural tractors, components for cars and trucks in Europe and North America, and car components including transmission systems. But GKN is also an example of a company which is 'diversifying'. Some of the companies which have been bought up by the group include: Chep™ pallets (used in transporting goods), Kwikform™ scaffolding – used in the building industry, Keller foundations, Vending services™ (automatic food and drink machines) and Cleanaway™ waste management. The company is also active in the area of 'defence': they produce tracked combat vehicles (the Warrior) for the British Army. They have factories in West Germany.

Extra activity

As a preliminary to the class discussion, have students work in pairs and encourage them to make a list of the likely companies they could compare with GKN – an engineering company in the UK, which has activities in a wide range of areas.

As an alternative, you may prefer to do the following:

You can give students homework of 'researching' similar companies in their own country (see the note above). Then they can be divided up into groups. Each individual student is then questioned by the others. The summary of the discussion can then be presented to the whole class.

If such preparation is not feasible, you could facilitate discussion in the whole class by asking students with experience of dealing with financial and annual reports or with knowledge of the field to give their opinions. They could be interviewed by the rest of the class. The engineering industry and its performance is the subject. So it would be a help to try and pick up information on some of the latest figures for the leading companies in the country you happen to be working in or which your students come from.

The focus is on financial success. Questions you could use to start discussion might include:

- Where would you get information about such a company and their profits and losses? Their trading performance?
- Which company earns as much as GKN, more than GKN?
- Where do they achieve their sales?

- Do they invest capital in this country or other countries?
- How big is their trading surplus?
- How big were their profits?
- How high were their dividends last financial year?
- Who are their biggest customers?

It might be a help to jog students' memories by referring back to sections 5.5 and 5.6. In those cases, the focus was on the development of a company and on what it does.

Which company in your own country could you compare with GKN? In what way is or was its performance similar or different?

At the end, allow time for feedback.

7.8 Where the money is ...   *Discussion*

This section provides the opportunity to talk about the wider implications of making money. The issue of ownership of industry and commerce is one which is likely to come up in business transactions. As well as being a topic people in business may be expected to talk about, it is also something which affects the 'normal consumer', whether as customer or user as well as employee or even shareholder.

A   This section can be steered by asking the students to keep a checklist of the areas of business mentioned. They first work in pairs. When they have finished, give them time to report back to the class as a whole and to raise queries and compare possibly unanswered questions. It goes without saying that it will help, if you, as a teacher, can provide some answers about the relevant sectors of industry in the country you are teaching in. You can then compare it with the UK and the US. You are advised to seek up-to-date information, as ownership can sometimes change hands pretty rapidly! This was more or less the situation in 1988 for each sector:

	UK	USA
POST	state	state
TELEPHONES	private	private
'NATIONAL' AIRLINE	private	private
RAILWAY SYSTEM	state	private
BUS TRANSPORT	private	private
MOTORWAYS/FREEWAYS	state	state and private Turnpikes
GAS	private	private
WATER	state	private
ELECTRICITY	state	private
STEEL PRODUCTION	state	private

155

COAL	state	private
TV	mixed	private
RADIO ...	mixed	private

B   Students first work in pairs. Then get students to form groups of four or six and compare the answers and opinions they arrived at. The class as a whole may then re-form.

A guiding question for the discussion might include the following: who do they think are the 'typical' shareholders in the various countries mentioned in the charts? What is the situation like in their own countries?

NOTE   The figures in the chart need to be taken with some caution. How many shares a shareholder owns varies very widely. The accounts for 1986 of British Telecom show that 1.2 million of the 1.3 million individual shareholders had holdings of fewer than 800 shares, worth less than £1,500 and owned just 7.3 per cent of the company.

Extra activity

If this topic proves of interest, you can divide the class up into two teams: A 'public control/nationalized' team and a 'private/commercial' team. Ask each team to gather arguments in favour of their positions. Then let them report back. Toss up to decide which team begins: One student must put forward a pro argument for his/her position then a student from the other team must put forward a counter argument. Then change sides and let a student from the other team put forward a pro argument, and so on until everyone has had a turn. Finally, ask the students to summarize their impressions of the discussion.

7.9   Financial terms   *Vocabulary*

This exercise can be done by students working in pairs. It can be done at any stage during the unit if you have time available, or done as homework.

1. royalties   5. overheads   9. standing order
2. proceeds   6. lack   10. subsidies
3. incur   7. funds
4. write off   8. endorse

Workbook

Other important vocabulary is introduced throughout this unit and in Workbook exercise 7.7.

7.10   Dealing with foreign exchange and money abroad

The purpose of this activity is to give students the opportunity to learn and practise useful terms concerning foreign currency and the kinds of payment situation abroad they may find themselves in either on business or as tourists.

Procedure

For the whole of this section students can work in pairs. Although you may find it helpful to let the class as a whole compare notes after each step.

A   This is a scene-setting step for the reading tasks in step B. Introduce the general topic of paying for things when travelling abroad and ask students to work in pairs and to make a list of the different ways you can pay for things when you travel abroad.

Write up a checklist in three columns which students should copy into their notes for this activity.

	Methods	Pros	Cons
1	. . .	. . .	too much cash on person is dangerous
2	. . .	takes up less space in personal luggage	. . .
3 etc...			

B   Students now follow the instructions and read the article. Remind them to read questions 1 and 2 before they read the article for the first time.

Then get them to read the article again and answer the detailed questions.

Suggested answers:
1. There are six methods discussed: traveller's cheques; foreign currency; postcheques; credit cards; charge cards and Euro-cheques.
2. The Eurocheque: is implicitly recommended very highly for Europe, where it is shown to be quite versatile. No *single* method is explicitly recommended as better than the others.
3. They will be replaced if lost or stolen, theoretically within 24 hours.
4. At a (foreign) bank. Elsewhere the rate is less favourable.
5. For necessary expenses when they return.
6. In most of Europe and around the Mediterranean as well as Hong Kong, the Bahamas and Japan.

7. They are accepted in nearly 5 million outlets. They may also be used for cash advances instead of a deposit on car hire.
8. They are less widely accepted than credit cards. One might also mention that like credit cards they charge a one per cent processing charge for bills converted back into sterling.
9. They are then debited in the same way as a domestic cheque.
10. Individual cheques can be cashed for up to a maximum of £100 or the equivalent in local currency. But there is no limit to the number of cheques you can use to make a purchase.

C This step is done in pairs. Then students tell each other what differences there are between their original list and the items in the article. This can be done in groups of four. If there is sufficient time, the whole class can then compare notes on what they consider advantages and disadvantages.

D This exercise gives students more practice in using numbers and amounts of money. For this conversion of currencies using the exchange rates table, students should work in pairs and take alternate items. It may help to take a pocket calculator along to the class for the follow-up session when students should compare their answers either with a member of another pair or with other members of the class.

It is in the nature of exchange rates that they fluctuate and will be markedly different by the time you read this in print. Hence you are advised to use the *Financial Times* or another easily available newspaper to get up-to-date rates for your students. The ones printed in the book are given to serve as a model.

Finally, students can be asked to convert the amounts given into the equivalent in their own currency using the table above.

E The questions are first done in pairs. Then students compare their answers with another pair. For this discussion, you are advised to look at current or recent economic and financial developments – in newspapers and magazines – which your students are likely to have heard or read about. The development subsequent to the period indicated in the graph may well be characterized by substantial fluctuations in exchange rates. Hence question 4 may need some extension. How much has the dollar, pound, DM or Yen fallen or risen against the other currencies in the intervening period?

Extra activity

BUSINESS SITUATIONS If there is time you can ask students to work out how they would react in the following business situations:
● Your firm receives an invoice from a supplier, Mr Robertson. You find he has changed the method of payment. He wants you to pay

by letter of credit instead of by cheque. What do you say when you ring him up about this?

(Really, Mr Robertson, we didn't at all expect / we can't accept a change in / You never informed us / should have told us there was going to be change.)

- Your company have received a bill for a large sum of money. Your account will not have sufficient money in it to pay by cheque. You ring the credit controller of your supplier to ask to delay payment. What do you say to her?

(Step 7.4A contains examples of what might be said if students find difficulty in getting started.)

Workbook

Contents for this unit:

7.1	Reported speech	Grammar
7.2	Numbers and figures	Reading aloud
7.3	Request for extension of credit and reminder	Letter writing
7.4	Suffixes	Word-building
7.5	Reminding customers of non-payment of bills	Listening
7.6	Prepositions – 3	
7.7	Vocabulary	
7.8	Taking a message – numbers	Listening

Background information: Delivery and after-sales

In business, dealing with a supplier isn't quite the same as buying groceries from a supermarket! A regular supplier, particularly if he is your sole supplier, will probably be someone whose good-will you depend on:

- you may be getting a good discount from him
- you may be getting favourable terms of payment and even extended credit from him
- he will be ready to help you out with an urgent order at short notice
- he may be working closely with you to tailor his products to your needs
- he may be able to offer you technical advice and support whenever you need it
- you know that you can rely on him to deliver goods of the quality you require
- and you know that he will deliver them on time.

A new supplier, even if his prices are low and he is keen to make a good impression and secure further orders, may not be able to work with you so well and may even let you down on his delivery dates.

Delivery

Goods may be shipped by air, sea, rail or road. Carriage and insurance may be:

- the supplier's responsibility – for example, with a 'CIF' (Cost, Insurance and Freight) contract, the price paid by the buyer includes shipment and insurance of the goods to an agreed point of delivery in the buyer's country.
- or the buyer's responsibility – for example, with an 'ex-works' or 'ex-warehouse' contract, the buyer will arrange for the goods to be collected from the supplier's premises.
- or the responsibility may be shared – for example, with an 'FOB' (Free on Board) contract, the supplier is responsible for the goods up to the time they have been loaded on a ship, and then the buyer takes responsibility.

Goods are always insured in transit, through an insurance company or insurance brokers. Claims for damage or loss may be made if the goods have been damaged, lost or interfered with in transit. When a consignment is received, it is examined and the delivery note is signed to confirm that the goods have been received and that they are undamaged. However, damage and errors are often noticed later when the container or package is unpacked and re-checked.

Problems may be due to mistakes made by the suppliers and these may be rectified by offering the dissatisfied customer a replacement, a refund or a credit note (to be used as part-payment of the next order).

After-sales

A buyer's contract with a supplier often includes installation of equipment by qualified personnel, regular servicing for a limited period after delivery, having a service person on call at 24 hours' notice to fix breakdowns, etc.

Once a service or goods have been paid for, the customer may be in a weak position: he can't refuse to pay if he is dissatisfied! Usually after-sales service is provided freely and without demur, because it is an important aspect of marketing strategy. A company that refuses to provide good service is going to get itself a bad reputation, which will affect all its sales in the future. But some customers are 'professional complainers' and suppliers develop special ways of detecting such people and then dealing with them in special ways. Genuine complaints receive more sympathetic attention!

8 Delivery and after-sales

This unit deals with some of the problems that may arise when goods have been delivered. There are a series of integrated activities where students become involved in 'cases' in which delivery or after-sales problems have to be resolved. This unit's functions are complaining and apologizing and the grammar topic is the use of conditional sentences.

8.1 We all make mistakes – sometimes!

The purpose of this activity is to make students aware of the difficulties of dealing with a big mistake that has been made – particularly when people may be upset or disgruntled. The work they have done in Units 6 and 7 will have prepared them for this activity. The theme of dealing with mistakes is continued in 8.2 and 8.3. Students should discuss various solutions to the problem, the best of which will result in nobody feeling as if they have 'lost' in the deal.

Procedure

Arrange the class into an *even* number of pairs or groups of three. Students who have little or no work experience should be placed with a more experienced colleague. If most of the class have no work experience, then groups of three or four may be more effective.

The groups will be rearranged at step 5 for the role play.

1. Students should read the notes and form their own impressions of what has happened. (Young Max has confused the two companies and placed a big order with the wrong company.)

2. 🔲 After step one, *without* discussing the problem with the class, play the recorded telephone message:

This is ... er ... Lucia Donato at UNIFLEX in La Spezia. Er ... we've been expecting your order this month and it hasn't arrived yet. I must admit that I ... I'm a bit surprised by this but I'm assuming that you want to repeat last month's quantities. I ... if you want to make any changes, you'd better let me know. We'll be loading tomorrow afternoon, so could you contact me first thing tomorrow please?

[Time: 30 seconds]

3. Then tell everyone to look at File 99, where they will discover that Mr Conti of Uniplex in Pisa is delighted to have received this unexpectedly large order. Just to make it quite clear what has gone wrong, they also see their own files about UNIFLEX and Uniplex.

4. While the groups are discussing the questions, go round giving advice and hints. There are no 'correct answers' to these questions, though members of the class may have strong feelings about what should be done!
   - If necessary, point out that as the order has been placed with Uniplex by Zenith, there is now a binding contract between the companies which can only be revoked by mutual agreement.
   - Get an impression of how far the groups have progressed in making their decision, so that you can tell everyone to begin the telephone/visit role play at the same time.

5. ☎ or 📺 Rearrange the groups so that the conversations take place between students who haven't been together so far. The conversations may be on the phone or face to face.
   - Point out that there are two role plays: one conversation between the Zenith buyer and Piero Conti and another between the Zenith buyer and Lucia Donato.
   - Remind everyone to make notes before the call, because the situations are delicate: both Conti and Donato may be disgruntled or indignant.
   - The third person, if there is one, should listen to the call as an 'observer' and make notes of what the speakers might have done differently or better.
   - Make sure *both* partners have a turn at being the Zenith person, so that no one has to play the role of both Mr Conti and Ms Donato.
   - If there's time, the third person can re-play one of the roles, with the benefit of his/her experience and observations.

6. The original groups should reassemble to draft their telexes or faxes. The MODEL VERSIONS on the page 165 may give some ideas to less imaginative or less experienced groups – but point out that these documents may not represent the wisest decisions!

   More experienced groups may well disapprove of the way the situation has been handled in these versions.

7 Collect the completed drafts and 'deliver' them to another group for comments.

8 Reassemble the class and ask each group to report on what they did. Encourage the others to ask questions, particularly on their reasons for making their decision.

9 The report can be started in class and then completed as homework. Suggest that each group makes notes together first. They should decide how the facts may need to be 'slanted' so as not to cast too bad a light on Max (your boss's favourite son, who is perhaps being groomed to take over his father's job?!).

Before you collect the homework, encourage students to read each other's reports.

Follow-up discussion

Ask the class what they learned from doing this activity:
- How important is it to apologize for mistakes?
- Is it desirable to establish a friendly relationship with your suppliers?
- Why should suppliers be treated with politeness and consideration, if they're just out to make a profit by selling you things? (See Background Information above.)

[YOU MAY PHOTOCOPY THESE DOCUMENTS]

```
TO: PIERO CONTI
FROM: ZENITH INTERNATIONAL

RE: OUR ORDER FOR MCL CABLE

WE REGRET THAT WE SHALL HAVE TO CANCEL THIS ORDER.
UNFORTUNATELY, A TEMPORARY MEMBER OF OUR STAFF PLACED THE
ORDER BY MISTAKE WHILE I WAS ON HOLIDAY.

HOWEVER, WE ARE STILL VERY INTERESTED IN YOUR PRODUCTS. WE
DO HOPE THAT WE MAY BE ABLE TO DO BUSINESS WITH YOU IN
FUTURE. PERHAPS YOU COULD CONTACT US TO DISCUSS THIS SOON?

WE ARE VERY SORRY ABOUT THE INCONVENIENCE THIS MAY HAVE
CAUSED.
REGARDS,
BBBB CCCC, ZENITH INTERNATIONAL
```

To Lucia Donato, UNIFLEX SpA., La Spezia
From Zenith International

MCL88 Cable

Dear Ms Donato,

We are very sorry about the confusion about our order
this month. There was a slip-up in our buying
department during the holidays, which resulted in a
number of errors.
    Page 2 of this fax is a copy of the order that
should have been sent to you. As you will see, this is
exactly the same as last month's order. I hope that
you will be able to fill the order in spite of our
delay.
    I apologize again for the inconvenience caused.
Thank you for drawing our attention to the situation
and for your patience.
    Looking forward to seeing you next time you are in
Aaaaa.

Best wishes,

Bbbb Ccccccc,
Zenith International.

© Cambridge University Press, 1989

8.2 Complaints and apologies

As the style of complaining is different in other languages, it's important for students to realize that a cool, direct criticism may be interpreted by British or American people as aggressive or even as insulting. In some cultures, a direct complaint may be even more hurtful. As the purpose of complaining is often to get someone to change or improve things (and not simply to apologize humbly), it is counter-productive to antagonize them, even if they have made a stupid mistake.

Presentation

If possible, students should look at the presentation section *before* they come to class. This will give them a better chance of remembering the expressions, will save time in class and will lead to a more informed and interesting discussion of the topic in class.

1. Begin by getting the class to look at the examples in speech balloons. Discuss the points made in the text.

   Do a quick repetition exercise with the expressions, emphasizing the *tone of voice* that should be used: a polite, slightly tentative tone is preferable to a cold, unfriendly or angry one. Ask the class to suggest how the incomplete sentences might continue.

2. 🔲 Play the recording. It may be best to pause between each conversation so that partners can discuss their notes as they go, while they can still remember what happened in each part.

   If you anticipate having to play the cassette several times, perhaps get students to note down the PROBLEMS only on the first listening – noting down the SOLUTIONS can be done on the second listening.

ONE

Customer: Er ... good morning. Er ... I bought this box of computer paper last week but it's not the right size – it should be A4.

Assistant: Oh, sorry about that. Um ... it says A4 on the box.

Customer: Oh, yes I know, but ... here ... if you look inside you'll see: it's a smaller size.

Assistant: Oh yeah, so it is. I'm very sorry ... er ... I'll get you another box.

Customer: Right, thanks.

. . .

Assistant: Er ... I'm very sorry but we haven't got another box in stock.

Customer: Oh no!

Assistant: Yeah, I am sorry about that. Er ... if you like, I'll just call our other branch to see if they have any.

Customer: Oh, no ... er ... don't bother. Um ... I'd prefer a refund.

Assistant: Of course. That's £11.95. Here you are. Sorry about that.

Customer: Oh, that's all right, thanks anyway. Bye.

Assistant: Bye.

TWO

Mr South: I'm ...er ... I'm sorry to bother you, Mrs West.

Mrs West: Yes, Mr South?

Mr South: Er ... it may have slipped your mind, but you told me last week that ... that *you*'d send in the orders to Compass International.

Mrs West: Yes, that's right, yes, I did send in the order. Er ... on Friday afternoon.

Mr South: Well, the ... the thing is, did ... did you realize there were two separate orders? O ... one for northern region and another for eastern region?

Mrs West: Oh dear! Jeez, I'm sorry. I didn't realize the eastern region had ... had to be done too.

Mr South: Oh, it really doesn't matter, there's still just time.

Mrs West: Well, I'll phone Compass and explain, shall I?

Mr South: Er ... no, no, I think it'd be best to send the order by telex, don't ... don't you?

Mrs West: Yeah, yeah, all right. I'll do that right away. Sorry again!

Mr South: Oh ... oh, that's all right.

THREE

Mr Joiner: Good morning. Carpenter and Sons, can I help you?

Miss Zimmermann: Hello, this is Heidi Zimm ᵣmann of Schreiner International.

Mr Joiner: Hello, Miss Zimmermann. This is Ted Joiner. What can I do for you?

Miss Zimmermann: Well, I think there may have been some ... a misunderstanding about our last order.

Mr Joiner: Oh dear, what seems to be the problem?

Miss Zimmermann: We've just started unloading the truck and the quality of the goods doesn't appear to be Class A1, which is what we ordered.

Mr Joiner: Oh dear, I'm very sorry. Let me just check this on the computer ...... Er ... oh dear, yes, I'm afraid there has been a slip-up in our shipping department. I'm very sorry, it's certainly our fault. Wh ... what would you like us to do about it?

Miss Zimmermann: Well, we can keep the goods and ... and use them for another order of ours, *if* you will charge us 20% less for the load and ship us a load of Class A1 right away.

Mr Joiner: That sounds fair enough. Let me just check the stock position ... Yes, we can ship tomorrow morning, if that's all right?

Miss Zimmermann: Oh yes, that will be fine.

Mr Joiner: Oh good. Er ... thank you very much, Miss Zimmermann. I'm very sorry that this happened.

Miss Zimmermann: That's quite all right. Goodbye.

FOUR

Telephonist: Good afternoon. Windsor Products.

Mr Wong: May I speak with Tina Castle in marketing please?

Telephonist: Tina Castle, certainly. One moment please.

Miss Castle: Tina Castle.

Mr Wong: Hello, this is Henry Wong of ArrowPrint.

Miss Castle: Hi, Mr Wong. What can I do for you?

Mr Wong: It's about the order for your new packaging. I think you may have forgotten to send us the colour negatives.

Miss Castle: I sent the complete set of negatives by airmail on the 14th, I remember packing them up myself. They should have arrived by now.

Mr Wong: Yes, well we did get a package from you on the 18th, but the problem is that the *colour* negatives were missing.

Miss Castle: Are you sure?

Mr Wong: Yes, we only got the black and white ones.

......

Miss Castle: Oh dear, I've just been

through my out-tray and I've found them here! I'm very sorry, it's my fault. I'll send them by courier at once.

Mr Wong: No, no, no, that's not neces-sary. My assistant, Mr Patel is coming to your office tomorrow, so you can give them to him and he can bring them back.

Miss Castle: Right. I'll make sure he gets them. I'm sorry this happened.

Mr Wong: It's perfectly all right, Miss Castle. Goodbye.

[Time: 4 minutes 20 seconds]

Find out if any members of the class have been in similar situations. Was the outcome different for them?

Afterwards, if there's time, play the recording again: with no questions to answer, students can sit back and enjoy listening to the conversations again. They will be receptive to the language used in the conversations and will be in the right mood to assimilate useful expressions – and they will be able to notice how the speakers complain and apologize.

3. Ask everyone to look at the speech balloons that show exponents of the functions of apologizing and forgiving. Then ask them to look at the section on reasons and excuses. Ask the class to suggest other excuses that may be used to cover up for a mistake: bad weather delaying delivery, your suppliers letting you down, sabotage by a disgruntled employee, a clumsy employee dropping something fragile, etc.

Exercises and activities

A After the pairs have completed the sentences, it might be wise to check their work. Then get them to work out how they would reply to each letter.

These are suggested completions and replies (all of which are open to discussion):

```
...Could you please confirm that you have received the order and
that you have the goods in stock?

REPLY...Please accept our apologies for not having confirmed
your order. The reason is that we have been understaffed
this month as there has been a flu epidemic here. We can
confirm that the order has been received and will be shipped
to you tomorrow, in accordance with your instructions.


...Would you please look into this matter? We can only assume that
this shipping note was sent in error and that the goods have not
been dispatched.

REPLY...We are very sorry for this mistake. Our dispatch
manager discovered at the last moment that your order was
incomplete and he delayed the shipment until the missing
parts had been found. Unfortunately, the shipping advice had
```

168

already been posted and we failed to inform you of the delay.
   I am pleased to inform you that the missing parts have now
been packed and left our works yesterday.

...Will you please refund the difference, which I calculate to be
$72.50 for 5 nights.

REPLY...We wish to apologize for our mistake in overcharging
you for your room. I have looked into the matter and
discover that you were charged at the double room rate by
mistake. I have refunded the sum of $72.50 to your
MasterCard account and enclose the refund slip.
   In view of our error and in the hope that you will stay
with us again, may I offer you a special discount of 15% for
your next stay at our hotel?

...Will you please arrange for the missing items to be shipped to us
at once?

REPLY...Please accept our apologies for this mistake. Since
your order was placed, we have begun using new boxes which
contain 100 items. Your order was short by 3520 items.
A further 36 boxes are on their way to you now.

B   In this activity the same situations are dealt with on the
phone. Students, working in pairs, should sit back-to-back as usual so
that they only use their voices to communicate. Each call must be
ended to both parties' satisfaction.

C   Student A should look at File 24, student B at 61. They
should imagine that they are colleagues, working in the same office. In
each file there are some things they should apologize for doing (or for
forgetting to do) and some things they want to criticize their colleague
for doing (or for forgetting to do).
   Point out that the expressions given in this section may help them to
start a complaint or apology but that they must use their own ideas to
continue.

Follow-up discussion

How is the British/US behaviour in making complaints and apologies
   different from that in your students' country – and in other countries
   they know?
In what other circumstances is it customary to complain or apologize
   in business *and* in social life?
Why is complaining sometimes rather risky? – see the first paragraph
   of this section above.

Finally, perhaps ...
Tell the class the story about the man who was travelling in a sleeping
car on an American railway train who found a bedbug in his bunk. He

169

was furious and complained to the company. He got back a long, beautifully typed letter saying that this was the first time anything like this had ever happened, they would be doing a thorough check of every sleeping car in their trains, they were truly sorry, they were really grateful to the man for bringing this to their attention, and so on for a whole page. As he was reading the letter, a little slip of paper fell out of the envelope and onto the floor. He picked it up and on it he read the words: 'Send this bum the bug letter'.

Workbook

Workbook exercise 8.2 provides further work on this function.

8.3 Friday afternoon: delivery problems

These case studies will give students a chance to exchange ideas and experiences in dealing with problems. Each text in this section, as well as giving information for the task, is a model for subsequent written work students will have to do – for example the telex to Medco in the 2nd problem can be based on the telex to Ocean View in the 1st problem.

The three problems should be dealt with in sequence, as they get harder. Allow time for groups to compare ideas after each problem. If you anticipate that your students will have difficulty with the listening and reading, perhaps check that everyone has understood exactly what each problem is before they discuss how to solve it. You could ask, for example: 'So what exactly has gone wrong in this situation?'

1st problem

▶ Begin by playing the recording of a telephone message from Mr Robinson, the production manager:

This is Ted Robinson. Um ... it's about these new alloy components. Now, when the components were unpacked and inspected, we found that although most of the parts are OK, the screw adaptors don't meet our specifications. Now, they ... the ones that you sent us are GJ 501s and we need JG 507s. I'll say that again: JG 507s. Now, I've checked your order and that was correct and so was the pro-forma the suppliers sent, so it seems to be the fault of the supplier's export packing department. Now, the problem is: if the right parts don't arrive by next Wednesday, part of the production line will have to stop and in all 5000 screw adaptors have to be replaced, of which 500 are needed for next week's production. So, can you do something about this and let me know what you propose to do? OK? Goodbye.

[Time: 1 minute]

Before they begin the 2nd problem, perhaps ask one or two groups to report their solutions to the whole class and ask them to justify any action they took.

2nd and 3rd problems

Follow the steps in the Student's Book.

Suggested solutions

Be prepared for members of the class (who will by now have discussed these problems at length!) to argue with these. It may be best to preface each one with 'Do you think it might be a good idea if . . . ?' if you're asked what *you* would do – after all you're an English language expert, not an experienced business person.

1st Problem:
Phone Ocean View and ask for all or part of the order to be airfreighted or shipped at once. Or maybe find another supplier locally who can deliver more quickly?

2nd Problem:
Try to persuade Medco to bring forward their delivery to Thursday, explaining your problem in the warehouse on Friday. Otherwise, make a special arrangement with your warehouse manager to have extra staff on duty that day to unload the truck from Medco.

3rd Problem:
Either placate Arctic Refrigeration by accepting responsibility (if you think $255/285 isn't a sum worth bothering about), but find out if the correct amount to credit is $255 or $285, preferably by checking with your delivery manager.

Or (if you think it's a significant sum and that Arctic really are trying it on this time and are likely to do so again) fax a letter to Arctic disclaiming responsibility and implying that they can whistle for their money.

Extra activity: A 4th problem

If there is time, students can be given another, more difficult problem to solve in addition to the three in the Student's Book.

Explain this situation to the class:
'You are a supplier. You are going to have to delay your delivery to Atlantic Imports of Miami by two to three weeks. This is due to staff shortages in your warehouse and to a late change that the customer made to the order, which required a lot of extra work. The order will arrive in Miami some time during the second half of February.'

1. Decide together what you're going to do this time. Will you inform Atlantic Imports of the delay? What will you say or write?
2. Draft a letter or telex – or write notes for the phone call you will make.
3. When you have decided, join another pair or group and compare your solutions. Look at each other's drafts.
4. You are about to get in touch with Atlantic Imports when this fax message arrives:

[YOU MAY PHOTOCOPY THIS DOCUMENT]

<u>Our order ref 4498</u>

I am writing to you regarding your delay in shipping this order.

As you will appreciate, we have commitments to our own customers who are depending on these goods. We require this order to arrive in our warehouse by February 14 at the latest. If you are unable to keep to this date we will deduct 5% from your invoice for each week of delay that we experience.

If we do not receive confirmation of this revised shipping date by return, we will be obliged to cancel this order and will seek another supplier.

Please acknowledge that you have received and understood this letter.

Sincerely,

Felipe Castro

Felipe Castro
Atlantic Imports

© Cambridge University Press 1989

5. Write the letter or telex you would send to Mr Castro (if you didn't want to phone him).

Follow-up discussion

At the end, ask the class what they learned from the activities:
- Do they prefer to deal with problems like these in person, in writing or on the phone – and why?
- Is it best to tell the truth, to lie or to tell a white lie?
- Is it best to take the blame or to blame someone else for your mistakes?

Finally, give students a chance to talk about their bad experiences. Even students without work experience may have been on the receiving end of a delivery problem, by mail order perhaps.

Workbook

Workbook exercise 8.5 provides further work on this topic.

8.4 What if ... ?   *Grammar*

Almost all students of English have difficulties with conditionals: using the correct verb forms and also choosing the appropriate type of conditional to express their meaning precisely. The use of *if, when, in case* and *unless* may also be confusing. The brief explanations in this section won't cure these difficulties once and for all and further work may be necessary using the Workbook and/or exercises from other sources (*Use of English* Units 24 & 25 are recommended).

Draw attention to the use of commas in the examples – but reassure (?) students that there are no fixed rules about this in English.

Exercises A to C in the Student's Book are designed to concentrate on the correct grammatical forms that are used in conditional sentences. Activity D is more open-ended. Further communicative activities are suggested in the Extra Activities below.

Presentation

If possible, students should read this section through before the lesson.

The examples ('If our flight isn't delayed, ...' etc) are recorded, so that students can hear, as well as see, the sentences that are used. Make sure any queries are cleared up before students begin exercise A in pairs – though it is to be expected that doing the exercise will give rise to further questions.

Exercises and activity

Exercises A to C should be done by students together in pairs, with time after each exercise for discussion and questions. In exercise A, they don't have to use the verbs given if they have any better ideas (see the suggested answers below). If time is short, the exercises can be set as homework, but should still be discussed in class afterwards to clear up any doubts or misunderstandings.

For D, the activity on newspaper headlines, students should work in groups of four or five, so that there are plenty of different ideas in each group.

To set the ball rolling, it might be best to start by picking one of the headlines and asking everyone in the class to speculate on consequences of the event – more fanciful consequences can be mentioned like this, using *might*:

'If unemployment ever rose to 50%, there might be a revolution in this
country.'
The idea is that the *possible* events will be discussed like this:
'If income tax rises to 50%, ...'
whilst *very unlikely* events are discussed like this:
'If there was/were a computer on every school pupil's desk, ...'

These are suggested answers to the exercises:

A 1. *example: make sure everyone understands what they have to do*
2. breaks down   will/shall call *or* contact
3. remains   will be carried out
4. had made   would have accepted
5. realized   would understand / would realize
6. would you do (*or* action would you take)   saw (*or* found/caught)
7. decline   shall/will (have to) send them
8. had foreseen   would have checked
9. arise   contact (*or* call) me
10. flourishes   will become

B 1. *example: make sure everyone knows what they have to do*
2. ... unless there is a breakdown or it requires servicing.
3. ... in case any unforeseen difficulties arise.
4. ... when my plane arrives.
5. ... if the machine is still under guarantee.
6. ... when he calls to carry out the first service.
7. ... in case the weather turns cold while I'm away.
8. ... unless the matter is extremely urgent.

C 1. will not   you are
2. I will *or* I shall   have not
3. What will   are not
4. What would   could not
5. I would   he had
6. I would have   I had
7. would not   had   would
8. had   would

Extra activities

These activities are more open-ended and communicative. Students
should work in pairs or small groups.

1. Just imagine that both of you were born in a completely different
country OR that you were born in a different century. Ask your

partner to speculate by asking:
> What would have been different about your childhood and your life so far?
> What would be different about your work and personal life now?

2. Find out from your partner if there have been any 'turning points' in his or her life (e.g. a chance meeting that led to an important relationship, or success at an interview that led to an interesting job). Then ask your partner to speculate by asking:
> What would have been different about your life if these events hadn't happened?

Workbook

Workbook exercise 8.6 provides further work on this topic.

8.5 Shipping and delivery   *Vocabulary*

This exercise can be done by students working in pairs. It can be done at any stage during the unit if you have time available, or as homework.

Answers:
1. merchandise   reject   refund
2. compensate   claim
3. negligence   take legal action   lawsuit
4. attorneys/solicitors   sue
5. truck   load   rebate
6. minor   major   modification
7. expired   void
8. circumstances   storage
9. overseas   regulations   quotas   boycotts
10. cash against documents   documents against payment
    Chamber of Commerce

Workbook

Other important vocabulary is introduced throughout this unit and revised in Workbook exercise 8.3.

8.6 After-sales problems

These case studies will give students a chance to exchange ideas and experiences in dealing with problems, both as customers and suppliers. Each text in this section, as well as giving information for the task, is a model for subsequent written work students will have to do – for example a letter to Coyote Enterprises in the 2nd problem can be based on the letter to Mr Reynard in the 1st problem.

In business, customers are sometimes dissatisfied with a product or service after it has been delivered and paid for – maybe because they have unreasonable expectations, maybe because the service really is bad. Often, it's six of one and half a dozen of the other, though!

The four problems should be dealt with in sequence, as they get harder. Allow time for groups to compare ideas after each problem. If you anticipate that your students will have difficulty with the listening or reading, perhaps check that everyone has understood exactly what each problem is before they discuss how to solve it. You could ask, for example: 'So what exactly has gone wrong in this situation?'

In each problem, if students have decided to make notes for a phone call, allow time for them to role-play the call – possibly with another group listening in as observers.

1st Problem

Follow steps 1 to 3.
In step 4, students look at File 116, where they will see an unexpectedly apologetic, placatory telex from Mr Reynard, which they must respond to.

Before they begin the 2nd Problem, perhaps ask one or two groups to report their solutions to the whole class and ask them to justify any action they took.

2nd Problem

1. 🔲 Play the first part of the recording to the whole class. Note that the woman's voice is very indistinct, as if it's heard down the line. Students are 'eavesdropping' on Mr Kellerman's phone call:

Bob: Good morning. Buying department.
Michelle: Hello, can I speak to Bob Kellerman?
Bob: Speaking. Hi Michelle. How are you?
Michelle: Fine. It's about those new components.

Bob: You mean the X77's – the ones from Coyote Enterprises?
Michelle: Yes.
Bob: Uhuh, why, are there any problems with them?
Michelle: There's a big problem with the quality of the wiring.
Bob: Yeah, but we tested all the

samples and my assistant told me there were no problems at all with the wiring. And the price is very good, Michelle. No, it ... it may be Coyote's ... er ... quality control that's at fault. Er ... is it just the wiring that's faulty?

Michelle: No, there have been problems with the switches too.

Bob: No, not the switches! What, is there a safety problem or something?

Michelle: The assembly people are having to reject 20% of them.

Bob: Wait a minute, did you say 20%?

Michelle: Yes.

Bob: Well, if you're rejecting that many, then there's no cost saving i ... in getting the components from Coyote. A ... and if any switches don't work properly, well, then we'll be getting some customer complaints.

Michelle: We already have had. There's obviously a design fault.

Bob: A design fault in the switches? But if there *is* a design fault, I'm ... Geoff

– you know Geoff in Assembly – well, he would have told me. So, are you sure?

Michelle: Yes.

Bob: Oh no! All right, I'll look into it. I ... is there any ... anything else?

Michelle: Well, the paint matching isn't quite right.

Bob: Well, if the paint doesn't match, that's not so serious, we can deal with that. But with everything else – well, OK, I'll get onto this right away. Um ... I'll get my assistant to look into it and ... er ... I'll get back to you ... um ... well, I'm not sure, but as soon as I can, is that all right?

Michelle: As soon as you can, Bob.

Bob: OK, Michelle. Listen, I'm really sorry about all this. I'll clear it up.

Michelle: Bye.

Bob: Bye-bye. I'll talk to you later. Bye-bye

[Time: 1 minute 40 seconds]

2., 3. and 4. Follow the procedure in the Student's Book. Allow time for the phone calls to be role-played, if necessary.

5. 🔲 Play the second part of the recording to the whole class:

Secretary: Bob, it's Mr Wiley of Coyote Enterprises. Are you free?

Bob: Mr Wiley?

Secretary: Yes, you know, the sales rep. from Coyote Enterprises.

Bob: Haha. Right! Yeah! Wheel him in, he's ... he's picked just the right day to call!
......
Ah, well, Mr Wiley, how ... er ... it's nice to ... er ... to see you again. Come on in, sit down.

Mr Wiley: Mr Kellerman, how are you?

Bob: I'm fine, I'm fine. Well now, about these components ... er ... we've been getting from you.

Mr Wiley: What the ... er ... the X77's? Yeah, well, they've been extremely popular – good value too, I think you'll agree.

Bob: Have you had any problems with ... er ... reliability?

Mr Wiley: Er ... no, none at all, why?

Bob: Well ... er ... you see, our sales people have been getting all sorts of complaints. First: about the wiring.

Mr Wiley: Well, I mean, that's very strange because as far as I know the X77's are completely reliable.

Bob: Well, that's not the information we've got. Now, where is the wiring manufactured?

Mr Wiley: Well, I'm ... now we do all the wiring in our own factory. Er ... but ... er ... now, let's see, because you got some of the *first* batch, didn't you?

Bob: First batch, yeah.

Mr Wiley: Which I believe were manu-

177

factured by our ... one of our sub-
contractors.

Bob: Ah, well, that's very interesting.
So, who was responsible for quality
control: was it their people or was it
yours?

Mr Wiley: Er ... well, I'm not sure

about that, normally of course we'd be
responsible, but in this case, well, I'm
not sure you see. It's some time ago ...

[Time: 1 minute 20 seconds]

6. Get everyone to decide what questions they'd like to ask Mr Wiley.

Problems 3 and 4

Ideally, everyone would have a go at both these problems, but if time is
short, different groups could be directed to deal with a different
problem. Then, at the end, the class will have covered both problems
and can explain to the other what they decided, giving their reasons.

Allow time for any phone calls to be role-played.

Extra activity: A 5th problem

If there is time, students can be given another problem to solve in
addition to the four in the Student's Book.

Explain this situation to the class:

'Six weeks ago, you ordered a computer software package from
Lemon Inc. by mail order. It arrived promptly but now you have
discovered that there is a serious bug in the program. You have
written to Lemon and got no reply. You have tried telephoning
Lemon, but they don't answer the phone.'

1. What action are you going to take?
2. Draft a suitable letter or telex – or notes for the phone call you will
make.
3. Role-play the phone call (if you decided to make one).
4. What would you do if you were marketing manager of Lemon Inc.
and you found out what had happened?
5. Draft a suitable letter or telex – or notes for a phone call.

Follow-up discussion

At the end, ask the class what they learned from this activity. Do they
feel more confident about dealing with problems in writing, over the
phone and face to face?

8.7 Satisfaction and loyalty? *Discussion*

This section provides a foretaste of Unit 10: Marketing and sales.
Students should work in groups of four or five for the three parts of
this discussion.

A Point out that this follows up the work done in 8.6.

B Students who have strong feelings about whether marketing
should or should not pervade all aspects of business life will find plenty
to say in this discussion.

C Get each group to show their work to the other. You may prefer
to have students work on this in pairs, or even do it as homework.

Extra discussion ideas

Many large companies publish 'Corporate Objectives', explaining
their principles to the public.
How do the members of the class react to each of these quotes?

1. from HEWLETT-PACKARD CORPORATE OBJECTIVES:
   'Objective #2: To provide products and services of the greatest
   possible value to our customers, thereby gaining and holding their
   respect and loyalty.'
2. ICI corporate objectives, 1984:
   'ICI's principal objective is to improve the effectiveness of wealth
   creation within the group and hence its financial performance, to
   the benefit of shareholders, employees, customers and the communities in which it operates.'

3. Chairman's Statement, Marks and Spencer, 1979:
   'We recognize our social responsibilities and help the communities
   in which our customers and staff live. We shall make progress so
   long as we pay attention to people and continue to be sensitive to
   the needs of our customers.'

4. Well-known saying (first coined as a slogan by the founder of
   Selfridges department store in London):
   'The customer is always right.'

5. Professor Theodore Levitt, Harvard Business School, 1960:
   'The customer is king.'

- Do companies have a social responsibility to the community in
  which they operate?

- Do companies have responsibility for the health and welfare of their workers and their families?
- Should Ethics be taught as part of a management course (as it is in some business schools in the USA)? Or is 'dog eat dog' or 'survival of the fittest' the name of the game in business life?

Workbook

Contents for this unit:

8.1	What's the problem	Listening 📼
8.2	What would you say?	Functions
8.3	Vocabulary	
8.4	Only the best is good enough ...	Listening 📼
8.5	I am writing to you to explain ...	Grammar
8.6	What if ...	Writing
8.7	Prepositions – 4	
8.8	Take a message	Listening 📼

9 Visits and travel

This unit covers many of the situations in which students may find themselves if they are travelling abroad on business *or* dealing with visitors from abroad: making travel arrangements, flying or travelling abroad by road or rail, arranging accommodation and dealing with hotels, looking after visitors and having a meal with an English-speaking person. We also deal with the situation of organizing a small conference or symposium.

This unit's function is narrating and the grammar topic is the use of gerunds and infinitives.

9.1 'A trip to the States ...'   *Listening*

To enhance the realism of the location recordings, it might be a good idea to take in a collection of English-language travel realia: airline tickets, street plans and underground/subway maps, an immigration card, menus, brochures, etc.

The three parts of this section involve first listening to some typical situations (recorded on location in the USA) and then re-enacting the situations. In each section we hear the same person, 'The Traveller' coping with the different situations.

1 Going by air

There are two parts to the recording: 'At the travel agent's' (where The Traveller books a flight) and 'At the airport' (where The Traveller checks in for an internal flight). The recordings are quite long and if time is limited we suggest that you just get the class to note down the missing information and don't spend too long going into the vocabulary or otherwise exploiting the texts.

Answers:
At the travel agent's
    London   29   7-day $595 $1190   15   immediately
At the airport
    San Francisco   317   17A   window   22   6.40
    7 o'clock

Part 1   Going by air

Travel agent: ... what can I help you with today? My name's Steve.

Traveller: My name's Mr Sanchez.

Travel agent: Mr Sanchez, what can I do for you today?

Traveller: I would like to go on a business trip to London.

Travel agent: To London? When are you planning on travelling:

Traveller: I plan on travelling at the end of the month. Today is September 10 and I wish to travel on September 29.

Travel agent: On September 29, let's see. Oh, that's within 21 days. Er ... most of the best airline rates just now are with a 21-day or a 30-day advance purchase. If you're travelling within 21 days the rates might tend to be a little higher. But let me check for you and see what's available ...... If you must leave on the 29th the only advance purchase available would be a 7-day advance purchase. A 7-day advance purchase right now to London would be ... let me check one moment for you ...... If you're travelling within 21 days the only rate available would be $595 in each direction, so that would make a total of ... $1190 round trip.

Traveller: OK, that's OK.

Travel agent: That's OK? That is OK with you? 1190? OK. Um ... if that ... if that rate is available ... if that rate is available for those dates, let me go ahead and see if I can get that. One moment please. ... You said you wanted to leave on 29 September and what was your return date?

Traveller: October 15.

Travel agent: OK, October 15. Um, let me see, do you have any preference to airline or ... Most of the rates are fairly similar on all the airlines, there really isn't much of a difference. Um, do you have a preference on airlines?

Traveller: If possible, British Airways.

Travel agent: British Airways, OK. Let me check one moment, let me give them a call. ...... OK. Um, this is Steve calling from ... ah ... NTC Travel Club. I was wondering if you could tell me if you have one seat available for travel from San Francisco to London on 29 September. ...... Oh, OK you do, thank you. Is there a return available for 15 October? ...... Great, thank you very much, I'd like to hold that reservation if I can. Um, last name will be Sanchez ... and excuse me, what was your first name?

Traveller: Roberto.

Travel agent: OK. First name is Roberto, Mr. ... OK, and what was the rate on that? 1190 round trip, thank you. And what is the ticketing deadline for that? OK, ticketing deadline is set for 15 September. OK, thank you very much, we'll be calling you back with ticket numbers on that. Thank you. As of right now if you want to go ahead and pay for it today, we can go ahead and take care of it right now or if you want a couple of days to think about it, we can hold the reservation until then.

Traveller: No, I can complete immediately.

Travel agent: OK, would you be paying by cash ... um ... or credit card?

Traveller: Visa.

Travel agent: A Visa card, OK. Let me just go ahead and run the authorization through to make sure that everything's OK and we can get the ticket issued for you. Hold on just one moment ..

———

Clerk: Can I help you this evening, sir?

Traveller: Yes please ... um, I'd like ... I'm travelling to San Francisco.

Clerk: OK, do you have your tickets already this evening?

Traveller: Yes, I do.

Clerk: ...... OK, sir, would you like smoking or non-smoking seats this evening?

Traveller: Er, no smoking please.

Clerk: OK. ...... OK, this evening you're going to be travelling out on flight 317. Your seat is 17A, non-smoking, window.

Traveller: Thank you very much indeed. Do you need to see my passport?

Clerk: Ah, no sir.

Traveller: Thank you very much.

Clerk: Was there any bags you'd like checked this evening?

Traveller: Yes please, one.

Clerk: OK ... Is your name and address on your bag, sir?

Traveller: Yes, it is.

Clerk: OK, that'll be one bag checked to San Francisco this evening. Your claim check is stapled in the back of your ticket jacket. Your flight'll be departing out of Gate 22 this evening. Boarding time is 6.40 and your flight leaves at 7 o'clock.

Traveller: Thank you very much indeed.

Clerk: OK, have an enjoyable flight this evening.

[Time: 4 minutes 30 seconds]

In the role play, the passengers keep coming and going to ask their questions about when their flights leave, returning soon after in a new role with a different query. Alternatively, passengers can visit different information counters around the class.

The clerks need to stand or sit behind an information counter, the passengers walk to and fro.

The information for passengers is in File 39 and the timetable for information clerks is in File 60.

Change roles half-way through, so that everyone has a turn at asking the questions. In the first half of the role play the time is 07.30 and in the second half it's 10.00, thus different information is required and given in each part of the role play.

2 Accommodation

We hear The Traveller checking into a motel first and then checking into the Royalton Hotel, New York and later checking out. Again, if time is limited it may be best to get students to concentrate on just doing the straightforward tasks in the Student's Book, and not to exploit the vocabulary in the texts. Reassure students that they don't need to catch every word that's spoken to be able to fill the gaps in the summaries.

Answers:

At the motel

$41.80	double bed	direct dialing	deposit	$10
license	car	coffee and donuts	6 to 10	116

$51.80 (i.e. $41.80 + $10) in cash

At the Royalton Hotel

$55 to $75	breakfast ($5 extra)	quiet	middle	$65
3 nights	519	$516.72	Visa	

(He seems to have stayed for longer than three nights – or maybe he made some very long phone calls!)

Part 2 Accommodation

Traveller: Excuse me, I'd like to check in for a room here.

Motel clerk: OK, how many in your party?

Traveller: Just myself.

Motel clerk: OK, the single rate is $38 plus tax.

Traveller: That's $38 for a single room.

Motel clerk: Mhm. Yes, that's correct.

Traveller: And what do I get in the single room?

Motel clerk: Well, it has the color TV, telephone – direct dialing, and a double bed.

Traveller: Is there breakfast?

Motel clerk: We have coffee and donuts in the morning.

Traveller: Right, so that's $38 plus tax, how much...

Motel clerk: That's right, 10% tax ... 10% tax.

Traveller: So what will the total be?

Motel clerk: 41.80.

Traveller: Per night. OK. Um ... I'd like to check in tonight.

Motel clerk: OK, would you fill out the register please?

Traveller: Right, OK. What do you require me to fill out?

Motel clerk: OK, just fill out your name, address, er ... your license number of your car. And your signature right here. And then I'll do the rest.

Traveller: OK, do you want to see my passport?

Motel clerk: Ah ... that's not necessary.

Traveller: OK, would you like me to pay now?

Motel clerk: Er, yes, pay in advance.

Traveller: Um ... what about telephone calls? Do I pay for those now, or ... ?

Motel clerk: Er, no, you can leave a $10 deposit. If your calls exceed that, then we'll call you and you can come in and take care of them or leave another deposit.

Traveller: OK, well, I'll pay by cash and I'll give you a $10 deposit for telephone calls.

Motel clerk: OK, that'll be fine. That's 10, 20...

Traveller: 30, 40.

Motel clerk: 1.80.

Traveller: That's $1 and ... 80 cents.

Motel clerk: OK, that's exactly right.

Traveller: And that's a $10 deposit for telephone.

Motel clerk: OK ... thank you very much.

Just a moment, let me get you the key. OK, and your room will be located right over there on the first level.

Traveller: So, it's room number...

Motel clerk: 116.

Traveller: 116. Thank you very much indeed.

Motel clerk: You're quite welcome. Coffee and donuts in the morning from 6 till 10. OK, if you're needing any help, just give us a call.

——

Traveller: Excuse me, do you have any accommodation?

Hotel clerk: Yes, we do. How many would you like?

Traveller: Um. I'd like some accommodation just for myself, please.

Hotel clerk: Sure, we have rooms at $55, $65 and $75 a night.

Traveller: Right, um ... I'd like a room that ... a quiet room away from the front of the hotel if possible.

Hotel clerk: Is the middle of the hotel OK, the middle ... you know ... better for you?

Traveller: Yes.

Hotel clerk: Sure. We have it.

Traveller: So how much will that cost?

Hotel clerk: $65.

Traveller: $65. Um ... does it have a bath?

Hotel clerk: Yes, they all have baths and showers, TV sets, radios, wall-to-wall carpeting, lamps: you name it, they has it.

Traveller: And ... um ... breakfast.

Hotel clerk: No breakfast, no ... you ... there's a restaurant here in the hotel, which is separate from the hotel bill.

Traveller: I see, how much is breakfast? Is it ...

Hotel clerk: Well ... $5 ... think so.

Traveller: Fine. I would like to stay for three days, if that's possible.

Hotel clerk: No problem, we have it.

Traveller: Fine, could I ... um ... check in ...

Hotel clerk: Just sign right in right here. Just fill this out: your name and address,

184

and your credit card. And ... er ... what kind of credit card are you using?

Traveller: Visa.

Hotel clerk: Visa, OK, we have it. Thank you. Do you have any ... do you have your passport with you?

Traveller: Yes I do.

Hotel clerk: Some ID? OK, let me have it. Oh, oh very good. There you go, here ... take it back with you. Don't forget your credit card. Er ... bellman, please, would you come here ...... Here's the key, don't forget the key.

Traveller: Thank you very much indeed.

Hotel clerk: OK, bye now. Enjoy your stay.

Hotel clerk: Checking out?

Traveller: Yes, please, yes.

Hotel clerk: Which room number?

Traveller: Um, 519.

Hotel clerk: 519. One moment ...... OK, here's your bill. $516.72. Sign here.

Traveller: Thank you.

Hotel clerk: OK. Thank you. There's your bill ...... Thank you very much for staying. Enjoy your trip. Would you like to make a reservation for next time you're here?

Traveller: No, thank you. But I've enjoyed my stay very much. Thank you.

Hotel clerk: Fine. Thank you very much. Come again.

[Time: 4 minutes 55 seconds]

In the role play, the guests keep coming and going to ask their questions, returning soon after in a new role with a different query. Alternatively, guests can visit different reception desks around the class.

The reception clerks need to stand behind a reception desk, the guests walk to and fro.

The information about the hotel for receptionists is in File 58, the questions for guests to ask in File 44.

Change roles half-way through, so that everyone has a turn at asking the questions. The guests in the second half could choose their questions from the bottom of the list in File 44.

3 Arriving at the office

This recording is different: it works rather like a drill. You will need to PAUSE THE TAPE at the six places indicated by ■ in the transcript, while the members of the class suggest suitable replies to J.R.'s questions. Then start the tape again so that they can hear The Traveller's actual reply to each question. J.R. is the same person we heard describing his job in 1.3 and The Traveller is posing as a Japanese visitor.

Part 3   Arriving at the office

J.R.: Hello, Mr Takahashi. I'm Jim Randall from First of Lake Forest, how are you? ■

Traveller: I'm very well, thank you. Pleased to meet you.

J.R.: Did you have a good flight? ■

Traveller: It was very comfortable thank you.

J.R.: I imagine it was quite long. Have you had the chance to make accommodations in the city? ■

Traveller: Yes, I have. I'm staying at the Holiday Inn and the room is very good.

J.R.: OK. I know right where that is and I'd be very happy to drop you off ... er ... as soon as we possibly have dinner. Have you had dinner on the plane? ■

Traveller: I did, but it was not very good. I would like to have something more substantial if possible.

J.R.: All right, we'd be very happy to ... to do that and show you part of Downtown Chicago as well. Uh ... how long will you be staying with us? ■

Traveller: I anticipate being here for five days.

J.R.: Very good, that will give us appropriate time for us to go over your request and I hope show you a very enjoyable part of the city and our banking facilities at the same time. Er ... would you like to make a call to your family or business associates? ■

Traveller: That's very kind of you, but I've already done so at the hotel.

[Time: 1 minute 34 seconds]

In the role play, one partner plays the role of visitor, the other the role of host or hostess. This time the visitor is not arriving in Chicago, but in the host's/hostess's own city. To give both partners a turn, the role play can be repeated with roles reversed.

9.2   International travel

Presentation

The phrases in the speech balloon are recorded, to show how they might be spoken. All the variations are not spoken, however. Allow time for questions and discussion about when the various phrases might be used.

Activities

A   Students work in pairs as they decide who they'd speak to and what they might say. After a while, get the pairs to compare ideas and discuss this as a class.

B   Now rearrange the class as groups. If time is limited, different groups can be assigned different problems to discuss. Again, allow a little time for each group to report on its discussion to the whole class.

9.3   Narrating   *Functions*

In this Functions section, the Presentation step comes *after* the listening exercise in step A.

A   The stories should be played with a break between them, so that students can discuss their answers after each story.

Answers:
The odd-numbered statements are all false.
The even-numbered statements are all true.

Man: ... anyway, I felt pretty upset, I can tell you!

Woman: Haha. Well, something even worse happened to some friends of a colleague of mine in New York. The husband was on ... on an extended business trip and the idea was that his wife would come over in the middle of it to spend a long weekend with him. He was flying in from Boston, and the wife from Europe and they were going to meet up on the Friday evening and stay the weekend together at one of those very big hotels near Central Park.

Well, the hotel computer had got the first letter of their name wrong – their name began with a B (I think it was Berry) but it was spelt on the computer with a P. So the wife arrived at the hotel, gave her name and asked 'Has my husband arrived yet?' and the reception clerk looked her up on the computer said no, not yet and so she said she'd wait in their room and she was shown to the room. So she turned on the TV and, you know, started waiting. Well, then about half an hour later the husband arrived and gave his name and spelt it out carefully to the reception clerk and asked 'Has my wife arrived yet?' and she looked up the name on the computer and said 'No, not yet', so he said he'd wait in the room and the clerk promised to send his wife up to him when she arrived and he was shown up to a different room. So he turned on the TV and started waiting.

Well, they both waited for a couple of hours and then the wife called reception, was told her husband still hadn't arrived so she went down to the restaurant and had a meal and then, being tired, you know, she went to bed. The husband was now quite hungry so, after calling reception and being told his wife still hadn't arrived, he went down to have his dinner, and then went to bed.

Well, the next day, they narrowly missed each other at breakfast, so they decided there was no point in sitting around waiting so they both went out shopping or sightseeing, missed each other again that evening and didn't finally meet up again till the next afternoon. By this time the husband had to fly off to Washington for a meeting first thing on Monday!

Man: Oh, that's amazing! Always strange in a new city. I ... I remember once I was going to a conference in Norway, I landed at Oslo Airport and as I didn't know the city I picked up a whole lot of leaflets and a street map at the airport before catching the bus into town. Well, one of the leaflets was quite fat, about 100 pages long and it was called 'Where to eat in Oslo', so I started looking at it to find a nice restaurant to go to that evening – I always prefer to eat out rather than in my hotel. And I soon realised that the same restaurant was being described again, I looked all the way through the leaflet and every page was a description of the same restaurant! There were no others in there! 100 pages all about the same restaurant.

Woman: What was the name of the restaurant?

Man: I can't remember!

Woman: Haha! Oh, that reminds me. Ha! A colleague of mine was in Sweden. He was at the end of a tough series of meetings in Stockholm and about to fly back home to London. Well, he checked his suitcase in and went through to the departure lounge, had a drink and caught his plane back to Heathrow. Unfortunately, the check-in clerk had put the wrong label on his case and it had the tag for a different flight on it...

Man: So *he* went to London and his luggage went somewhere else?

Woman: No, no, no, no, worse than that. They did a security check on all the

187

luggage that was being loaded onto the other flight and found that there was no passenger name on that manifesto to match that particular suitcase. So they very carefully took the case off to the far corner of the airport and the security police blew it up! Haha. Luckily it only contained dirty clothes and a toothbrush and stuff like that. And he got fully compensated by the airline.

Man: Er ... I remember my boss telling me about something that happened a few years ago when he was in China, I think – somewhere in the Far East anyway. There was a long delay at the airport, which apparently was quite common then, and then there came an announcement over the loudspeaker: 'We are sorry but the plane is sick, we will find a new one'. So they all settled down for a long wait, feeling reassured that they weren't having to fly in a faulty plane.

Two hours later there was another announcement 'We have found a new plane. But the new plane is more sick than the first one, so we will take the first one.' And they were all escorted to the first plane and it took off but they all felt very nervous and everyone started knocking back the gin and the whisky. Anyway eventually they arrived at their destination and by this time everyone had managed to forget that the plane was 'sick' but instead of landing the plane kept circling round and round and round. Everyone started to get worried again. Mhm. And then a man in uniform came out of the little door leading to the flight deck with a screwdriver. He walked half way down the aisle, stopped and lifted up the carpet. Then he raised a metal flap and reached inside with the screwdriver. There was a loud click and then they heard the landing gear going down. The man in uniform went back to the flight deck. The plane made its final approach and landed safely. As they all came down the steps he said you could literally see everyone still shaking with fear.

[Time: 5 minutes 20 seconds]

Presentation

Get everyone to study the expressions in the speech balloons. These are not recorded. Answer any queries.

B   The sequence of steps should be followed according to the instructions in the Student's Book.

1. Step 1 has to be done alone. IF POSSIBLE, THIS SHOULD BE DONE AT HOME BEFORE THE LESSON. As a variation, they might be asked to think of some true stories *and* some invented ones.
2. Students swop stories in groups. (Using the variation, they would also have to guess which stories were true or invented.)
3. The picture story is deliberately enigmatic, including ambiguous clocks and baffling icons, so as to provoke discussion in pairs and different versions of the story.
4. Rearrange the class into groups of four (each pair with another pair). Allow enough time for both pairs to tell their stories and for the others to ask questions.

9.4 Looking after a visitor

This section is in four equally important steps. They could each be
done in a different lesson as they are not interdependent. Note that
'looking after a visitor' in this case also involves 'being a visitor' as
both roles are considered.

A   This step should be done first by students working alone. Perhaps
emphasize that we are not just considering what they currently have to
do, but what they may have to do in the future too. The activities listed
may be the responsibility of high-powered or more low-powered
employees, depending on the status of the visitor.

When they have ticked all the boxes, they should form groups to find
out if the others are likely to have to do similar things.

B   MEETING A VISITOR

The recorded conversation illustrates some of the phrases in the
speech balloons being used. Play the tape and ask for questions. Allow
students time to study the phrases silently for a few moments and ask
any questions they wish to.

Sandra: Hello, are ... are you Mr Brown?
Mr Brown: Yeah.
Sandra: Oh, I'm Sandra Ellis.
Mr Brown: Hi Sandra.
Sandra: I ... er ... welcome to Man-
chester.
Mr Brown: Well, I'm sorry I'm so late.
You see, there was fog at Amsterdam and
we were delayed there. I hope you
haven't been waiting long.
Sandra: No, no, it's OK. I was able to
catch up on some of my notes.
Mr Brown: Oh good.
Sandra: Well, it's a great pleasure to meet
you, Mr Brown.
Mr Brown: Yeah, I've been looking
forward to meeting you too, Sandra.
Sandra: How was your flight?
Mr Brown: Not too bad, thanks.
Sandra: Oh good, well I think the best

thing is we'll go to your hotel first if
that's OK. My car's outside.
Mr Brown: Terrific.
Sandra: Can I take one of your bags?
Mr Brown: Oh thanks, yeah, here you are,
Sandra.
Sandra: Right now, is there anything you'd
like to do before we set off?
Mr Brown: Well, I'd just like to make a
quick phone call, if ... er ... that's all
right.
Sandra: Yes, sure. Look, there are some
phone booths over there. Um ... would
you like a drink or something to eat
before we go into town or ... ?
Mr Brown: Well, er ... maybe just a coffee
if we've got time.

[Time: 1 minute]

For this role play students should be in pairs – if possible there
should be an even number of pairs (pairs of pairs).
1. Allow everyone enough time to decide who they are and why they
   are where they are.

189

2. For the role play, where they are enacting an 'arrival at the airport', everyone should STAND UP and move around realistically.
3. Rearrange the pairs so that students who 'arrived' in step 2 can now be the ones who are 'waiting'. This is quite straightforward if there are pairs of pairs.

C GIVING DIRECTIONS

Three recorded conversations illustrate the words in the speech balloon being used. Play the tape and allow time for everyone to ask questions, make notes or discuss the situations.

Who are the people speaking, and what is their relationship?

It may be necessary to spend a little time revising 'giving directions' in English before students take part in the role play.

Man: Um, can you tell me how to get to the restaurant for the meal tonight?

Woman: Well, it's a bit complicated ... um ... I'd better show you on the map. It'll take about 20 minutes on foot.

Man: Oh, that's OK, I've got enough time and it's a lovely evening.

Woman: Right then. Now let's see, um ... well, first of all you go to the right as you leave this building, OK? And turn left when you get to the town hall.

Man: Right.

Woman: Mm, then you keep straight on and you just cross the river. Er ... oh, you'll see the railway station on your right, got it?

Man: Yeah.

Woman: OK, now you continue along that road for about three blocks till you come to a church. Um ... and opposite the church there's a big square. Now, the restaurant is down a little back street on the other side of the square. It's called the Black Bear — it's just there on the map.

Man: Oh, I see. Yes.

Woman: Do you see?

Man: Yes, that's fine, no problem. Thanks very much.

Woman: You're very welcome. Enjoy your evening.

Man: Thanks.

———

Woman: Can you tell me how to get to the restaurant where the lunch is being held?

Man: Oh, yes, sure. Well, er ... you can take a taxi or you can take the tram, that's the best idea, yes. It's the number 89 which says 'ZOO' on the front.

Woman: 89: Zoo.

Man: You'll need to get a ticket from the machine before you get on. Right now, at the fifth stop you get off, cross the road, walk on for about 100 metres.

Woman: OK.

Man: OK, now ... now, the restaurant is on the left. And you can't miss it because it's called the Black Eagle.

Woman: Black Eagle. OK fine, thanks very much.

Man: That's all right, not at all. Enjoy your lunch!

Woman: Thanks.

———

Woman: Can you tell me how to get to the restaurant where we're meeting tomorrow?

Man: Certainly. When you come out of the car park, turn left, OK?

Woman: Left. Right, fine.

Man: Drive straight on until you see blue signs that say 'CITY'. Now, follow these signs as far as the lake and then turn right and drive along the lake for about 5 km. Now, the restaurant is on the right

just after the first village, you can't miss
it. It's called the White Swan.

Woman: Oh, fine. OK, I'll see you there

tomorrow at about 11, then.

Man: At 11, fine.

[Time: 2 minutes 10 seconds]

🔳 As preparation for the role play, it might be helpful to draw on
the board or OHP a rough street plan of the town or city your class are
studying in – with their assistance, as they call out suggestions. Then
they can use this as the basis of their role play. Write up a list of the
important tourist sights and commercial sites in the town. Or you
could try to get enough copies of a real street plan for each pair to have
one. Alternatively, as suggested in the Student's Book, get the 'host' to
actually draw a rough map as he or she is giving directions – this is
more challenging but a very realistic demand of this type of situation.

D   LOCAL KNOWLEDGE

Although these discussion activities come last, please don't omit
them – an essential element of looking after a visitor is putting yourself
in his or her shoes!

Point out that many of the things you take for granted about your
own country and hometown are unfamiliar to foreigners. The names of
people and products that are 'household names' in your country may be
a closed book to other nationalities. By contrast, paradoxically, what a
visitor may need to know about (museums, bus routes, renting a car,
etc.) may be unknown territory for someone who actually lives in a place.

First, go through the 'What do you know about your own city?'
questions with the whole class contributing ideas. (If your class all
come from different places, you may need to agree on a single place to
discuss for this activity.)

Then divide the class into an even number of pairs (pairs of pairs
again). There can be a couple of groups of three, if necessary. If time is
limited, do steps 1 to 3 now and return to 4 and 5 in the next lesson.

1. During the preparatory discussion in pairs, go round offering advice
   and encouragement.
2. 🔳 Each pair joins another pair. One pair plays the role of
   'visitors' the other the role of 'hosts'.
3. The roles are reversed.
4. This part can be done in pairs. If you have different nationalities in the
   class, rearrange the pairs to have the same nationalities working together.
5. Now each pair joins another pair – or they can form larger groups.
   Make it clear to everyone that the idea of this activity is to explain
   to 'foreigners' what each of the 'household names' listed represents:
   What are the people famous for?
   What kind of image do they have?
   Are they admired or regarded with affection?
   Are they feared or considered to be comical?

9.5   To be or not to be ... or be-ing??   *Grammar*

A perennial problem for students: hopefully the examples and rules presented in this section will help to reassure students that this is not an insurmountable barrier to their learning! The presentation section takes the form of an exercise, which can be prepared at home.

Presentation

The 'exercise' part of this section can be prepared at home, done in pairs – or done with the whole class suggesting what to put in the gaps.

Suggested answers (many variations are possible):

Visiting / Arriving in
Staying / Living / Spending night after night
Getting/Driving

going to / visiting / flying to
making / making sure you have / confirming
phoning/calling

going/travelling
waiting / sitting / having to wait
trying/tasting/sampling

to stay / to spend a night
to spend
to get / to book / to obtain

eating/sitting / to eat / to sit
to catch / to take / catching / taking
to chat / to discuss our families / to talk / chatting / discussing our
   families / talking

making/taking
to answer / to pick up
to send
meeting / seeing / being introduced to / bumping into

to reach / to get / to contact / to get in touch with
   calling/phoning

to meet / to see
to discover / to find out / to read

to get
to meet / to come to meet / to wait for

heavy/expensive/bulky
to get / to find / to be sure of getting

Exercises

Both exercises are best done by students working in pairs. Afterwards, answer any queries they may have.

A This exercise draws attention to some cases where the -ing form is *not* used.

Answers:
1. *example: make sure everyone understands what they'll have to do*
2. to find out
3. to post
4. to avoid
5. to buy
6. having
7. to get
8. to get

B Students will have to use their own ideas to fill the gaps here. Questions 15 and 16 are very open-ended and may provoke some revealing ideas!

Suggested answers:
1. *example: make sure everyone knows what they'll have to do*
2. to stay at
3. to get / to have   to visit
4. to spend
5. to find
6. going to / visiting
7. Smoking/Advertising
8. playing   sleeping / getting to sleep
9. to have
10. to meet
11. to catch
12. to pay for
13. to invite / to look after / to see
14. to give you
15. spending time on my own / being by myself
16. seeing new places / meeting different people / catching up on my reading

Extra activity

Students can be put into teams and challenge the others to complete more sentences like 15 and 16 above, each using a structure similar to the ones presented in this section.

Workbook

Exercise 9.4 in the Workbook gives more practice on this topic. Supplementary work can also be found in *Use of English* units 13, 14 and 15.

9.6 Accommodation

This section deals with making hotel bookings and discussing accommodation facilities. Students who don't actually ever travel abroad on business may well have experience of travelling abroad for pleasure.

A ▭ The recording shows a fairly typical phone call to a hotel. Students may need to hear the tape more than once: first to get the gist of the conversation and again to note down their answers. Point out that the notes that the students are making simulate the kind of notes Vera Müller would make, in order to relay the information to her boss.

Vera Müller phones because she has special requirements – one of the people she's booking for is unable to climb stairs – and she needs the information very urgently.

The relevant information she gets from the hotel is <u>underlined</u> in the transcript below.

Receptionist: Hotel Concorde.
Vera Müller: Good morning. My name's Vera Müller. I'd like to book some accommodation for tomorrow for five nights.
Receptionist: April 1st to 5th. Just one moment, madam. We are rather full at the moment, because of the trade fair. What kind of rooms would you like?
Vera Müller: I'd like three single rooms, all on the same floor.
Receptionist: I have three double rooms but not three singles available, sorry.
Vera Müller: What's the difference in price?

Receptionist: <u>Single rooms are 400 francs, doubles are 700 francs.</u>
Vera Müller: I see, um ... what kind of rooms are the double rooms?
Receptionist: Very nice rooms, madam. I can give you three doubles on the sixth floor overlooking the city. They have balconies and bathrooms.
Vera Müller: Now, one of the guests is in a wheelchair. Are these rooms accessible by wheelchair?
Receptionist: Ah, no, madam. The lift goes to the 5th floor only. In this case <u>you could have three rooms on the ground floor one single and two doubles. No view of the city, but close to the garden.</u>

Vera Müller: And do you have a small conference room I can reserve for April 3rd all day?

Receptionist: Er ... yes, we have a nice quiet room that will take about 12 people, would that be suitable?

Vera Müller: Yes, that would be fine. And ... um ... are the public rooms all accessible without having to go up or down steps?

Receptionist: Yes, madam. The restaurant is on the first floor – there's a lift. Otherwise everything, including the conference room is on the ground floor.

Vera Müller: All right, fine. Um ... then I'd like to book the three rooms on the ground floor for Acme International. The guests' names are: Mr H. Meier, Miss A. Schwarz and Mr D. Negri.

Receptionist: Thank you, so that's three rooms on the ground floor arriving on April 1st and departing on April 6th. And the conference room all day on April 3rd.

Vera Müller: Right

Receptionist: OK. Can I have your telephone number please?

Vera Müller: Yes it's 41 (that's Switzerland) 22 34 89 23. And I'm Vera Müller. I'll confirm this by telex.

Receptionist: Fine, thank you Ms Müller. Goodbye.

Vera Müller: Goodbye.

....

It's OK Mr Meier. I've booked the rooms in Toulouse.

Mr Meier: Great. Thanks, Vera.

[Time: 2 minutes 50 seconds]

B   Before starting the role play, get everyone to read and comment on the two hotel advertisements. If The Ritz is normally out of their price range, encourage them to daydream a little here!

1. ☎ Student A calls the hotel to book rooms and his or her requirements are given in File 76; Student B is Reservations Manager and has all the necessary information in File 68. Make sure both partners read their information through BEFORE they begin the call.
2. Same again, but with reversed roles. In this case the *other* hotel should be phoned.
3. Both partners work together to draft a letter or telex to one of the hotels, confirming what was agreed on the phone. This task can be set as homework.

C   For this group discussion activity, try to arrange the groups so that each group contains at least one member with experience of staying in hotels – preferably as a business traveller, though not necessarily abroad.

Each step is explained in the Student's Book.

For step 4, every two groups can be combined into a larger group, or each group can report to the whole class.

9.7 At a restaurant

One essential task that students may have to perform when eating with a foreigner is explaining dishes on the menu – it makes more sense if these are national dishes of their own country.

■ Encourage students to get hold of menus from restaurants that they frequent, to add a local flavour to the activity. If they can't or won't do this, perhaps you could supply these for them – most restaurants are delighted to allow customers to advertise for them!

A 🏆 For this role play, the pairs should use the menus they have gathered or which you have provided.

If none are available, begin this step by composing (with the help of the class) a typical menu of national dishes from your students' country on the board or OHP – then they can refer to this, as if it was a menu on a chalkboard in the restaurant.

▭ The useful expressions are illustrated in a recorded conversation, which takes place in a restaurant in the USA. Students may need to hear this more than once.

Man: Mmm, that was delicious!
Woman: Mmm, would you like a dessert?
Man: Yes please. Can you ... um ... help me with the menu?
Woman: Yes, certainly. These are starters, and these are main courses and these are desserts. See?
Man: Ah, yes, um ... hmm, can you tell me what Boston Indian Pudding is?
Woman: Yes, it's a specialty of this region. It's a sort of ... mm ... dark cake which contains dried fruit soaked in tea.
Man: Tea?
Woman: It's hot and you have it with ice-cream. Very nice.
Man: I see. And ... um ... what's Hot fudge sundae?
Woman: That's something rather special. It's a kind of ice cream with a hot sticky sauce over the top – very sweet and fattening!
Man: I don't really like the sound of that. What about Zabaglione?
Woman: Well, that's difficult to explain, it's a bit like a warm mousse. It's made of egg yolks, sugar and Marsala wine. It's an Italian specialty.
Man: That sounds very nice, I'll have that, please.
Waitress: Are you ready to order your desserts?
Woman: Yes, John?
Man: I'd like to have the Zabaglione and a large black coffee, please.
Woman: Just an iced tea for me, please.

[Time: 1 minute 10 seconds]

B 🏆 The menu is a traditional English Christmas menu, served at the King's Head Hotel in Wimborne (amazing value at £9.95!). You may be asked to explain some of the items. Note that the 'novelty crackers' are not to be eaten (as they might be in the USA) but to be pulled – inside there's a paper hat and a cheap novelty gift!

The groups should be arranged at 'tables' and one or two members

of the class might be given the role of 'waiters' or 'waitresses' −
however, it might be best if you were the *maître d'* yourself! In this
case, you can explain the unfamiliar dishes in your role as head waiter.
In a small class you can be the restaurant proprietor and there won't be
any need for waiters.

Encourage everyone to enter into the spirit of the situation and
indulge in 'small talk' while they're waiting to order.

9.8 Organizing a conference

This integrated activity involves resolving problems, making arrangements, and correspondence with speakers: here students will be practising
their letter- and telex-writing skills. The three stages can be done on
different days − then the passage of time may seem more realistic.

The groups should consist of three or four members. A more
advanced or experienced class may be able to do the activity in pairs.
There should be an even number of groups. All the necessary instructions for the integrated activity are given in the Student's Book, but a
few additional pieces of information are given below. Note that
students should show their draft correspondence to another pair for
comments − you should also check some of this as you pass from
group to group.

First of all, the groups should agree what kind of arrangements need
to be made. Even if no-one has organized a conference or a weekend
course, many students may have participated in them. The arrangements being made would be fairly similar if you were organizing a sales
conference or a training course. If necessary, this could become a
whole-class discussion.

March 16

The three steps include writing a final draft letter − this could be done
as homework.

March 30

Three of the speakers have replied in writing, the fourth has left a
recorded message on the answerphone:

'Er ... this is Madeleine Tennant. Um ...
I'm calling about the conference in May.
Um ... I'd like to have my expenses paid in
cash in dollars, not by cheque in your
currency. Um ... I haven't had time to
book a flight yet so I don't know how
much the tickets'll cost, but ... um ... I'll
let you know the amount when I arrive for
the conference.'

[Time: 25 seconds]

April 13

At the end, allow time for each group to give feedback to the other before the follow-up discussion.

Follow-up discussion

What tasks did you find difficult in doing the activity?
How similar were the tasks to the ones you really have to do in your
    work?
If you could do the whole thing again, what would you do differently?
Which of the tasks should the organizer of a small conference or
    weekend course delegate or perform personally?

9.9 Flying down to Rio

This integrated activity begins with a problem-solving activity, involv-ing a considerable amount of discussion about dates and times – saying times, dates and numbers aloud is a skill that even more advanced students need to practise frequently – and continues with letters and telexes to write in steps 1 to 4.

There should be an even number of groups, with about three students in each group. If you have a large wall map of South America that you can pin or stick up in class, this will make the task more realistic and appealing. Dealing with maps and timetables is a process that some people find intimidating – while others relish it. If possible, try to mix both these 'types' up in different groups.

The procedure is fully explained in the Student's Book. Don't get too worried if no one seems to be producing a perfect solution – it's the *process of discussing* that is the point of the exercise as far as language practice is concerned.

If a group is having a lot of trouble with the schedules, you can WHISPER this clue to one member of the group:
'If you arrange all the people in alphabetical order, you can get the meetings to come out right!'

Solution

The following schedule will work out OK, but it's just a suggestion and your students may be able to do the whole thing differently and/or better.

AUGUST
16   Getting over the flight and confirming meetings by phone
17   Meeting in Rio with Antonio Almeida

18   Meeting in Rio with Bruno Baena
19   Flight to Lima at 11.00
20   Meeting in Lima with Carlos Castro
21   Flight to Rio at 11.50
22   Shuttle flight to São Paulo, meeting with Doris Dias and back to
      Rio
23   Meeting in Rio with Edison Echevarria
24   Flight to Florianópolis at 07.00: trade exhibition begins in the
      afternoon
25   Trade exhibition in Florianópolis
26   Trade exhibition in Florianópolis
27   Trade exhibition in Florianópolis
28   Taxi to Blumenau for meeting with Fritz Fischer
29   Flight from Florianópolis to Montevideo at 10.15
30   Meeting in Montevideo with Gregorio García and flight to Buenos
      Aires at 16.20
31   Meeting in Buenos Aires with Hectór Hudson and flight to
      Iguassu Falls at 18.00

SEPTEMBER
 1   Sight-seeing in Iguassu – the Falls are incredible and it'd be a
      shame to have to miss them out!
 2   Flight to Rio at 17.30
 3   Shuttle flight to Brasilia for meeting with Ivan Itaparica and back
      to Rio
 4   Flight to Belo Horizonte at 08.00 for meeting with João Jardim
      and back to Rio afterwards
 5   Flight to Bogotá at 12.00
 6   Meeting in Bogotá with Klaus König and flight at 21.40 to
      Santiago via Rio
 7   12.50 arrival in Santiago
 8   Meeting in Santiago with Lucia Lluch
 9   Flight to Rio at 14.15
10   Shuttle to São Paulo, meeting with Mario Martin and back to Rio
11   Meeting in Rio with Nélson Neves and flight home at 22.30

9.10   The romance of travel?   *Discussion*

A [cassette] To start the discussion off, there is a recording of some
comments from experienced business travellers.

'My advice would be: only take hand baggage, not a large suitcase.'
'Well ... er ... I think it's essential to organize everything before you travel.'
'You know, it's a good idea to take plenty of office work to catch up on.'
'Well, you should take a Walkman and plenty of reading matter.'

'Er ... I'd advise you to learn as much as you can about the customs of the people.'

'Um ... well, I think it's important to arrive a day early ... er ... to give yourself time to adjust and acclimatize.'

'Well, foreign customs are difficult to get used to: you should only do what you feel comfortable doing.'

'Mmm ... well, my advice would be to be very careful about local food and drink.'

'Oh, one very important thing: don't get involved in a political discussion.'

'When you're abroad treat everyone you meet with respect.'

'An old friend once told me this: never forget that you're a foreigner. That's a piece of advice I've always remembered!'

[Time: 55 seconds]

B   To participate in the discussion, students need only have experience of travelling abroad on holiday or use their imagination.

C   Get everyone to do the discussion and role play tasks, following the instructions in the Student's Book.

Were 'the good old days' really better? What was it really like in the golden days of civilized foreign travel?

Workbook

Contents for this unit:

9.1 Did I ever tell you about ... ?   Functions listening 📼
9.2 Prepositions – 5
9.3 Air travel in the USA   Read and listen 📼
9.4 -ing v. to ...   Grammar
9.5 What would you say?
9.6 Vocabulary
9.7 What the clever traveller knows   Listening 📼
9.8 Negative prefixes   Word-building

Background information: Marketing

In recent years marketing has become a driving force in most companies. Underlying all marketing strategy is 'The Marketing Concept', explained in this diagram:

THE MARKETING CONCEPT
(We must produce what people want, not what we want to produce)
↓
This means that we PUT THE CUSTOMER FIRST
(We organize the company so that this happens)
↓
We must FIND OUT WHAT THE CUSTOMER WANTS
(We carry out market research)
↓
We must SUPPLY exactly what the customer wants
↓
We can do this by offering the right MARKETING MIX: "The Four P's"
= the right PRODUCT
at the right PRICE
available through the right channels of distribution: PLACE
presented in the right way: PROMOTION

Nowadays, all divisions of a company are urged to 'Think Marketing':

To think marketing we must have a clear idea of:
↓
what the customers need
what the customers want
what causes them to buy
what the product is to the customer: functional, technological, economic +
aesthetic, emotional, psychological aspects
↓
'FEATURES' (what the product is)+'BENEFITS' (which means that . . .)

A company that believes in marketing is forward-thinking and doesn't rest on its past achievements: it must be aware of its **strengths** and **weaknesses** as well as the **opportunities** and **threats** it faces in the market (remember the letters: 'SWOT').

More about 'The Marketing Mix' and the '4 P's':

PRODUCT = the goods or service that you are marketing. The product is not just a collection of components, but includes its design, quality and reliability. ⟫→

Products have a life-cycle, and forward-thinking companies are continually developing new products to replace products whose sales are declining and coming to the end of their lives. A **'total product'** includes the **image** of the product as well as its features and benefits (see below). In marketing terms, political candidates and non-profit-making public services are also 'products' that people must be persuaded to 'buy' and which have to be presented and packaged attractively (see Promotion below).

PRICE = making it easy for the customer to buy. The marketing view of pricing takes account of the value of a product, its quality, the ability of the customer to pay, the volume of sales required, the level of market saturation and the prices charged by the competition. Too low a price can reduce the number of sales just as significantly as too high a price. A low price may increase sales but not as profitably as fixing a high, yet still popular, price. As fixed costs stay fixed whatever the volume of sales, there is usually no such thing as a 'profit margin' on any single product.

PLACE = getting the product to the customer. Decisions have to be made about the channels of distribution and delivery arrangements. Retail products may go through various channels of distribution:
1. Producer → sells directly to end users via own sales force, direct response advertising or direct mail (mail order)
2. Producer → retailers → end users
3. Producer → wholesalers/agents → retailers → end-users
4. Producer → wholesalers → directly to end-users
5. Producer → multiple store groups/department stores/mail order houses → end-users
6. Producer → market → wholesalers → retailers → end-users

Each stage must add 'value' to the product to justify the costs: the middle-man is not normally someone who just takes his 'cut' but someone whose own sales force and delivery system can make the product more easily and cost-effectively available to the largest number of customers. One principle behind this is 'breaking down the bulk': the producer may sell in minimum quantities of, say, 10,000 to the wholesaler, who sells in minimum quantities of 100 to the retailer, who sells in mimimum quantities of 1 to the end-user. A confectionery manufacturer doesn't deliver individual bars of chocolate to consumers: distribution is done through wholesalers and then retailers who each 'add value' to the product by providing a good service to their customers and stocking a wide range of similar products.

PROMOTION = presenting the product to the customer. Promotion involves considering the packaging and presentation of the product, its image, the product name, advertising and slogans, brochures, literature, price lists, after-sales service and training, trade exhibitions or fairs, public relations, publicity, and personal selling, where the seller develops a relationship with the customer.

Every product must possess a **'unique selling proposition'** (USP) – features and benefits that make it unlike any other product in its market.

In promoting a product, the **attention** of potential customers is attracted and an **interest** in the product aroused, creating a **desire** for the product and encouraging customers to take prompt **action** ('AIDA').

Background information: Sales

Some people believe that you have to be a special kind of person to sell a product. But although it is clear that a successful sales rep does need special talents and an outgoing personality, many of the skills he uses are used by us all: we build and maintain relationships with different kinds of people, we listen to and take note of what they tell us and don't just enjoy the sound of our own voices, and we explain things to them or discuss ideas with them.

A firm may depend on their own sales team and/or on the salesmanship of their distributors, wholesalers or retailers. But any company needs to establish a personal relationship with its major clients ('key accounts') and potential customers ('prospects'). It is often said that 'people do business with people': a firm doesn't just deal impersonally with another firm, but a person in the buying department receives personal visits from people representing the firm's suppliers on a regular basis – or in the case of department stores or chain stores, a team of buyers may travel around visiting suppliers.

Keeping sales people 'on the road' is much more expensive than employing them to work in the office and much of their time is spent unproductively travelling. Telephone selling may use this time more productively (though in some countries this is illegal), but a face-to-face meeting and discussion is much more effective. Companies involved in the export trade often have a separate export sales force, whose travel and accommodation expenses may be very high. Servicing overseas customers may consequently often be done by phone, telex or letter and personal visits may be infrequent. Many firms appoint an overseas agent or distributor whose own sales force takes over responsibility for selling their products in another country.

A sales department consists of many people who are based in different parts of the country or the world, who don't have the day-to-day contact and opportunities for communicating with each other that office-based staff have. For this reason, firms hold regular sales conferences where their entire sales force can meet, receive information and ask questions about new products and receive training.

© Cambridge University Press, 1989

10 Marketing and sales

Marketing and selling are aspects of business that influence, and often actually control, almost every part of a company's activities. For this reason, we feel justified in dealing with a number of rather specialized concepts and ideas in a way we have avoided in other units.

This unit covers various aspects of marketing and sales: market research, applying marketing principles, arranging and participating in a sales meeting and sales demonstration, and promotion and advertising. Students with expertise in these areas are encouraged to contribute their ideas and knowledge throughout the unit, particularly in the discussions, integrated activities and case studies.

The high-level, subtle skills of negotiating, which are particularly demanding and delicate when dealing with people from other countries and using another language, are beyond the scope of this course.

The functions in this unit are possibility, probability and certainty and the grammar topic is comparing and contrasting.

10.1 Local products

Discussion

This discussion sets the scene for the unit. Students will be discussing how all kinds of products and services are actively marketed these days, even public services and monopolies that have captive customers.

Students should think of specific examples of local products and services, including the brand name and the producer or provider of the service.

To start everyone off you could discuss with the class just one of the items listed – a particular local cinema, for example:

What competition does the local cinema face from other cinemas, from other leisure industry products, from non-leisure related products?
Does it have an up-market or a down-market image?
Where do customers receive their information about its product?
Is promotional material generated by the owner of the cinema or by the distributors of the films he shows? Are its customers regular customers or one-time customers?
If you were running the cinema, would you market it more strongly and if so how?

After the group discussions, ask each group to report to the class on one or two of the more interesting products they have discussed.

10.2   What is marketing?   *Vocabulary*

The vocabulary exercise leads on to a discussion about marketing strategy (for students who are working in a firm).

A   The exercise could be prepared at home or done in class by students working in pairs.

Answers:
1. creative process   profitably
2. Product   Price   Promotion   Place
3. satisfy   need   image   design
4. rival
5. posters   labels
6. distribution   end-users   outlets   hire purchase
   mail order
7. Strength   weaknesses   opportunities   threats
8. production-orientated   patterns   range   first

B   In a class of students with and without business experience, arrange the pairs so that each one has an experienced student. It may be necessary to arrange larger groups to achieve this. Students who are currently unemployed can talk about the company they used to work for.

10.3   Comparing and contrasting   *Grammar*

As there are quite a number of pitfalls involved in forming comparatives and superlatives and using the various structures connected with this topic, it is probably best to 'see what goes wrong' and correct the mistakes that are made, rather than try to explain everything. Although we are concerned with revising grammar here, this topic has clear 'functional' applications too.

   In this section, presentation, exercises and activities overlap, but first of all students should begin by studying the rules – or they could do this at home before the lesson.

A   This mechanical exercise could also be done at home or by students working in groups or pairs. Clear up any problems before going on to the next presentation step.

B ⌷▭ The examples are recorded. Allow time for questions before continuing with step C.
C Students should do this exercise in pairs. It must be done in writing. Encourage them to use a variety of structures, using the examples in B as their models. You might set a deadline for this, asking students to write as many sentences as possible in the time available.

D Back to marketing here, as we consider the features and benefits of a product. In this case, students should work in pairs or groups and first discuss the three fans, using the structures presented in B above. Towards the end of the discussion, students should write down some of their ideas.

E Finally, in groups, students consider their own companies' products and competing products. Again, if necessary, make sure each group has at least one student who is working at the moment.

There is more practice on these grammar points in Workbook exercise 10.1.

10.4   Arranging a sales meeting

In this integrated activity, students work in pairs to draft a letter, reply to a letter by telex and then role-play a phone call.

A Some of this information is irrelevant: the task involves deciding which of it *is* relevant. Note that 'Jean' could be an English name (female) or French (male).

B Perhaps go round checking each pair's draft before you 'deliver' it to another pair. If you happen to have pairs of pairs, this is straightforward. Otherwise deliver each letter to the pair on the right, passing it anti-clockwise.

C Each pair receives a letter. Now they change role and play the part of JEAN MEYER, René van Hoorn's assistant. They have to draft a reply by telex on behalf of Mr van Hoorn.

D ☎ In the telephone role play, one partner looks at File 114 and plays the role of Mr Müller's assistant, the other looks at File 70 and plays the role of Jean Meyer. There are a number of problems to sort out over the phone and each partner has a list of points and queries to make.

At the end, ask each pair to report briefly on what they did. Are there any questions arising from the activities they have done in this section?

10.5 Sales talk

A [cassette] We begin with a listening exercise, in which we hear a sales person at work with a client.

Students should be encouraged to find fault with both speakers' performance. Note that there are no 'correct answers' to the questions in the Student's Book – these require students to interpret and evaluate what went on.

Miss Ashley: Hello Mr Ray. And thanks for seeing me.

Mr Ray: Good afternoon, Miss Ashley, how are you?

Miss Ashley: Mm, fine thanks, Mr Ray.

Mr Ray: Have a seat.

Miss Ashley: Ah ... thanks.

Mr Ray: Er ... let me see, we last talked on the phone some time ago, didn't we?

Miss Ashley: Y ... mm ... yes, it was about the Hamburg order in June. That all went through all right, I think?

Mr Ray: Yes, yes. The 404X's have been working very well in our factory there. Er ... I was thinking ... ah ... we might take another 20 for Amsterdam.

Miss Ashley: Er ... well, a ... actually ... mm ... the 404X's have been so popular that we're supplying two versions now: the original beige 404X and a platinum grey model 404PS ... er ... with a newly designed case.

Mr Ray: Ah yes, but are there any modifications to the engineering?

Miss Ashley: No, the hardware is exactly the same. It's a more attractive case, a ... as you can see from this photo in the catalogue. And it's much stronger, as it's made of ... a ... steel, not plastic.

Mr Ray: Hey, hey, why haven't you sent me the catalogue?

Miss Ashley: Oh, they only arrived from the printers yesterday. I'll leave this one with you.

Mr Ray: Yeah, what's the price difference?

Miss Ashley: The price is only 3% more. We think the original 404P will be bought by some people who are using the original X808 and want to add on a matching 404X. New buyers will probably go for the 404PS.

Mr Ray: And will you be phasing out the 404X then?

Miss Ashley: Mm ... er ... although we'll probably stop production in ... a year or so, we guarantee to maintain stocks for 24 months.

Mr Ray: Hmm, yes, so why should I go for the more expensive version? Our 404Xs haven't shown any signs of wear or damage – even if they have got plastic cases!

Miss Ashley: Haha, well, our market research shows a significant preference for the new model. Although the 404X works perfectly well of course, people often mistake its appearance for an old ... er ... 201A.

Mr Ray: Oh goodness, yeah!

Miss Ashley: The new 404PS, on the other hand: it looks much more streamlined and modern.

Mr Ray: Yes, yes, mm, I remember last time I was in Hamburg I had to explain to some visitors that we weren't still using 201As!

Miss Ashley: Mhm. Anyway, perhaps we can come ... ah ... back to that. I thought ... I thought you might be interested in knowing about our upgrade path for the 706J. I th ... think you're using one of those in the warehouse here?

Mr Ray: Yes. It would be good if we could speed up its processing speed – and ... er ... improve the reliability. We can't afford to have it break down on us again.

Miss Ashley: Well, that's certainly what the upgrade would achieve, but it would also prolong its working life.

Mr Ray: Good, good.

Miss Ashley: If you're still having a problem with reliability, maybe it'd be best to go down and ... and have a look at it. Is it operating now?

Mr Ray: Oh yes, we have it going all day.

Miss Ashley: Well, a ... and then perhaps we could come back and ... and discuss your order for the 404PSs.

Mr Ray: Ah, 404Xs.

Miss Ashley: OK, let's talk about that later!

[Time: 3 minutes 20 seconds]

B   Again, with this reading text, taken from a training manual, students should be encouraged to disagree as well as agree with what is written. Make it clear that what is written here is not necessarily 'true' or definitive information.

C   Hopefully students will agree that open questions are less effective than closed questions. In considering answers to the questions here, students might be advised to think about their own firm's products or one of the local products they discussed in 10.1.

D   In this role play students will be acting out two sales meetings and writing a short report. Arrange a class into an even number of pairs (pairs of pairs). Any groups of three can share roles and become a 'double act' in each part of the role play.

1. Student A, looking at File 22, plays the role of salesperson, representing an importer. Student B, looking at File 8, plays the role of customer: chief buyer for a mail order house. The sales rep has to describe the features and benefits of a new product, while the customer has a list of queries. The product described and illustrated in File 22 is a tiny radio.
2. After the meeting the partners separate and find a 'colleague' in the corresponding pair. They have to report on the meeting they have just had.
3. Now the roles are reversed: Student A becomes the customer and looks at File 8 while Student B becomes the salesperson and looks at File 30. The product described and illustrated in File 30 is a miniature stationery set.
4. After the meeting, the partners separate again and report to their 'colleagues' on the meeting they've had.
5. Finally, perhaps as homework, each student should draft a report on one of the meetings and its outcome – either in the role of salesperson or in the role of customer.

10.6   Marketing your own region

In this integrated activity, students will be considering the different
stages of marketing a product: analyzing statistics, conducting market
research, devising a questionnaire and carrying out a market survey,
considering the strengths and weaknesses of the product, devising a
marketing strategy and drafting an advertisement. In real life, of
course, all these processes would take a lot more time and require more
specialized skills than may be available in class.

One has to have an enormous amount of information about a
product to market it. This is why we have chosen a product that
everyone is familiar with – even students with no business experience
can participate actively in the simulation.

Procedure

Begin by asking students to read and comment on the advertisements
shown in the Student's Book. This makes it clear that even a country or
a region is a product.

Decide with the class exactly what 'product' everyone will be
marketing. If several regions are represented in the class, agree on just
one as the 'product' for the activity – or the whole country might be
considered as a single product.

In a multi-national class, the class could be divided into several
groups, each dealing with a different country. But not too many, or the
activity will become unwieldy.

Make sure everyone is clear what they will have to do, perhaps by
briefly previewing what will happen in steps A and B.

A   Students working in pairs consider what kind of information they
need to obtain in order to carry out the tasks in B. After a while, ask
the pairs to report to the class and pool everyone's good ideas.

B   The three groups each have different information to obtain by
devising and later administering their questionnaire.

Group A look at File 62: their questionnaire will find out people's
attitude to the region and also their attitude to competing countries or
regions.

Group B look at File 28: their questionnaire will find out what
factors people take into account when choosing a holiday destination
for both a main holiday and a second holiday.

Group C look at File 46: their questionnaire will find out people's
attitudes to the unattractive features of five competing countries or regions
as well as to the unattractive features of the region under consideration.

From now on, follow steps 1 to 8 in the Student's Book. Here are some additional ideas and comments:

1. First the groups discuss what to do (this may take a few minutes) and then get down to drafting their questionnaire.
2. Make sure everyone is involved here. Point out that it's up to each person to find members of other groups to interview – the ideal is for everyone to be interviewed twice. For the sake of realism, each encounter should end with a 'Thank you for helping me' not 'Now it's my turn to ask you some questions'. If students are getting involved in the activity and have invested a lot of time in devising their questionnaires, the interviews could be continued out of class with neighbours, colleagues and friends (in their own language).
3. The results are collated and tabulated before being evaluated in steps 4 and 6.
4. In a small class, this can be a whole-class discussion. In a larger class, form groups of three (one member from each original group).
5. This can be done alone (perhaps as homework) or by the original groups back together again.
6. Another change-round: groups of three, with members drawn from each original group, as in step 4, perhaps.
7. Having considered the questions in step 6, a small class or two groups of a larger class (or even more groups of a huge class) devise a marketing strategy. A class with little business experience should skip this step and go on to step 8.
8. Make sure there's time for everyone to discuss this before they draft an advertisement (maybe based on the ones at the beginning of the section).

Follow-up discussion

What is different about marketing your own company's product?
What is similar about marketing your firm's product?
What important steps were missed out in the simulation we did?
Which of the processes require specialist skills from outside agencies or consultants?
How is export marketing handled differently from domestic marketing in your own firm?
What are the differences between marketing a region, marketing a manufactured product and marketing a service?

10.7 Promoting a Total Product

This section covers four main areas: brand names, instruction leaflets or booklets, advertisements and commercials.

A We begin by hearing part of a lecture. After completing the task, students are encouraged to suggest some foreign brand names that are unsuitable in their country – in this case, maybe, British or American brands. This may have a lot to do with pronunciation problems as well as cultural connotations – GM cars in Europe are marketed under the Opel badge, not as Vauxhalls. And translation can also lead to hazard: an air freshener marketed with the evocative brand name 'Alpine Mist', would not go down too well in a German-speaking country (in German *Mist* means *manure*)!

'... Now, on the subject of brand names: English names often used in foreign countries to make products sound more 'international'. Here are a few examples of products whose names would *have* to be changed for the British market. Er ... how about *Pocari Sweat*? That's a drink for sports people. Then there's ... er ... *Calpis*, *Pschitt* and *Sic* – these are soft drinks as well. There's *Mother*, a brand of biscuits, and would you believe *Bum*, a brand of potato crisps. And how about *Cedric* and *Gloria*? Those are both cars. But a good product can succeed even if the name does sound a little bit strange. Look at the Japanese cars: you've got *Sunny, Camry, Cherry* – all very successful in the UK. By the way, I've always been puzzled by how many Japanese cars have an R or L in their name: there's *Bluebird, Prairie, Corolla, Starion* – I think this is supposed to sound like 'stallion' – like the *Ford Mustang*.

Now, here are some portable radio brand names: *Party Boy, Yacht Boy, Tiny 320, Weekend 360* – these are all marketed in the UK under those names, but they do sound a bit silly, don't they? Still, they're very successful. Brand names are important if you're exporting a product. You may have to change the brand name to make it acceptable because people in different countries react in different ways. Here are some more cars as an example: the European *Ritmo* becomes *Strada* in the UK – Ritmo sounds like a grass-cutting machine, a lawnmower. In Europe the *Kadett* becomes in the UK the *Astra* – 'cadet' sounds too military for us. In the USA and

in Britain, we have the *Nova*, in Europe it becomes the *Corsa* because in Spanish and Italian 'No va' means 'Doesn't go' – very appropriate, you may think! Now in the USA they have a thing called the *Rabbit*, a sort of light-hearted, amusing image, hasn't it? That believe it or not is our *Golf*, because in Europe we prefer a sporty but still a serious image. Even a ... fashionable product like a computer has to have a marketable, and a memorable brand name – and fashions do change quite quickly, of course. The names *Einstein* and *Dragon* are very much last season's names – much too unsophisticated and ... and primitive ... um ... for us now. Er ... now we seem to prefer ... um ... fruity, clean, fresh sort of names to suit our current image of computers. So we have ... er ... the *Apricot* and *Apple*. Er ... but *Banana* or *Lemon* probably wouldn't have worked so well! And then there's *Macintosh*, which is actually also a type of apple, er ... though *Golden Delicious* or ... or *Granny Smith* probably wouldn't have succeeded and then of course they wouldn't have been able to call the software *MacWrite, Mac-Paint, MacDraw* and *MacEverything else*! Then you have sort of unpronounceable names like the *Compaq* – the last letter is Q – this of course makes it a very memorable name.

Er ... one more example: my vacuum cleaner is called a *Vampire* on the Continent. Um ... for us that's far too frightening, of course, sounds like 'Dracula' – so we call it, rather boringly I think, the *Compact Electronic*.

Now, having said all that, what I'd like

you to do is to think of some foreign brand names that you think are unsuitable for the market in your country. Er ... get together with a colleague and you've got three minutes to make notes. OK? ...'

[Time: 3 minutes 15 seconds

B   The activity involves considering different ways of dealing with the same ideas: in a letter or telex, over the phone and by internal memo.

First, working in pairs, students read the fax from Mme. Duvalier. Any comments or queries? It's based on an authentic letter, by the way, which was even more sarcastic!

1. ☎ First, they role-play a phone call conveying the same ideas that were in the faxed letter.
2. Then they work together (in the role of Herr Gebhardt) to draft a telex or letter in reply to the fax from France.
3. Finally, they draft a memo to all members of staff (or to those it may concern).
   At the end get the pairs to show their draft memos to another pair and ask for comments.

C   The five extracts have not been modified: they are quite typical of what can be found in such leaflets. To show that this kind of thing is not restricted to places like Taiwan, we have shown the country of origin in the Answers below.

Maybe the cause of all this is that instructions are written by a technical specialist, who then uses a dictionary to translate them into other languages. The moral presumably is to have all printed material checked by a native speaker before it goes to the printers. And later to have the printer's proofs checked too!

Answers – these are corrected versions with more suggested amendments in brackets:

1. If the iron is standing on its heel (base?), pull the tank (water container?) away from the iron   *W. Germany*
2. Position the stabilisation shelf on the pins and tighten them clockwise (?). Prevent the shelf from snapping (slipping) out by screwing the locking bolt.   *W. Germany*
3. Even if (Even though??) the oven is self-ventilating, the room should be equipped with a chimney for natural ventilation so that the heat passing through the oven's thermal insulation disperses.   *Italy*
4. Consequently no readjustment is usually required if the unit is used in the country of purchase.   *Japan*
5. Finally, here is a summary of advice for successful (?) and safe operation:
   – Clean away any grease or paint which covers the part (unit?)
   – Never lay the various cables on parts which have just been welded   *not known*

D   The ads in the Student's Book should be treated as 'starters'. If you bring to class your own selection of large, colourful, up-to-date magazine ads in English, these will be more motivating. The text of the ads should be readable from a distance if you're planning to display them in the classroom. Better still, encourage the members of the class to seek out some of their own favourite advertisements (in English and/or in their own language) and bring them to class. Maybe include some ads that are terrible or tasteless as well.

It will be particularly revealing to compare different national styles and conventions in advertisements: for example, the use of visual or verbal humour and the use of 'knocking copy' in Britain and the USA (criticising competing products is illegal in some countries).

E   Again, if this is possible, the recorded commercials can be supplemented by your own collection of commercials – preferably British or American TV commercials.

Man: Choose any Philips washing machine, dishwasher or fridge-freezer at Allders and get a £25 voucher free.

Woman: That's £25 off your choice of groceries at Sainsbury, Tesco, Marks and Spencer and other stores.

Man: There's more!

Woman: Choose your Philips washing machine, dishwasher or fridge-freezer now and you'll also get a bonus gift absolutely free.

Singers: 'Altogether a better choice – it's all, all, altogether: Allders.'

Man: Choose Philips at Allders for your £25 voucher and bonus gift.

Woman: Don't miss it!

Voice 1: In 1936, television broadcasts began with one channel.

Voice 2: In 1955, we got a second.

Voice 3: By 1982, we had a grand total of four.

Voice 4: But now you can get up to 16 channels from Telecom Satellite Systems. We can install a complete satellite system for under £900 and you'll receive showing movies, sport, music, the arts, news – even a channel for kids. For further information and a free site survey, call Telecom Satellite Systems on 01 446 4444. That's 446 4444.

Man: Interested in a Peugeot?

Woman: Mm.

Man: Vilton Cars have a fantastic deal for you on the Peugeot 205 range.

Woman: Oh, I like the 205s.

Man: When you buy a Peugeot 205 from Vilton Cars, not only will you get a great price for your old car but – would you believe it – they guarantee to exchange it within 12 months and credit the original price you paid.

Woman: No depreciation?

Man: And no depreciation.

Woman: Oh, I'll take it. What's the phone number?

Man: For details, ring Vilton Cars, Southgate, on 882 2707.

Woman: 882 2707, 882 2707, 882 2707 …

Customer (Smith): Morning.

Shopkeeper (Jones): Morning.

Customer: I'd like to buy a selling spot, please.

Shopkeeper: A radio commercial, yes sir. What did you have in mind?

Customer: Well, something with plenty of 'oomph'.

Shopkeeper: I see, 'oomph'.

Customer: Lots of noise and somebody shouting.

Shopkeeper: Somebody shouting?

Customer: Yes, 'Come, come, come to Mankie Motors!' – you know the sort of thing.

Shopkeeper: Yes, you're looking for a used model, then?

Customer: Oh, yes. Don't want anything modern.

Shopkeeper: No, of course not.

Customer: Got to cram in all my bits ...

Shopkeeper: All your bits?

Customer: You know, name of the company, name of the manager, my name, addresses, outlets, price lists, plenty of telephone numbers ... And if we could mention everything twice, so much the better. Oh, and I nearly forgot: I'd like it sung.

Shopkeeper: You'd like it sung?

Customer: Yes, sort of late 70s glam rock.

Shopkeeper: Oh, of course, yes. Well, how about this model? Only twenty previous owners and it comes complete with a deep voice at the end.

Customer: Mm, yes. Sounds a bit subtle.

Shopkeeper: Well, it could always be done in a funny voice like this.

Customer: Oh, yes, I like that. I'll take it.

Deep voice: Why buy a secondhand advertising idea when your agency should be able to give you a brand new one? Radio advertising: it's only dull if you are.

Customer: Oh, look at this!

Shopkeeper: I'm afraid that one's taken, sir.

Customer: Oh.

Deep voice: It's even possible to come up with a better idea than using Smith and Jones.

Men: 'Doowahbeketchup, bedoowah, bedoowiedoowie ...'

Girls: Gee, Lucy, was that Dirk Studebaker outside your house last night?

Lucy: Uhuh.

Girls: What on earth did you do to get him out of his car?

Lucy: Can't you guess?

Girls: Oh, Lucy, you didn't!

Lucy: Yes, I did!
    'I cooked him dinner: frankfurters and fries,
    with two hamburgers and for a surprise,
    we had some gammon with a pineapple ring,
    that's what I cooked him –

Girls: Did you miss anything?

Lucy: Don't think so.

Girls: Was the ketchup on the side of his plate?

Lucy: It was Heinz, it was Heinz on his plate.

Girls: Well, oh, well, oh well, oh
    give me more, give me more
    of that Heinz Ketchup taste.
    Eat it all, eat it all,
    'cause it's too good to waste.'

Men: 'I do like a dollop of ketchup, of Heinz ...'

Girl: Are you seeing Dirk again tonight, Lucy?

Lucy: You betcha!

All: 'Heinz is the ketchup, so thick and so smooth
    Heinz is the ketchup for dinner for two ...'

[Time: 3 minutes 45 seconds]

10.8 Promotion   *Vocabulary*

A   This rather long vocabulary exercise may be best done at home before the lesson and discussed in class afterwards. Suggest that any elusive gaps can be left till later and then filled by process of elimination.

Answers:
1. brochures   catalogues   leaflets   direct mail
2. Point of sale
3. Packaging   impact
4. contribute   trademark
5. Showrooms   display   hands-on
6. Trade fairs and exhibitions   stand   representatives
7. Publicity   press releases   press conference
8. Public relations   reputation   image
9. Word of mouth   recommend
10. toll-free   specific
11. effective   key accounts
12. extent

B   The pairwork discussion gives everyone a chance to use the vocabulary introduced in A above.

10.9   A sales demonstration

The activity in step B requires students to do preparation at home. Announce this in good time – or postpone the demonstrations to another lesson, perhaps after doing 10.10.

A   ⬛ The two parts of the listening task can be done on separate hearings. The notes of customer questions will be of use when hearing the demonstrations in step B3.

Answers:
depth and realism
£100   trade discount
sale or return
computer-controlled   laboratory
five   35mm
special   material
button   automatic   system
advertising campaign   buy it / try it out / have a go with it

Salesman: ... yes, well, the best thing to do is to take a look at this print here. You see you get an amazing feeling of depth and realism. And, well, I mean it's as if you're really there, isn't it? You don't need any special glasses, you know, anything like that.

Customer: Hmm. That's very impressive. Mm ... what's the price and ... and what sort of discount are you offering?

Salesman: The cost to the end-user would be under £100. And we're obviously offering you the usual trade discount.

Customer: Mhm, I see. Well, I might be prepared to take ... er ... let's see, well, 10 on a sale or return basis for each branch ... er ... that's 50 altogether.

Salesman: Ah, er ... problem: I'm afraid

... er ... can't let you have the goods on sale or return because, well, the demand's going to be very heavy.

Customer: Now, the problem is, you see, it does look a bit complicated for the beginner to use.

Salesman: Oh no, not at all, no. Look, if I could just show you, you see, you just look through the viewfinder here, press the button and ... er ... the automatic exposure and focusing system takes care of the rest.

Customer: Mm ... er ... do you have any point of sale advertising material?

Salesman: Yes, we have this showcard and a nice colourful poster.

Customer: Oh yes, that's very good, I like that, yeah.

Salesman: And we're running a national advertising campaign, so ... er ... end-users will be fully aware of the product. And ... oh ... there'll be this double-page spread in the Sunday colour magazines next month. You see, it answers all the questions people may want to ask about the product.

Customer: Mm, I see. Well now, presumably the camera needs a special film?

Salesman: No, no, it uses normal 35 mm colour print film. Er ... the films are processed by us in our computer-controlled laboratory. The four images ... er ... from the four lenses are printed onto a special micro-lens material to form one single image. And ... oh ... and we're running a special introductory offer: End-users' first three films are processed free.

Customer: Yeah, that's good. And I'd like to know ... mm ... what'll happen if the product doesn't take off and ... er ... you stop manufacturing it – will the laboratory still operate? Um ... I mean, will my customers be left with a piece of equipment that they can't use?

Salesman: No, there's absolutely no danger of that whatsoever. This product is going to be a big success. Er ... the reviews in the trade press have been fantastic. Take a look at this one, for instance...

[Time: 2 minutes 10 seconds]

Before starting the next part, ask everyone to study the useful expressions in the speech balloons.

B   As suggested above, steps 1 and 2 of this should be done at home before the lesson. Students who wish to work together on this should be encouraged to do so. Maybe demonstrate a product you have 'recently' acquired to start the ball rolling (perhaps a toy belonging to your child, or a cassette or CD from your collection).

As step 3 may be intimidating and very time-consuming in a large class, it should be done in groups.

10.10   Possibility, probability and certainty   *Functions*

10.3 was a rather functional grammar section – this is a rather grammatical functions section! Many different structures are used in English to describe degrees of certainty.

Presentation

📼 After looking at the 'simple' structures using modal verbs (see also 12.4 Grammar), students can hear a recording of the more precise expressions in the speech balloons. Students sometimes get confused between the concepts involved: for example, if I'm not certain that something is true that doesn't mean that I'm certain that it is not true!

Answer any questions that may arise and, in a more advanced class, maybe consider shades of meaning and emphasis among the recorded examples.

A 📼 We hear some predictions. Students make notes and then discuss with a partner the likelihood of each event occurring. Finally they write a sentence giving their own view on each prediction.

Interviewer: What do you think might happen in the business world in the next 20 years or so?

Woman: Um ... there'll be no more telexes, businesses will only use fax and electronic mail.

Man: Mm ... office cleaning will be done by robots.

Woman: Well, there will be much more unemployment

Man: Well, I think, people will have to retrain for new skills every ten years.

Woman: I think robots will replace production workers.

Woman: Computers will replace clerical workers.

Man: People will buy their food from home.

Woman: There'll be less need for transport, as people will work from home.

Man: Most consumer advertising will be delivered directly to the home.

Woman: Well, business travel will be replaced by live video meetings, there won't be any need to go to see the client any more.

[Time: 45 seconds]

B Groups of three look into their crystal balls and try to foresee trends in marketing the products listed. To start everyone off, a couple of the products can be discussed as a class.

C In the same groups, students evaluate the 'truth value' of the trivial facts given. Encourage them to use the expressions presented earlier and not to say just 'Probably true' or 'May be true'.

Answers:
all the odd-numbered facts are untrue
all the even-numbered facts are true

Further information about each statement:
1. It's British – Saatchi & Saatchi, which owns a major US agency. Dentsu (Japan) is No. 2.
2. – eight kilos per person per year

217

3. Indian National Railways with two million employees is the West's biggest employer. In most countries, the state is the largest employer of both civilian staff and military personnel.
4. – and in Italy 99% of businesses have an average of eight employees
5. It's Japan
6. – and in the rest of the world it's over $1.5 billion
7. It's Jeddah (by area) or Chicago (by number of passengers)
8. – otherwise the meeting is sure to be disrupted
9. It's Gatwick (No. 1 is Heathrow)
10. – state monopolies make over half the world's cigarettes, most of the others are manufactured by six multi-national companies.
11. It's West Germany
12. – company name consultants in the USA gross $25 to $40 million a year
13. It's actually 15 million a day
14. – Nestlé. (A Nestlé executive was once looking for companies to acquire in Italy and began negotiations with a pasta manufacturer, only to find that Nestlé already owned it!)
15. It's actually Rotterdam, in terms of tonnage handled
16. – of course: 150 litres per head per year!

There is more work on this topic in Workbook exercise 10.6.

10.11   What would *you* do?   *Discussion*

The case studies can be shared out among the groups if time is limited. There are no 'correct answers' – if in doubt call on your most experienced students to decide which of the suggested courses of action are unwise or wise.

  As homework, students could be asked to select one of the cases and 'write up' their explanation of what they would do.

Workbook

Contents for this unit:

10.1 Comparison	Grammar
10.2 Vocabulary – 1	
10.3 Prepositions – 6	
10.4 Vocabulary – 2	
10.5 The three stages of a sales interview	Listening 📼
10.6 How certain are they?	Functions

Background information: Meetings

Business people spend quite a lot of time in meetings and meetings come in all shapes and sizes: ranging from formal committee meetings to informal one-to-one meetings.

There are several reasons why meetings are held:

- Reaching decisions in a meeting means that all the participants can feel more committed to the decision
- More information is available
- different ideas can be contributed

Meetings can lead to more imaginative and informed decisions – often more courageous decisions than one person might feel brave enough to make.

Some of the drawbacks are that:

- more time is required
- there's more talk (sometimes irrelevant and repetitive)
- and more group pressure.

The more people there are at a meeting, the longer it may take to reach a decision. There seem to be ideal sizes for meetings, depending on the purpose – a meeting where information is being given to people can be quite large, as questions from the floor may be asked by a few individuals on everyone else's behalf.

The way a committee operates often depends on the style of its leader or chairperson: he or she may control the proceedings very strictly, or let everyone speak whenever they want. An effective chairman should be flexible. In some meetings the members have to take a vote before a decision can be made: formal proposals or 'motions' may have to be tabled, seconded and discussed before a vote can be taken. Other meetings may require a consensus of the members – everyone has to agree.

Most meetings have an agenda. For a formal meeting, this document may be circulated in advance to all participants. For an informal meeting, the agenda may be simply a list of the points that have to be dealt with. The purpose of an agenda is to speed up the meeting and keep everyone to the point. The agenda for a formal meeting must be organized in logical order. Often the agenda shows not only the topics but the meeting's function regarding each topic ('to receive a report on ... ', 'to confirm ... ', 'to approve ... ', etc). All items on which a decision is to be taken should appear on the agenda, which would usually have this format:

》》》→

1	Minutes of last meeting
2	Matters arising
3 – n	Items
n + 1	Any other business (AOB)

Taking minutes – and writing them up later – are special skills, involving decisions like 'Do we need to know which person made every point?' and 'Is this point worth mentioning?' Minutes usually report details of the time, date and duration of the meeting and the names of those present, but the content of the report itself may be detailed or brief, depending on the anticipated readership

One-to-one or small informal meetings also tend to be structured (usually with an agenda) and planned. They are different from chance conversations in a corridor or over coffee. Small informal meetings may also take place or continue during a meal.

© Cambridge University Press, 1989

11 Meetings

All business people spend a fair amount of their time attending meetings. This unit revises some of the skills that are required when participating in meetings of different kinds and sizes. Students will be considering and taking part in both formal and informal meetings. The relationships and behaviour at meetings where many people are involved, as in a committee, or where just two people are involved, as in one-to-one meetings, are also discussed and practised. We have avoided the use of the term 'interview' for one-to-one meetings and have reserved this term to describe job interviews, progress interviews and promotion interviews (see Unit 13).

This unit's functions are discussion techniques and the grammar topic is using prepositions and prepositional phrases to describe location and direction.

11.1 Discussion techniques   *Functions*

This section extends some of the ideas introduced in 5.2 Agreeing and disagreeing. To begin with, perhaps, refer students back to the expressions presented there.

The exponents are not recorded, but the recorded meeting in A shows the expressions used in a real meeting. Students should study the Presentation section before they hear the recording.

A [cassette icon] Students will need to hear the recording twice: the first time they could just sit back and listen. The second time, they may have to make notes on the points made in order to be able to discuss them later. Students who are not working may not have much to say about this. By the way, don't spend too long discussing flexitime, as this will be the subject of an integrated activity in 14.5 – this meeting provides a foretaste of that.

The exponents that are used in the meeting are <u>underlined</u> in the transcript.

All: ... yes ... it took an hour and a half for my bags to come through ... yes, but it ... it's always the same ... the last time I saw you I...

Chair (Mr Brown): Er ... OK, it's 10 o'clock, everybody, so I think we'll ... er ... make a start. Now, the first item on the agenda is a discussion of the

221

management's proposals on flexitime. Now, you've all discussed the proposals within your departments, haven't you?

All: Yes. We have, yes.

Chair: Er ... Miss Garcia, would you like to start, then?

Anna-Maria: OK, well, most of my people are perfectly happy with the present non-flexible system. They think a change would be dangerous.

Carla: <u>I'm sorry, I'm not quite with you.</u> Dangerous?

Anna-Maria: Well, they feel more flexible hours would make it difficult to cover for each other. We all have quite clearly defined responsibilities. Some people would benefit more than others.

Enzo: <u>It seems to me that</u> your people can just agree together to go on working from nine to five, they don't have to work later.

Anna-Maria: Yes, but the problem is that if one or two people opt for the new system, the others will have to cover for them when they're not there.

Chair: Ah, Mr Bergman, <u>what are your views on this?</u>

Alex: Well ... um ... the thing is that ... er ...

Carla: Look, <u>I'm really sorry to interrupt.</u> <u>I'd just like to say that</u> any department can vote to opt out. They can just vote on it and the majority wins.

Chair: Thank you, Mrs Baldini. Ah ... Ms Legrand, yes.

Tina: Um ... c ... <u>could I make a suggestion?</u> Wouldn't it be ... um ... be best to hear what each member has to say about the proposals ... er ... from the point of view of his or her department?

Chair: Yes, all right. Er ... Ms Legrand, wh ... <u>what are your views?</u>

Tina: Well, the main problem is ... is the decision about ... about basic core times.

Enzo: <u>I'm sorry, I didn't catch what you said.</u>

Tina: I'm talking about core times – that's ... er ... the basic hours that would not

be flexible. It's been suggested that these be ten to three, but this seems much too restricted, don't you agree, Carla?

Carla: Absolutely. In fact I'd say that there should be flexible days.

Anna-Maria: <u>Sorry, I'm not quite with you.</u>

Carla: Well, staff should be allowed to build up a credit of hours to entitle them to take whole days off, not just fewer hours on other days.

Chair: Ah ... Mr Rossini, <u>what do you think about this?</u>

Enzo: Yes, I'd go along with that. As for cover, in my own case it's no problem, there are three of us in the Export Department and we work as a team, so it's easy for us to cover for each other as long as there are still two of us in the office.

Alex: Er ... Mr Brown?

Chair: Yes, Mr Bergman?

Alex: Er ... <u>If I could just make a point here</u> ... er ... in our case, we do a lot of dealing on the phone with the States and ... er ... sending messages to and fro by fax in the afternoon. Er ... if we had anyone off then we wouldn't be able to manage. That means our core times would have to be one to five. Maybe, each department should set its own core times.

Chair: Mm ... er ... yeah, Mrs Baldini?

Carla: That's all very well, Alex, but then no-one in any other department would know who was in at what time, I mean there'd be chaos. There has to be a standard for all departments.

Chair: Er ... yes, Mr Rossini?

Enzo: Yes, coming back to the flexible days idea, this just wouldn't work. People phoning the company or visiting would get terribly confused.

Tina: No, no, that ... that's not true, Enzo. I mean, when people take holiday or ... or when people are sick, cover arrangements are made. Well, with flexible days, exactly the same kind of arrangements would be made.

Chair: Well, any other points?

All: No ... don't think so ... covered it all ...
Chair: Have you got everything down, Mr Johnson?
Johnson: Yes.

Chair: Then I think we'll move on to the next item on the agenda ...

[Time: 3 minutes 30 seconds]

B   This discussion is best done in groups of about four – preferably sitting round a table as if holding a meeting. To start everyone off, use the exponents yourself as you ask various members of the class for their views on the first couple of opinions. Or maybe write up this one on the board and use the exponents to elicit the class's views:

What is a meeting?
A meeting is a group of people who take minutes but waste hours.

There is no further practice in using the exponents in this section, as opportunities to practise them further occur throughout this unit.

11.2 Planning a meeting

In this integrated activity, students will have to make arrangements for a meeting, decide on a suitable venue, write memos and draft an agenda. The activity includes listening to recording messages and role-playing telephone calls.
    Make sure everyone understands their role.
    Arrange the class into an even number of pairs (pairs of pairs).

1. The fax messages are from head office and from two people who will be attending the meeting.

2. The recorded messages are from two more people who will be attending the meeting and from Michele Lombardini, 'your assistant' in Paris.

This is Hans-Ruedi Frommer, calling from Archimedes AG in Zurich. About the meeting next month: If the choice of venues is between Turin and Munich, we are in favour of Munich as this fits in with our trip to key accounts in Austria during the last week of the month. If the meeting was in Turin, we would have to cut this trip short.

This is Montserrat Farres Escovet of Archimedes SA in Barcelona. I believe that the change of venue for our

meeting from Paris to another city is most inconvenient and a bad move. Meeting in Paris gives us a chance to talk to our other colleagues in the main European office. If the meeting is somewhere else, we'll still have to visit Paris on another occasion! So please, let's have the meeting in Paris as usual.

This is Michele Lombardini. I forgot to leave a note on your desk about the arrangements for the meeting next month. I've telexed all our European

223

managers and so far the voting is: For Munich four votes, For Torino four votes. Against both Munich and Turin (in other words in favour of Paris) seven votes. See you on Thursday.

[Time: 1 minute 10 seconds]

3. Now everyone has to decide on a suitable venue, trying to placate all the participants.

4. [cassette] Now Ms Brewster gives her ruling – which may or may not conflict with the decision made in step 3.

Er ... this is Claire Brewster in Chicago. I've given more thought to the matter of the meeting in Europe next month. And it's got to be Turin, OK? Not Munich – the reason is that I've got another meeting in Rome that has to fit in with it. So can you let your people know, please?

[Time: 15 seconds]

5. Three memos have to be drafted – a different tone is required for each, depending on whether the recipient is likely to be inconvenienced or delighted with Turin as the venue.

6. [icon] Changing partners (each pair with another pair) means that the speakers won't be privy to what was discussed in the earlier steps. In each pair, one partner will have to play the Swiss role. Encourage everyone to make preparatory notes before the calls are made.

7. Back with his or her original partner, the person who called Switzerland reports on what happened.

8. The agenda is drafted.

9. Two pairs join to form a group and compare their agendas. Further discussion questions follow.

11.3   Speaking at meetings

This section takes the ideas introduced in 11.1 one step further. Ask the class to study the expressions in the speech balloons (not recorded). Draw attention to the more formal expressions noted with asterisks.

All three steps of this section concern the same topic: improving office working conditions. The meetings are likely to be fairly informal in these circumstances.

A   [icon] The groups should consist of four or more people. Everyone is a 'member of the staff committee'.
1. After deciding who will chair each meeting, the chairperson has some tips on how to conduct the meeting in File 47, while the others see the points they will have to make in Files 14, 65 or 100. In a larger group two members can share a file.

2. The meetings take place.
3. The group draft a short report on the meeting. This report will be the basis of the meeting that follows in step B. Once completed the report should be delivered to the group sitting on the left (anti-clockwise).

B The theme is the same, but now everyone is a 'member of the management committee'.

1. Again, after deciding who will chair the meeting, the chairperson (preferably a different member this time) has some tips in File 47, while the others discover the costs of carrying out any proposals suggested by the 'staff committee' in Files 88, 9 or 37.
2. The meeting is held.
3. A memo is drafted to the firm's staff. Once completed, the memo is delivered to the group sitting on the right (clockwise) and this is the management's reply to the report they sent in step B.

C Now in pairs, the roles change again with one partner playing role of 'staff rep' and the other the role of 'manager'. The management memo is discussed.

Finally, ask each pair to report to the class what happened in their tête-à-tête.
How is the situation of staff vis-à-vis management in your students' firms similar to the simulation in this integrated activity?
Would such matters be dealt with in such meetings or simply decided by a benevolent, paternalistic manager?

We return to the theme of staff-management relations in Unit 14.

11.4 Do we really need a meeting? *Discussion*

If possible, arrange the groups so that students with experience of meetings will be able to advise those without.

A Firstly, students should think of meetings they have attended themselves and evaluate them. One-to-one meetings should be considered, not just committees. This can be done as a whole-class warm-up, or by students working in pairs and later reporting to the whole class.

B Draw everyone's attention to the suggested 'If...' sentences at the end of this step. There are no 'correct answers' as the practice tends to vary from country to country and from firm to firm. In some countries decisions tend to be reached by consensus, whilst in others managers are more autocratic. In general, it may be better to meet individuals if the problems aren't shared by or relevant to anyone else, or if the problem is too delicate for a public airing.

Ask each group to suggest which members of staff should be involved to solve each of the eight problems.

C This can be done as a whole-class follow-up, or by students working in pairs or groups. Here everyone has a chance to say what they feel – see also below.

Follow-up discussions

- What advice can be given to people who feel too shy to speak their mind at meetings?
- What are the qualities of a good chairperson?
- What 'golden rules' can the class suggest to make sure meetings are successful?

Here are some suggestions, which the class could evaluate and then add to:

    Start on time
    Be punctual
    Make sure everyone has a chance to contribute
    Don't let anyone dominate
    Stick to the agenda
    Don't insist on everyone addressing the chair

11.5 Place and direction   *Grammar*

This section revises the use of prepositions, by means of a series of communication activities. The difficulties here are often connected with expressing **precisely** where something is located – language is a less efficient medium than a drawing in doing this and quite a lot of 'Do you mean...?' and 'Could you say that again?' questions are usually necessary in a conversation. The emphasis throughout this section should be on the need to describe location precisely, not approximately.

Begin by going through the prepositional phrases on the left-hand side. Any questions? Perhaps do the Extra activity (see below) as a warm-up exercise.

Steps A, B and C are all based on the office layout in the Student's Book. Here each worker's desk is identified by a different letter of the alphabet on the plan. You'll notice that the members of staff conveniently have surnames beginning with a different letter!

Students are asked to imagine that they are directing a visitor to different people's desks.

A First, the examples in the speech balloon are to be matched to particular desks in PrepCo's offices. Ask everyone to look at the list of personnel before they go on to step B.

B Working in pairs, students should write down what they'd say to direct a stranger to desks D to H. Follow this up by asking for some pairs to read out their directions.

C Now, in this information gap activity, one partner looks at File 90, where the locations of desks I, K, M, O, Q and S are shown. The other partner sees the location of desks J, L, N, R and T in File 101. Each has to find out what the other one knows.

D Students who are not yet in work could discuss different styles used in the illustrations in 2.4. Again make sure the details are given precisely (i.e. not 'Near the bottom' but '2 centimetres from the bottom of the page').

E This activity needs time to do it justice. Decide first what kind of meeting the classroom is to be rearranged and refurnished for. What other items are necessary – from paper clips up to a telephone and photocopier?
   At the end each group should describe to the class exactly where different items should be moved to.

Extra activity

Take a box of paperclips into class (preferably conspicuous coloured ones) and place them in different parts of the classroom. First call on members of the class to spot the paperclips, by explaining exactly where each one is. Then they should tell you where to move each one. Students will be saying things like this:'There's one just beside my chair, between the chair and the wall.'
'Pick up the one from under my chair and put it on top of your Teacher's Book.'

Workbook

There is more work in the Workbook on prepositions of location and direction in exercise 11.5. Further work on idiomatic prepositions and prepositional phrases can be found in Workbook exercises 5.1, 6.5, 7.6, 8.7, 9.2, 10.3, 11.4, 12.1, 13.7.

11.6   One-to-one meetings

In case the topic of the integrated activity in B seems a little mundane, reassure students that there are other meetings in later units and that we want to concentrate on the *techniques and skills*, rather than on the subject matter. The main advantage of this topic is that it doesn't require any elaborate preparation.

A   First we hear an illustrative example of a one-to-one meeting. Students may need to hear this twice.

Fisher: Ah, good morning, Ms Ross, do come in.

Ross: Hello, Mr Fisher. Nice to see you.

Fisher: Face to face instead of on the phone, what? Haha. How are you?

Ross: Fine, thanks, very well.

Fisher: Oh, do sit down. Would you like some coffee?

Ross: Oh, yes please, black.

Fisher: ...... Here you are.

Ross: Thanks. Well, how's it all going?

Fisher: Oh, not too bad, we're just about to open a branch in New Zealand.

Ross: Oho ... I'm hoping to – if I can justify it to the marketing director! How's your little boy, has he started school yet?

Ross: Oh, yes, he's in the second year now.

Fisher: What, already? Doesn't time fly! Is he enjoying it?

Ross: `Very much, it's much more fun than being home!

Fisher: Haha. Well, I suppose we'd better make a start. Shall we get down to business?

Ross: Right. First of all can I confirm the time and date of the presentation. It's Saturday 24 October in the morning. What time exactly?

Fisher: Well, on the invitations we've sent out we've said that the presentation itself will start at 11 and go on till 12.30.

Ross: So you'll need the room from about 10 till 2. Would you like us to serve coffee beforehand?

Fisher: Yes, yes – and drinks and snacks at the end.

Ross: Better to have buffet lunch?

Fisher: No, I ... people who are invited won't be expecting a free lunch, they might think that's overdoing it. They'll want to get back to their families, as it's Saturday.

Ross: All right, the normal pre-lunch snack buffet will be what you need – that's basically the same as what you had last February.

Fisher: Oh, that'll be fine.

Ross: OK, well, we'll charge for the room, coffee and snack buffet at the standard rate less 15%, as we agreed. And we'll charge for the drinks served on a pro-rata basis.

Fisher: Fine, fine, yes.

Ross: What type of ... um ... equipment, furniture would you like?

Fisher: Well, let's have ... um ... four ... no, no ... five tables for our display. Er ... we'll bring our own stands. Now, there's an overhead projector and sound system already in the room, I believe? Can you get someone to check that before we come, you know to see that it's working?

Ross: Oh, of course, the technician will be with you when you're setting everything up. Oh, the seats in that room have flap-over desk tops, will that be all right?

Fisher: Yes, yes, that's fine, sure.

Ross: You say you've sent out the invitations, any idea how many people there'll be? Um ... I think you know there's ... the capacity for the room is about 50, but 40 is ideal.

Fisher: Yes, ah ... the problem is that we

won't know exactly how many there'll be until shortly before.

Ross: Can you let me know definitely by the Thursday?

Fisher: Mm ... no. But I'll have a rough idea and we'll budget for the number I give you then. We've sent out 100 invitations ...

Ross: 100?!

Fisher: Yes, well, in theory that means that there could be 200 people.

Ross: Yes, but the room won't ...

Fisher: But of course ... haha ... I don't expect more than about 30 to come.

Ross: But what if they do? This room is the only one we have that day – there's a wedding reception in the banqueting rooms, so we ...

Fisher: Well, in that case, I suppose ...

[Time: 3 minutes]

B In this integrated activity students prepare and simulate a series of one-to-one meetings. The class should be arranged into an even number of pairs (pairs of pairs: Pair A and Pair B). To make the numbers match, there can be some 'pairs' of three.

The procedure is explained in the Student's Book, but here is an overview and some extra comments:

1. The two pairs decide who will play each role. Pair A will be the suppliers (supplying the services of their educational institution), while Pair B will be the customers (looking for a venue for their conference).
2. Pair A drafts a telex while Pair B makes a list of requirements. The telex is 'delivered' to Pair B.
3. Pair A consider their facilities while Pair B read and reply to the telex.

4. ☎ One partner from Pair B phones a member of Pair A: meanwhile the non-participating partners eavesdrop and make notes and comments afterwards.

   Alternatively, both partners could make simultaneous phone calls to their counterparts, so that everyone participates.

5. Pair A draft an agenda while Pair B list the questions they'll ask at the meeting in the next step. Maybe remind students of different kinds of questions they might ask or have to answer: open questions, probing questions, leading questions, etc.

6. 👥 Now we come to the climax of the activity: the two members of each pair split up and meet their counterparts. Two simultaneous meetings take place in each pair of pairs – everyone participates.

   Make sure everyone knows how long the meeting should last and draw their attention to the expressions in the speech balloons.

7. Everyone makes notes after their meeting.
8. Finally, the two partners in each pair report on their meetings.

Finish by asking the class what they learned from this activity – how different was the process to what might really happen?

11.7 Let's have a meeting!

A 🔲 First a discussion, based on these recorded comments. This is best done in smallish groups:

Interviewer: What can go wrong at meetings?

'Sometimes the participants aren't sure what the purpose of the meeting is.'

'People always start to argue and then they get angry with each other.'

'What often happens is that the chairperson dominates the group.'

'Yes, and the chairperson rushes through the agenda so that the meeting can finish on time.'

'Lots of meetings I go to have no written agenda.'

'Well, for a start, there are too many items on the agenda. We can't possibly cover everything.'

'Well, often some members are late and then the meeting doesn't start until everyone has arrived. So we just have to sit there waiting till they come.'

'Look, the meeting finishes late because too much time is allowed for discussion.'

'Yes, but not all the items on the agenda are dealt with.'

'Well, you see, the chairperson encourages everyone to speak when they want to and proposals aren't made "through the chair".'

'The chairperson doesn't control the discussion and everyone talks at once.'

'Because the chairperson asks the more senior people to speak first, the more junior ones are afraid to give their ideas.'

'No one is asked to take notes and keep the minutes of the meeting.'

[Time: 1 minute 10 seconds]

B The whole class should work together for this integrated activity. The purpose of the activity is to simulate the steps that are gone through to prepare a meeting from scratch and then hold it.

If possible, students should be encouraged to organize a REAL picnic, dinner or outing so that what is done in class has a direct, enjoyable outcome.

The procedure is explained in the Student's Book, but here is an overview of what happens:

1. Together, an agenda is drafted. The nature of the event needn't be decided until the meeting is held. Don't forget contingency plans in the event of rain, etc.
2. Half the class will participate in the activity, the rest will take notes. Who will be who can be decided randomly, as there will be two sessions to give everyone a turn.

   One student is assigned the role of Chairperson, who can be referred back to the 'tips for chairmen' in File 47.
3. The first session of the meeting is held. Set a deadline, making sure this allows enough time for the remaining steps.
4. Students work in pairs, arranged so that one note-taker can show his or her notes to one participant.

5. Now the roles are reversed for the second session. One student is assigned the role of Chairperson, who can be referred back to the 'tips for chairmen' in File 47. The second session of the meeting is held.
6. As in step 4, one participant is shown the draft minutes by one 'secretary'.
7. FOLLOW-UP: A discussion of what went wrong will help to focus attention on discussion skills and organizational skills that students can continue to improve. If you're aware of a shortcoming, that's usually the first step in overcoming it.
8. In this step students form pairs with another member of their own group to check notes for content. Then, probably as homework, everyone drafts a summary of the half of the meeting they made notes on – in the style of a report that will be circulated among both the participants and other people involved.
9. Enjoy the picnic!

Workbook

Contents for this unit:

11.1 What would you say   Functions
11.2 About this meeting ...   Listening
11.3 Vocabulary
11.4 Prepositional phrases – 1
11.5 Place and direction   Grammar
11.6 Choose the best summary   Listening
11.7 More suffixes   Word-building
11.8 We need some guidelines ... Listening

12 Operations and processes

This unit aims to present and practise English as it is used both in the description of simple and everyday operations as well as in more specialized work and business operations. While it is not the specific task of this course to prepare students to use 'technical English', there is an area of language where, for example, the giving of instructions and explaining how things work will need to be mastered. This is dealt with in the functions section.

In addition, the ability to cope with and refer in English to problems that arise in the course of production processes is a skill which students need some practice in. Furthermore, the rate of change in industry and business makes it important for students to be able to describe even fairly complex manufacturing processes involving automation, computerization and robotics. Finally, this unit also provides the opportunity for the introduction and discussion of topics and ideas connected with the general principles and motives behind business and commerce.

12.1   Explaining a process. How do you...?

The process dealt with is of a relatively concrete and everyday type. Most learners of English at this level can be expected to be familiar with, or may even have had experience of, the DIY-assembling of objects such as tables. Such a 'hands-on' and physical operation provides a gentle transition to the more abstract business-specific operations (in 12.2) and the subsequent manufacturing process in 12.5. In this way practice in the basic serially ordered stages and processes involved in such activities can be more readily understood and followed.

Procedure

Before starting step A check that the words for the processes and the words for the components of the table are understood by everyone. Go through the items in the box and those in the diagram.

A   For this step students work in pairs.

232

B   Rearrange the class into groups of two or three, so that the original pairs are not together. To help them they can look at File 112 which contains a photograph and diagram of the table.

C   ▱ Without stopping to discuss the table at this stage, play the recording. Remind the class that this is an exercise in listening for gist and that they should listen for the order in which the steps in the assembly process take place and take notes. It may help weaker students to tell them there are four major operations or steps to listen out for. The main points are <u>underlined</u> in the transcript.

Suggested answers:
These are the four major operations or steps which are mentioned:
1. the assembling of the legs,
2. the table assembly,
3. the assembling of the seats,
4. the screwing in of the braces on the underside of the table.

Now ladies and gentlemen, here before me we have the various components of this do-it-yourself, easy-to-assemble wooden table. This is just the kind of table you can use out in the garden on these long summer days we've all come to love in recent years. Hah, hah, haha ... Hm. You don't need to be an expert to put the component parts together. Everything is clearly explained ... er ... in these assembly instructions. And here too all the parts and the screws and everything, they're all quite clearly labelled.

Well, now ... um ... I'll just demonstrate how easy it all is. Now as you can see we've got four long pieces of wood like this. Now, these are the legs here. Now we start with the assembling of the legs and the framing ... er ... the frame is made of these two large pieces here ... um ... a long piece for the bottom and a short piece of wood for the top. <u>Each set of legs must be assembled to provide a pair</u>. So, first of all you ... you put a screw in each join. A ... and make sure everything's straightened up. And then you can put in all the other screws and tighten them up, like this. Now, remember: <u>use these thick, heavier gauge screws for the framing.</u> All right?

Now, the next thing that you do is to assemble the table. Now for this you will require seven slats. That's these long and

narrow bits of wood here. And they hang over at each end of the table. Now first of all you fit the two outer slats. So that you see how ... how wide the table is. Right? Now when the two outside slats are in position like so, you then take the central table bearer and screw it into place underneath the two table slats. There right, OK now, that's ... that's done. Now, then you take the remaining slats and you space them out and screw them into place to form the table top. <u>Now remember here: the centre bearer must be in the centre of the length of the table.</u>

Now at this stage we can fit the seats into place. Now follow the same procedure in assembling the seats. So screw a slat at the edge and one next to the leg and in the middle of the long seat bearer and ... and then we can then screw in the third slat, so. And we simply repeat the same procedure over here on this side. Right, now, we have something that's beginning to look like a table, haven't we?

Now we turn the table upside down, like this. We lay it on its top, so to speak. Now we take these last two pieces of wood. Er ... these are the braces and they're positioned across the table. <u>The braces should be positioned centrally across the width of the table.</u> And then we screw in first the notched block and then we screw in the

233

brace ... er ... in the notched block ... er ... here in the middle. Er ... first put in one screw and <u>then put in the other screws and tighten them all up.</u> Now we pull the leg frame up and screw in the screws at the other end. And, there we have it, ladies and gentlemen. One garden table.

[Time: 3 minutes 30 seconds]

If they have not already done so the students should be encouraged to look at File 112 to see a diagram of the table. Play the recording a second time, if necessary.

D   Students work in pairs for this activity. They take it in turns to describe a machine, gadget or an everyday process they know well, without naming the object. The listener has to try to guess what it is. Suggest that they think about what they are going to describe and write its name down, *before* they begin to describe it. This will avoid charges of 'cheating' later!

Extra activity

Perhaps ask some of the pairs to try out their explanations in front of the whole class.

12.2 Flowcharts

The purpose of this activity is to draw students' attention to the stages involved in typical business operations with which they are likely to come into contact. In particular, in this step, the focus is placed on interpreting or transferring material displayed in graphs or diagrams into a verbal format, both spoken and written.

Procedure

In steps A to D of this activity students are to work in pairs.

A ▣ The pairs should first look at the flowchart and the items which are listed in the box together before hearing the recording. Play the recording for the first time. Give the class a chance to look at the flowchart of the process and decide which boxes the operations should be placed in. Then play the recording a second time.

Well, the first thing that's got to happen in ... er ... the development of a book is that it has got to be commissioned, that someone has to have the idea for the book, and this can be the publisher, or it might be the author the book itself and this comes in to the publisher, usually in the form of a typescript. So the complete manuscript or typescript of the book comes in and at an early stage there will be a meeting between the authors and editor ... er ... which will be a briefing meeting ... erm ... the authors say how they would like the book to be produced and so on and how the editors ... er ... would like to see it done and ... er ... this ... er ... briefing meeting would probably also include a designer as well. After that, a small section of the book is probably taken away by the designer and he or she starts to specify how the book – how the material – should look on the page. Er ... they will decide on what typeface is used – what style of type – erm ... how the material should be placed on the page, erm ... what kind of illustrations are going to be needed and where they will be placed, and so on. When everyone's happy with the content, with how the style of the book is going to look ... we can proceed to a detailed editing phase. So the typescript is discussed with the author to see that he or she is happy with it and then it goes to the designer for the designer to ... er ... mark it up according to the style which has been established already and then it goes to a typesetter and the typesetter takes it and keyboards it. Erm – now this stage – they're called galley proofs – they are proofs ... er ... which are not laid out ... er ... in the form of the book page. Er ... the designer takes that material and pastes it up into the shape of the pages. At the same time the editor will be correcting the galley proofs, making sure that ... er ... they come out correctly and the author will also be correcting the proofs at the same time. When the designer has prepared the paste-up ... er ... we can then start to commission the artwork. if there are illustrations to be put in we have to go out and get the photographs, we have to get the illustrators to prepare the drawing or illustrations so that they will fit in the spaces that have been left by the designer.

The galley proofs are then sent back to the typesetter for them to correct and they will prepare a correct version of the typesetting. Er ... these are then made up into pages – so they will look at how the designer has set out the pages and they will ... erm ... cut up the typesetting and put it down according to that ... er ... arrangement. So we have page-proofs made up. The author and the editor can then check these page-proofs ... er ... any final corrections and changes are made and sometimes we have a final check at this stage ... er ... where we look at that latest material ... erm .... It's converted into film because printers work from ... er ... film of a book and they carry out the printing process through a photographic process. Er ... it goes to the printer ... er ... the printer puts it on the machine and the book is printed. It comes out in the form of sheets, which are glued and cut – and then it has to be bound – that is, the pages have to be stitched or glued together and the cover put on, whether it's a hard cover or a paperback. That's the binding stage and after the binding stage the books can be shipped from the printer to the publisher's warehouse to ... er ... perhaps, the wholesalers and then to the end-user ... er ... through the bookshop. So that basically is how a book ... er ... comes from the idea stage through the writing stage ... er ... through the publishing stages to your local bookshop.

[Time: 5 minutes 30 seconds]

This is the completed flowchart.

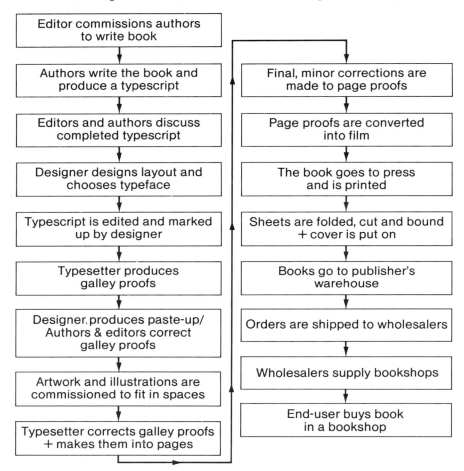

The Stages of Book Production: From Writing to Bookshop

Editor commissions authors to write book	Final, minor corrections are made to page proofs
Authors write the book and produce a typescript	Page proofs are converted into film
Editors and authors discuss completed typescript	The book goes to press and is printed
Designer designs layout and chooses typeface	Sheets are folded, cut and bound + cover is put on
Typescript is edited and marked up by designer	Books go to publisher's warehouse
Typesetter produces galley proofs	Orders are shipped to wholesalers
Designer produces paste-up/ Authors & editors correct galley proofs	Wholesalers supply bookshops
Artwork and illustrations are commissioned to fit in spaces	End-user buys book in a bookshop
Typesetter corrects galley proofs + makes them into pages	

B   Students compare their answers with those of their partner. They follow the instructions in the Student's Book and decide which points they should concentrate on when explaining the process to a foreign visitor. Then ask the class as a whole to share their decisions. What have they decided? Why are they going to concentrate on particular points? Allow time here for questions and queries concerning vocabulary and other language items. Refer to the completed flowchart.

C Students work in pairs and follow the instructions in the Student's Book. This time they will be looking at a diagram of another process – in this case booking a ticket for a flight. (The diagram the students are looking at is called an algorithm.)

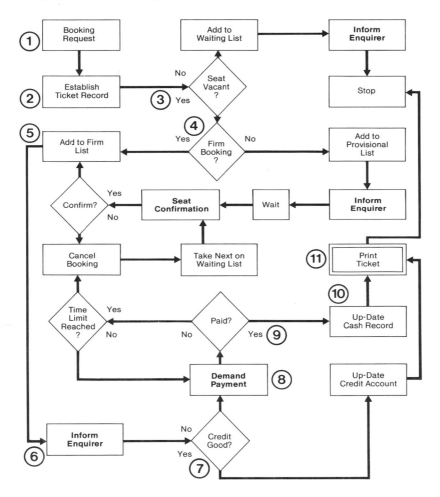

D Students work in pairs to draft a short set of explanations of the process of booking a flight.

E Re-arrange the pairs into groups of four. Students show their draft to another pair and look at the other pair's draft. Encourage them to say how helpful or otherwise they would find the explanation and to provide reasons for their opinions.

Allow time for the class to raise any questions concerning problems they may have had doing the activities.

12.3 Explaining, giving instructions   *Functions*

Presentation

If possible students should look at the presentation section *before* they come to class. This will give them a better chance of remembering the expressions and will lead to a more informed and interesting discussion of the topic in class.

Begin by getting the class to look at the examples in speech balloons. Discuss the points made in the text. Do a quick repetition exercise. Ask the class to suggest how the incomplete sentences might continue. Draw attention to the fact that some of the sentences given are more formal than others. Some will be used between friends and well-known acquaintances, while others are typical for people you know less well or strangers.

The examples ('First of all ...', etc) are recorded, so that students can hear as well as see the sentences that are used.

Make sure any queries are cleared up before students begin exercise A – though it is to be expected that doing the exercise will give rise to further questions.

Further exponents which can be mentioned:
1. To explain the order in which certain things are done to someone you know fairly well, but not to a stranger:
    '(Look) all you do is ...'
    'Watch. (First) you ...'
2. If you want to add a further point, you can say:
    'Make sure you remember to ...'
3. When asking someone to help you:
    'Sorry to bother you, but ...' is fairly informal and familiar; whereas
    'I wonder if I might trouble you for a moment? But ...' is quite formal.
4. A further expression to use if you've not understood the explanation is:
    'How do you do that again?'
5. When you think you've understood, you can say:
    'I'm sorry if I seem a little slow, but I'm not sure I understand.' (This is quite formal.)
    'What you're saying is ...' is more neutral, perhaps.

Exercises and activities

A   Play the recording. Stop after the first conversation. Students

should be listening for informality or formality, and whether the
people appear to know each other well or not.

FIRST CONVERSATION
Man: Avril.
Woman: Hm?
Man: Sorry to bother you. Um ... can you show me how this thing works?
Woman: Ha.
Man: It's not like the old one.
Woman: No ... no. It ... really ... it looks much more complicated than it is, Martin. Come over here. I'll show you how to do it.
Man: OK.
Woman: First of all, don't be worried about all these buttons.
Man: Ha.
Woman: It's really easy. OK. Now look. The first thing that you have to do ...... Well the first thing you have to do is you make sure that there's paper in it.
Man: Sure.
Woman: That's over here on the side.
Man: Yeah.
Woman: And if it runs out a light will go on there. And there's stacks of paper. See just right over here.
Man: Right. And does it go in that tray or that tray?
Woman: It goes in, it goes in that tray. If you use bigger paper, then you have to just adjust this little thing, see? Right ... right here?
Man: Yeah.
Woman: Yeah. To ... er ... you know ... to take different or bigger sized paper.
Man: Fine. Good. I've got that. Good.
Woman: OK. Then, the next thing you do is you take whatever you want ... done and you put it right here. You lift this thing. See?
Man: Right.
Woman: Lift this up. Put it down face down. That's very important.
Man: Yes.
Woman: Well the old machine did the same thing.
Man: Yes. It was much the same as that, wasn't it?

Woman: Now the next thing you have to do is to punch in right here ...
Man: Yeah.
Woman: ... this little digital display ...
Man: Hm.
Woman: ... how many copies you want.
Man: Sure.
Woman: OK? And then all you have to do is just push this button here.
Man: Right. But, yeah ... but the ... the ... the digital display....
Woman: Ahah?
Man: Um ... does it keep repeating? Does it store that in the memory. Or ... er ... I mean, if I put another sheet in?
Woman: No. Er ... what it ... er ... no ... then you have to do it again.
Man: Yeah.
Woman: Actually, no there's a button right here that you can, if you're going to do ... if you're going to do more than one copy ...
Man: Yeah.
Woman: ... then you can actually just feed them in here and the machine will do it automatically. That's why we got a new one. It's brilliant at this.
Man: Right ... right.
Woman: Um ... so you can ... you know ... if you're doing more than one ...... then use this right here and it just feeds them in and it'll take them and it'll do the same amount of copies for each one.
Man: Yes, that's fine. Right. Well. Um ... and ... um ...
Woman: Does that make sense?
Man: Well, yes I think it does. And the lid's got to come down too, hasn't it?
Woman: Right.
Man: To do for the tone, like the old one. Fine well, I think that's ... that's ... that's ... er ... all fairly clear, lovely. Thanks very much, Avril.
Woman: You're welcome.
Man: See you later.
Woman: Mmm mmm.

[Time: 2 minutes]

SECOND CONVERSATION

Woman: Um ... (Coughs) Excuse me ... um.

Man: Yes, Madam?

Woman: Er ... this looks like the ... the sort of machine I've ... I've been looking for. But I wonder ... um ...

Man: Ah. Yes.

Woman: ... could you tell me a bit about it? Tell me how it works?

Man: Certainly. Right. Well, the first thing you have to do is ... er ... to plug it in ... er ... to your supply.

Woman: Does it take an ordinary ... um ... you know an ordinary three-pin plug?

Man: Oh. Yes ... yes madam, indeed. Well we can supply that ...

Woman: Hm hm.

Man: ... with the ... with the machine. Er ... right, now then. Here are the instructions here. They're all quite clear. But, you want to set up the time first ...

Woman: Hm hm.

Man: ... which is displayed here. Now, this is the button you press. And you see the hour flash right through ...

Woman: Oh, yes.

Man: Until the correct hour is shown, there.

Woman: Yeah.

Man: Er ... and then you press this button.

Woman: Hm hm.

Man: ... until the correct minute is shown.

Woman: Yes.

Man: Now you are set up.

Woman: Oh, I see, yes.

Man: You see? Now ... er ... you can adjust that to the desired level by turning this.

Woman: Oh, I see, to make it brighter.

Man: Yes. There you are.

Woman: Oh, yes, that's good.

Man: Variable control there. Er ... now to operate the radio. Well it's ... it's rather like an ordinary radio. There's an ON/OFF switch, er ... your AM/FM band.

Woman: Hm.

Man: Whichever you want. Volume control. Er ... tuning control. There you are.

Woman: Hm.

Man: Select your station. Er ... now ... er ... to use the alarm you press this here – the AUTO/MANUAL switch – and you slide the MUSIC/ALARM switch to the 'music' position.

Woman: Yes.

Man: Yes, now you press the ALARM/OFF button and while the alarm button is depressed, you press the 'Fast' button here to the hour at which you wish to wake. And then ...

Woman: Yes.

Man: ... the 'Slow' button the exact minute of the hour which you wish to wake. I've just put ... er ... seven twenty-five.

Woman: Yes. Right, yes.

Man: Er ... now the wake-up time's entered into the timer memory. And if you want to check it, then you press the ALARM/OFF button. There you are.

Woman: Oh.

Man: And the pre-set wake-up time will be there in the timer memory. The radio will switch on the same time the next day.

Woman: Oh I see, so if ... if I want to see what time I've set it for, if I press that button ...

Man: Yes, if you suddenly think, oh my God, I haven't set the ... er ... alarm ... er ... you just press the ALARM/OFF and it will tell you.

Woman: Yes, yes I think ... yes, I think I understand that. Yes ... yes.

Man: Well, er ... you know, the ... the instructions are all there, so.

Woman: Yes. Well that ... that seems fine, thank you very much indeed.

Man: Right you are, madam.

[Time: 2 minutes 30 seconds]

B In this activity the same situations are dealt with in the form of
a problem-solving exercise. Students should look at the diagrams
and try to agree what is done in what order. Then student A should
look at File 94, student B at 36. This is the correct numbered order of
the figures for using the coffee machine.

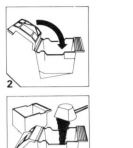

C 🔲 In this activity, students work in pairs.
1. They should imagine they are friends and attempt to explain how to
   do one of the activities listed in the book. Allow time for feedback
   as a class after this activity. There may be questions about how
   certain operations are actually carried out. Ask selected pairs to give
   the explanations they have worked out. Ask the class for their
   comments. Would they be able to carry out the operation now?
   Does anyone have an alternative, more complete or clearer explanation of the operation?
2. Students write down the main points which they feel can't be left
   out of the instructions.
3. Now students work in groups of 4 and compare each other's drafts
   and suggest improvements or alternatives.

Follow-up discussion

At the end, ask the class what they learned from this activity:
● Does it help if you use different forms with different people when
  explaining things? Or the same style for everybody?
● What kinds of things have happened to them when people have
  tried to explain things or they have explained things to people – e.g.
  using automatic ticket machines?
● What sort of help have they had from written instructions – such as
  operating manuals, etc?

241

Workbook

Exercise 12.2 in the Workbook provides further practice on this function.

12.4 Modal verbs   *Grammar*

Using modal verbs almost always presents difficulties to intermediate and upper-intermediate students.

   This section concentrates on giving examples of some of the commoner forms together with brief explanations of some of the verbs of obligation and possibility. Further work may be necessary using the Workbook or exercises from other sources (*Use of English* Units 10, 11 and 12 are recommended).

Presentation

If possible, students should read this section through before the lesson.

🔊 The examples ('He said he would not come to the meeting the next day.' etc) are recorded, so that students can hear as well as see the sentences that are used. Play the recording to the whole class. Make sure any queries are cleared up before students start exercise A in pairs – though it is to be expected that doing the exercise will give rise to further questions.

Exercises and activity

This exercise is to be done by students together in pairs, with time after each exercise for discussion and questions. If time is short, exercise A could be set as homework, but it still needs to be discussed in class to clear up possible misunderstandings.

A   Suggested answers:
 1. We must get that order.
 2. We can't help you this time.
 3. You should apply soon, if you want the job.
 4. Couldn't you pay promptly this time?
 5. If you have problems after the guarantee runs out, the supplier doesn't have to/needn't help.
 6. That company oughtn't to get the order.
 7. If a machine breaks down under guarantee, the company must repair it without extra charge.
 8. We could find the fault, if we look(ed).
 9. They might sell the shares.

10. You must have experience for this job.
11. The switch could be broken.
12. After the guarantee period they shouldn't charge the full price.

B   Students work in pairs. They then go through their suggestions as a whole class.

Suggested answers:
This means that hard hats must be worn.
You can picnic in this area.
The fuel can easily burn.
Radioactivity can be a hazard.
You can reach the motorway this way.
You must not smoke / ought not to smoke.
You can get/hire a taxi where you see this sign.
You can stop for a meal here.
You should use the alarm in case of fire.
You must keep to / shouldn't leave walkways.

C   Students work in pairs. They should follow the instructions in the Student's Book for this step.

Extra activity

After reporting their results to another group the whole class should try and decide which are the most important DOs and DON'Ts in their country. Why do they think so?

What do they think are the most important DOs and DON'Ts when visiting other countries? Do they consider it important to respect the customs and conventions of other countries or peoples? Why?

How do they feel about visitors to their own homes, countries who do not do so?

Workbook

Workbook exercise 12.3 provides further work on using modals.

12.5   Producing the goods

This exercise familiarizes students with a production process and its description. The topic chosen is deliberately non-technical – although clearly even crisp (American English: potato chip) manufacture has a series of technical terms associated with it.

Procedure

This exercise practices both reading for gist, reading for detail and reordering jumbled information with the help of the visual clues in the diagram. Emphasize that it is not important for them to understand every word in the diagram: the overall understanding of the production process and the various stages are the focus.

A   Students should work in pairs and follow the instructions in the Student's Book for this step.

Suggested answers:
Production capacity could not keep up with demand.
New machinery was available.

B   Before they attempt the true/false questions students should look at the statements.

Suggested answers:
1 false   2 false   3 true   4 false   5 true   6 true
7 false

C   Students should work in pairs, look at the diagram and then the jumbled text.

Suggested answers:
PEELING → G   GRADING → D   SLICING → C
WASHING → H   COOKING → B   FLAVOURING → E
WEIGHING → A   PACKING → F

So the stages of the process are: first peeling, then grading, followed by slicing, washing, cooking, flavouring, weighing and finally packing.

Extra activity

Students can draft a short written description of the process of making crisps in their own words after they have discussed the agreed order as a class.

Allow time for students to raise points or queries on the activity.

12.6 When things go wrong ... What do we do?

Students work in pairs for the first two steps. They first read the
newspaper extract. Ask them to try and decide what the difference is
between a 'breakdown' and a 'bottleneck'.

The newspaper article acts as a scene-setter for the subsequent documents. Be prepared to explain vocabulary and to answer queries
concerning the comprehension of the documents.

A   Students first read the documents. Ask them to locate what has
been going wrong and to attempt to find out what the cause could have
been.

B   Students make notes and draft a letter explaining what happened.

C   Reassemble the students in groups of four (each pair with another
pair) to compare notes. They read the report they have drafted and
offer suggestions for improvements.

This is a model report:

[YOU MAY PHOTOCOPY THIS DOCUMENT]

From the Chief Executive Officer   **DELTA TOOLS**
                                                  Southford
                                                  SF4 HK3

                                                     20 May, 19xx
Vance Ballard
European Regional Director
Delta Tools Inc.
Monsstraat
Brussels
BELGIUM

Dear Mr Ballard,

                    Problems at Southford Plant

You asked for a brief report concerning the recent events at
the Southford plant.
    We have consulted the files and spoken to relevant members
of the higher management and thus feel able to provide an
explanation for the breakdown reported in the press on 17 May
of this year.
    The cause of the breakdown was very simple. The handling

---

equipment used to deliver the components to the assembly line
has been known to be in need of an overhaul for the past six
months. The plant has been working to full capacity to finish
the American orders according to schedule.

As you know, we had commissioned a study by Industrial
Research Consultants. They submitted their report on April 5.
In it they warned that there was not enough space available
to store sufficient components. They also recommended
expanding the present two-shift system to a three-shift one.

We had decided to install a fully automated robot system.
However, at the same time it was clear to our production
director that given the present maintenance staff, we would
not have sufficient staff available if big problems were to
arise. The firm has been advertising for maintenance
engineers for some weeks. But we were still only working a
two-shift system so the machines were not getting the
necessary cover.

We all agree that the breakdown was extremely unfortunate
and yet we must admit that, under the circumstances, it was
not entirely unexpected.

We now believe that we have managed to sort out the major
problems which we had been having with the conveyor
equipment. And also when the new robots are installed in
September, we feel certain that such problems will become a
thing of the past. Added to this the fact that the personnel
department has been successful in recruiting some highly
qualified maintenance staff makes us confident that a
repetition of the 16 May now seems entirely unlikely.

Sincerely,
Hank Cruyff
Hank Cruyff

Extra activity

Look for words and phrases in the texts which mean the same as:
conveyor machines: (handling equipment)
service: (maintenance)
limit (v): (restrict)
present (a): (available)
propose (v): (put forward)
reserve: (standby)
another word for production: (output)

Allow time at the end for the class to raise any queries or difficulties
which may have arisen in the course of the activity.

12.7 Production and operations *Vocabulary*

This exercise can be done by students working in pairs. It can be done at any stage during the unit if you have time available, or done as homework.

Answers:

1. output	6. dismantled
2. manpower	7. apprentices
3. know-how	8. utilization
4. slowdown	9. setbacks
5. cut back	10. by-product

Workbook

Other important vocabulary is introduced throughout this unit and in Workbook exercise 12.6.

12.8 Robots and automation: the factory of the future

For the whole of this activity until the final step students should work in pairs. This is an integrated activity entailing briefing first through written material and then later by means of spoken material. Students should be encouraged to take notes. They will be expected to draw on their notes for the discussion at the end.

A For this step students work in pairs. They follow the instructions in the Student's Book. This is a warm-up discussion for the tasks that follow.

B Let the students read the advert.

Suggested answer:
The teaching method used is that of 'jog and log'. The robot is moved in a particular way and positioned to carry out a function. Then the function button is used.

C Students follow the instructions in the Student's Book.

Suggested answers:
Expressions likening robots to human workers and what they did are, among others: *iron men, joined the production line, have recruited, steel-collar workers, cleverer, touch* and *sight*.

The numbers refer to the following:

1961: the year the first industrial robot joined the production line at General Motors

20,000: steel-collar workers

28,000: the West European robot population of 28,000 units

6 per 10,000: number of robots per industrial worker

36 per 10,000: 36 robots per 10,000 industrial workers

80,000: industrial robots working around the clock

$1 billion: building robots has become a $1 billion business

D 🖭 Remind everyone to read through the statements before you start the recording. Play the recording for the first time.

Reporter: Now I'm with you in front of what looks almost like a ... a very complicated children's toy. Er ... there's a crane-like robot picking up a small white object and it's moving it across and placing it very precisely into a jig and that jig is just revolving.

Trainer: That's right.

Reporter: Now ... now the whole thing appears to be controlled by a micro-computer.

Trainer: Absolutely. We use this micro because it's a very significant tool for our purposes.

Reporter: Ah. It drives the robot?

Trainer: Exactly. The robot isn't a toy, of course. Indeed it's quite a sophisticated instrument. In fact, it can be used for a variety of purposes.

Reporter: And you use it for training purposes. Is that right?

Trainer: That's correct. Yes. It can be used for informing people of the possibilities of computing. Indeed, with our training programme we can actually take a person, an individual, and give them the basis of programming a computer to do the simple task that you're looking at.

Reporter: Er ... how long does it take to learn to programme a robot?

Trainer: Well, of course there are different things you can do with a robot. And our courses are of different lengths. So there's no real fixed time limit. I mean, well, it ... it varies, of course. This robot is actually simulating a quite complicated series of steps which are used in industry.

Reporter: And what sort of people can learn to programme robots in this way?

Trainer: Well, we work with different organizations. We work mostly in schools. But for young people aged 15 and 16 we use these methods.

Reporter: I see. And they would learn about robots at school, would they?

Trainer: Yes, we're talking about schools which cooperate very closely with industry. For example, the youngsters we train use engineering facilities from a factory which the factory has no further use for.

Reporter: So there is a very practical orientation to your training, is there?

Trainer: Exactly.

Reporter: Ah.

Trainer: We don't believe in theoretical studies. Particularly when you are training people to use computers to run robots, you must have practical experience. You must have hands-on experience of working with a computer.

Reporter: But also factory experience, you're saying?

Trainer: Our programme gives young people direct experience of working under factory conditions. So it's not just skills training. They also learn to work under actual manufacturing conditions.

Reporter: Working with computers and robots requires further training as well, doesn't it?

Trainer: Ah, certainly. We cannot neglect ordinary or academic subjects like mathematics and English. But the important thing to remember is that in the modern world we must give people skills which will prepare them for the changing world of manufacturing and production which is now upon us. It's no good training people in old-fashioned skills.

Reporter: You believe that your training in computing and robotics will make the young people more flexible?

Trainer: Oh, yes, of course. The individual knowledge of a particular computer or robot is not the main thing. It's the principles and the more general computer skills that matter. We must train a workforce that is flexible and mobile in the future.

[Time: 3 minutes]

Suggested answers:
1 false   2 true   3 true   4 false   5 true   6 false
7 false   8 false

E Play the recording a second time. Direct the students' attention to the questions:

What is the relevance of the training discussed in your opinion?
What is the point of the training programme according to the man interviewed?

Suggested answer:
To give people skills which will fit them for the changing world of manufacturing and production.

F Reassemble the students into larger groups, say four or six, to compare their answers to the questions.

Remind the students that they should be concerned with ways in which robots *may, might, can, could, should,* or *ought to* be utilized, or *if* they *should* be installed in a new plant or used more generally in industry. Each pair should formulate questions to ask the other pair(s) using the modal verbs. Refer them back to step A for examples of verbs to use.

Alternatively you can reassemble the class. You may wish to use these questions in a round-up session in which the several groups report back their conclusions to the rest of the class.

At the end, ask the class what they learned from the activity.

12.9 Business with a fairer face

This activity is centred around a straightforward reading task. It serves as input for a discussion of the possible rationales and motivations for doing business. Follow the steps as they are laid out in the Student's Book. Steps A and B serve as scene-setters for the reading task to come, in C, and to provide a point of reference for the discussion in D.

A Students should work in pairs. When they have completed their own list, they should join up with another pair, or else leave their original partner and form a group with two or three other people.

B In this step students should work in groups of three or four. You may wish to let the class as a whole share their views very briefly at this stage.

C Students work in pairs. Before they start reading the article remind them to look at the statements first.

Answers:

1 false	2 true	3 false	4 true	5 false	6 false
7 false	8 false	9 true	10 true	11 false	12 false

D Students should work in pairs and discuss answers to these questions. Then reassemble the class and let the pairs share their answers together.

Extra discussion questions

- Are there other ways people are or can be motivated to do business other than for profit? What do students think of moral incentives?
- What reasons do the members of the class have for doing business themselves?

You may want to remind students of the related question of social responsibility in the more narrow sense of maintaining customer loyalty as discussed in Unit 8. Do they see any connections between the kind of company described here and publicly expressed claims concerning business practice?

Workbook

Contents for this unit:

12.1 Prepositional phrases – 2
12.2 Explaining   Functions 🔲
12.3 Modal verbs   Grammar
12.4 A memorandum   Writing
12.5 How to fight noise   Listening 🔲
12.6 Vocabulary

Background information: A new job

In different countries, different conventions apply to the process of job application and interviews. In most parts of the world, it's common to submit a typed CV (curriculum vitae – British English) or resumé (American English). This contains all the unchanging information about you: your education, background and work experience. This usually accompanies a letter of application, which in some countries has to be handwritten, not typed. A supplementary information sheet containing information relevant to this particular job may also be required, though this is not used in some countries.

Many companies expect all your personal information to be entered on a standard application form. Unfortunately, no two application forms are alike, and filling in each one may present unexpected difficulties. Some personnel departments believe that the CV and application letter give a better impression of a candidate.

Interviews may take many forms in business today: from the traditional one-to-one interview, to panel interview where several candidates are interviewed by a panel of interviewers, to 'deep-end' interviews where applicants have to demonstrate how they can cope in actual business situations. Moreover, the atmosphere of an interview may vary from the informal to the formal and from the kindly to the sadistic. Fashions seem to change quite rapidly in interview techniques and the only rules that applicants should be aware of may be 'Expect the unexpected' and 'Be yourself'!

In different countries, different trades and different grades, the salary that goes with a job may be only part of the package: perks like a company car or cheap housing loans, bonuses paid in a 'thirteenth month', company pension schemes, generous holidays or flexible working hours may all contribute to the attractiveness of a job.

© Cambridge University Press, 1989

251

13 A new job

This unit covers all aspects of applying for a new or different job or for a promoted or transferred position within one's existing company. We consider the interview situation from the point of view of both interviewer and candidate and look at progress interviews.

The grammar topic in this unit is relative clauses and there is practice in reading job advertisements aloud.

13.1   Your career history

It's important to realize that different countries have different conventions when it comes to CVs (known as résumés in the USA), application letters and supplementary information sheets. It's important to observe these conventions, as not just the information, but also the style of each may be important: which has to be hand-written or typed, which can be dot matrix printed, etc?

A   This step gives students a chance to discuss what the conventions are in their country. If possible, arrange the pairs so that those with less knowledge have a more experienced partner — it may be preferable to have groups of three to achieve this.

B   Arrange the class into groups, each consisting of two pairs. Each pair sees a different File, which contains a complete CV. Following the directions in the Student's Book, they have to discuss what 'picture' they get from the CV in the File and then find out about the other pair's person by asking questions. The two CVs are later used as models for students' own work in C.

File 107 contains information about Mary Scott.
File 111 contains information about George Michaelides.

C   Now, working again in pairs, students discuss and make notes on their own career histories before drafting their own CVs. The drafts can be done in class, if there is time, or as homework. Once the drafts have been checked, students should produce a final version, preferably typed or word-processed.

13.2   Classified advertisements   *Reading aloud*

In this section we focus on the use of catenation in reading aloud. To
read fluently and clearly, one has to read smoothly. And, of course, the
important words must be pronounced correctly.

A   [cassette icon] We hear two readings of the same text. The first reading is
'bad' because the words aren't joined together:
there   is   a   pause   between   each   word.
   The second reading is better because catenation is used:
the wordsarejoinedup like this.

B   In a smallish class, you could go round the class, calling on each
student to read a different part of the ad aloud, with everyone listening
and offering advice. In a larger class, this would be best done in pairs
or groups of three. Play the recording again at the end of the step.

C   Students work in groups of three. Each looks at a different 'Help
Wanted' advertisement in the Files, which they will have to read aloud.
The Files contain the original ad and the first paragraph reprinted in
breath-sized pieces with catenation marked. Encourage everyone to
spend some time preparing themselves to read (looking up any
unfamiliar words, deciding how any difficult words should be pronounced, reading the text through under their breath, etc) before they
read it to their partners.

The ads all come from the *San Diego Union*:
   File 63:   'Sales Professionals'.
   File 75:   'Clerk Typist'.
   File 35:   'Sales Engineer'.

[cassette icon] Each text is recorded on the cassette, read aloud by an American
speaker. The recording can be used before students read the texts
themselves (to guide or encourage them) or after they have read the
texts (as a key to the exercise). Or before *and* after, perhaps.

Extra activity

Advertisements for jobs vary considerably in style. The modern,
dynamic style used in the ads we've chosen for this section may not be
considered appropriate in all fields and in all countries, where a more
traditional, sober style may be preferred.
   Go through a British or American newspaper and select, cut out and
photocopy some ads in different styles – if possible, ads that members
of the class might really consider applying for. Alternatively, you could
ask the class to search for such ads themselves.

Look at the selected ads together and consider any differences in style and content – comparing them with the four ads that have been read aloud in 13.2. Ask the class to compare these with ads that might appear in their own language.

What are the advantages and disadvantages of using a dynamic 'advertising style' in a classified job ad?

The ads you discuss here can be used again in 13.3.

Workbook exercise 13.1 contains more work on reading aloud, with a recorded key on the cassette.

13.3   Applying for a job

This section covers the writing of a job application letter and focuses on aspects of style that can be emulated or avoided in writing one's own letter.

A   When the groups have sorted the applications into 'piles', ask them to report to the others. They should explain **why** they have put them into particular piles.

B   Students should work in pairs for this step. If possible, they should use an advertisement for a job they might really apply for (see Extra Activity above). If you can arrange to have a pile of English-language newspapers to take into class, all the better. If this isn't feasible, students can 'apply' for one of the jobs in Files 63, 75 or 35.

The procedure for this step is clearly explained in the Student's Book. Although the final version would probably be done as homework, step 2 should be done in class so that students can give each other help and advice as they're preparing their first drafts.

Finally, there is a model application letter for students to study in File 87 – this is an application for the PR job in 13.2.

Extra activity

APPLICATION FORMS   We have not included an application form in this course, as forms are all so different from each other that showing an example would not be very helpful – it's much better if students can see a variety of authentic forms that they can relate to.

Ask each member of the class to bring an application form that is used in their firm – if they can find one in English that'd be wonderful. Also get some yourself (your Director of Studies may be able to let you have some) and show them to the class.

Look at these forms with the class and discuss how the various sections should be completed. Photocopy one or two of the forms you have discussed and get the class to practise filling them in.

13.4 Equal opportunities?   *Read and discuss*

A   For the first part of the discussion, the class should be divided into two or more groups. After discussing the questions, get each group to report to the whole class.

B   If possible, get everyone to read the newspaper article at home before the lesson. Then students should discuss their answers to the questions in pairs. The article may contain some tricky vocabulary, but the questions concentrate on the basic information and ideas given in the text.

Questions 1 to 10 are true or false comprehension questions. Questions 11 to 15 are discussion questions. These might be discussed in larger groups.

Even-numbered statements are all **true**
Odd-numbered statements are all **false**
    – note that Question 9 is partly true: you can get a job in the Civil Service at 32, and in the Probation Service at any age.

13.5 Relative clauses   *Grammar*

Although relative clauses are a minor aspect of English grammar, they cause such problems for students that we feel justified in devoting a complete section to them. The problem of punctuation is particularly troublesome.

Presentation

The examples are recorded: the first ones as dialogues, the others as if sentences read aloud. Make it clear that non-identifying relatives are less common in informal speech. Clear up any problems before going on to the exercises. Draw attention to the way that the non-identifying ones are pronounced (with the 'additional information' in the clause spoken in a monotone).

Exercises

A   There are two parts to this exercise: putting in any missing commas and also completing each sentence.

Do the first sentence with the class as an example to show everyone how to approach the tasks.

In these suggested answers, the sentences that require commas are shown with a • (bullet):

1. The qualifications that are mentioned in a job advertisement give you an idea whether you should apply for the job.
2. An interviewer who tries to frighten the candidate is abusing his superior position.
3. On the other hand, an interview which is too relaxed and friendly may not find out how a candidate reacts to stress.
4. • My friend Nick, who feels very nervous at an interview, finds it hard to put himself over effectively. •
5. • A handwritten letter of application, which many companies prefer to a typed one, can show the reader more of your personality than a typed one. •
6. A CV which gives too much information may not be read carefully.
7. • Your curriculum vitae, which you should always send a copy of, is a document you can use over and over again. •
8. • Your application for the post, which was mailed on 4 May, did not arrive till after the deadline for applications. •
9. Unfortunately, the envelope in which your documents were sent contained your letter and photograph, but not your CV.
10 • Mrs Mary O'Farrell, with whom you have been corresponding, is no longer working with our firm. •

B   Students, working in pairs, should discuss and then write down their sentences. Draw attention to the way sentences containing non-identifying relative clauses are read aloud with a slight pause and change of tone before the 'by the way' information in the relative clause.

Extra activity

Ask the class to compose further sentences about the other members of the class, or about the other people that work in their own department in their firm. They should use similar structures to the ones presented in this section.

There is more practice on using relative clauses in Workbook exercise 13.4.

13.6 Questions, questions!

Before students become involved in steps A, B and C of the activity, spend time studying the advice given about interviewing and the 24 difficult questions.

All the dialogues and expressions in speech balloons are recorded. A lot of advice given here is applicable to other situations where people are eliciting information.

Ask students to suggest how the incomplete sentences might continue – the first words of a suggested continuation is on the cassette and in the transcript below.

Woman: Have you written many reports and letters in English?
Man: Yes.
Woman: Are you an aggressive person?
Man: No.
Woman: Can you tell me about your experience in writing English?
Man: Yes, in my present job I've had to ...
Woman: What kind of person would you say you were?
Man: I'd say that I was quite a capable sort of chap...

Could you tell me why you want to leave your present job?
I wonder if you could tell me why you intend...?

Would you mind telling me why you think that...?
I'd also like to know how much experience you...?
I'd like to know how much time you...?
Do you happen to know how many people...?

Let me see, ...
I'm not sure about that.
I've no idea I'm afraid
That's a very good question!
Oh, let me think ...
I'm afraid I don't know.

[Time: 1 minute]

The 24 VERY difficult questions are recorded. Play them through before the pairs begin work on step A. A class with little experience of interviews may need some help with all three steps and some parts of the activity may need to be done as a whole class.

WARNING! Some of the questions are very challenging: you may feel you want to 'protect' some students from the experience of being put on the spot in this way.

A Some further difficult questions might be:
- What do you think my next question will be?
- Does your present employer know you've applied for this job?
- If you were me, what other questions would you ask?
- How would you describe the ideal person for this job?

B Pairs who can't answer some of the questions should ask another pair for advice. At the end, just check round the class which of the questions seemed the hardest.

C 🔳 This role play should be done with a different partner, so that the probing seems more realistic.

Finally, find out if any students have attended interviews where such difficult questions were asked. Do such questions serve a useful purpose, or is the difficulty self-defeating?

13.7 A good interview?

Here we look at interviews from the point of view of both the candidate and the interviewer. There are two recorded interviews to listen to and evaluate, which may later serve as models for 13.8 and 13.9. Both interviews are for the job described in the job ad in 13.2.

A 🔲 The first interview is fairly humane and affable. We hear the beginning of the interview, which fades out before the end. In the second interview, the interviewer is giving the candidate a harder time. We join the interview just before the end.

FIRST INTERVIEW

Interviewer: Good morning, Miss ...

Miss Jones: Miss Jones.

Interviewer: Miss Jones, yes, right. Hi. Um ... now, you'd like to join our team, I gather.

Miss Jones: Yes, I would.

Interviewer: That's ... that's very good. Er ... I'd like to know a little bit about you. Perhaps you could tell me ... perhaps we could start ... if you could tell me a little bit about your education. ■

Miss Jones: Oh yes, right. Well, I left school at 18 and for the first two years I went to Gibsons, you might know them, they're an engineering firm. Um ... and after that, I wanted to do a course, so I d ... I did a one-year full-time PA course and went back to Gibsons. I was PA to the Export Director. I stayed there for two years and ... and then moved on to my present company. Um ... that's Europa Marketing ... um ... Mr Adair, the marketing director, offered me a job because Gibson had ... had worked quite

a lot with Europa Marketing. And I've been with them for three years now ... um ... first working with the Marketing Director and ... and now I'm with the Sales Director.

Interviewer: That's all very interesting, Miss Jones. Um ... I ... I'd like to know, what did you enjoy most at school? What was the course that you enjoyed most? ■

Miss Jones: Ah ... foreign languages I liked best. We did French and German. Yes.

Interviewer: Mhm. And are you quite fluent in those now or ... ?

Miss Jones: Yes, a bit rusty now, but ... um ... obviously the more travel I can do the more I can use my languages and I'd like to learn another language. I'd like to add Italian as well.

Interviewer: Italian?

Miss Jones: Yes.

Interviewer: Very good, very good, that ... that might be very useful. Now ... er ... tell me a little bit about ... er ... the work you're doing at present. ■

Miss Jones: Um ... well ... er ... Europa Marketing is a marketing and public relations company and they do consultancy work for companies operating in the UK and European markets. Er ... our clients come from all over the world ... um ... we deal with some of them by ... by post, but most of them come to our offices and at least once during a project. I assist the sales director by arranging these visits, setting up meetings and presentations and I ... I deal with her correspondence. I've not been able to go with her on any ... on any of her trips abroad, but I ... I've been to firms in this country, several times on my own ... um ... to make these arrangements.

Interviewer: It sounds as if you're very happy there, Miss Jones. I'm curious why you'd like to leave them and join our company. ■

Miss Jones: Well ... um ... I know the reputation of Anglo-European and it has a very good reputation. And I feel that I would have more scope and opportunity in your company and that the work will be more challenging for me. I might be able to possibly travel and use my languages because at the moment most of my work is ... is rather routine secretarial-type work and I like the idea of more ... um ... challenges in my life really....

[Time: 2 minutes 55 seconds]

SECOND INTERVIEW

Interviewer: ... yes, well, your CV seems pretty well up to scratch. Now, I wonder, can you tell me about yourself? ■

Candidate: Um ... well, I ...

Interviewer: Yes?

Candidate: I ... I'm ... I think I'm serious ... serious-minded, I ... calm ...

Interviewer: You're calm?

Candidate: Yes, well, yes, I like a joke, though, good sense of humour. I don't panic in a crisis and I ... I enjoy working with all kinds of people. I ... I even like ... um ... p ... people who are, you know, bad-tempered or something like that.

Interviewer: Yes, but wh ... where do you see yourself in let's say five years' time? ■

Candidate: Um ... well, I ... sort of a long-range thing. Well, I see myself in the public relations and ... er ... one day I must admit I would rather like to open up my own consultancy in my home town.

Interviewer: Mhm, what is it specifically about Anglo-European PR that attracted you? ■

Candidate: Er ... well, first of all, I want to leave my present employers because they're a small company and ... er ... I know about Anglo-European PR, I mean, they're a ... they're a good company, larger. I think I'll have more scope ... er ... the work will be more challenging. I mean, quite a lot of what I do at present is quite boring, it's ... it's routine secretarial work.

Interviewer: And ... and you'd like to move on?

Candidate: Yes, if I could, you know, hopefully to a job that gives me more opportunity. So I can use my initiative.

Interviewer: Mhm.

Candidate: Can I just ask you this question ... cough ... excuse me ... I'd like to know if I get this job with Anglo-European, would I be able to ... um ... work abroad in one of your overseas branches?

Interviewer: Oh yes, certainly. Um ... our staff regularly do six-month placements in other branches. So I'm sure you might ...

Candidate: Six ... oh well, that's good ... um ... that's what I'm interested in.

Interviewer: Mhm. Can I ... d ... I know we're all human beings here and I'd like to know wh ... what you consider your strengths and your weaknesses. ■

Candidate: Um ... strengths and weaknesses? Haha. Well, I ... I mentioned before, I think my sense of humour ... er

... and my ability to work with all types of people is a particular strength.

Interviewer: Yes.

Candidate: My weakness? I don't know, I suppose I'm a bit of a perfectionist ... I ... I'm quite often dissatisfied with what I've done. I always think I can do it better or, you know, in a different way.

Interviewer: I wouldn't call that a weakness, I'd call that a strength. ■

Candidate: Well ... ah ... well, that's good, well ... I mean, I ... apart from that I ... I suppose I get a little bit sort of full of the Wanderlust and that's why I want to travel. I'm easily bored with repetition and ... er ... and procedure.

Interviewer: Do you have a lack of commitment? ■

Candidate: No, not at all. No ...er ... once my goals are set and I've got the right sort of initiative then ... er ... I ... I'm as committed as anybody.

Interviewer: Not one of these people who wanders off? ■

Candidate: No, not at all.

Interviewer: Now ... um ... i ... is there anything else you'd like to ask me? ■

Candidate: Aha ... yes, if I can just get down to the nitty-gritty: would the salary be reviewed at the end of the year?

Interviewer: Yes, the salary wi ... the salary would be reviewed every six months. And after six months you'd also be eligible to share in the company's bonus scheme.

Candidate: Oh, I didn't know that. Oh, that's good, yes.

Interviewer: Right, well ... um ... time is pressing on, I'm afraid, so thank you very much for coming to see me and we'll be in touch with you before the end of the week.

Candidate: Good. Well, thank you for seeing me.

Interviewer: Goodbye.

Candidate: Bye.

[Time: 3 minutes 15 seconds]

B Now play the two interviews again, but this time with pauses. Pause the tape at the places shown by ■ in the transcripts. Ask students to suggest how they might answer each question. Then play the real response so that they can compare what they said with the answer on the tape.

C When the groups have decided on the best and worst advice for interviewers, ask them to report to the rest of the class which they considered to be the TWO BEST – and the TWO WORST pieces of advice.

D Now everyone thinks of advice they would give to a novice interviewee: get the groups to compare ideas afterwards.

13.8 A progress interview

The overt topic of this section disguises its underlying purpose: to give students a preparatory 'dry run' for the Real Thing in 13.9. Decide first whether a job progress interview *or* a mid-course feedback interview will be most appropriate for your class.

A Everyone, working in pairs, makes a list of some suitable questions. Discuss these with the whole class before beginning step B.

B [🔀] This step depends on having groups of three (or four) – the pair who are participating in the interview are 'observed' by their partner(s), who afterwards make comments and evaluate both participants. The observer(s) should sit slightly apart from the participants so as not to put them off. Perhaps point out that in business, it's not uncommon for there to be an observer who disconcertingly doesn't participate in the interview.

File 81 contains role information for the interviewer.
File 53 contains role information for the interviewee.
File 71 contains guidelines for the observer.

As there may need to be four interviews (in groups of four), allow plenty of time for this.

Finish by asking everyone to say what they learned from this activity.

Some of the ideas about progress interviews raised in this section are followed up in 14.2.

13.9 The Real Thing

This simulation may appear, at first glance, to be very complicated. However, if you work out a realistic timetable on the basis of the suggestions below, it will go very smoothly.
   If you think all your students should have experience of both interviewing and being interviewed, you will need to do the simulation twice – but this may not be necessary as the 'interviewers' can learn a great deal about being interviewed by being an interviewer.

Arranging the room

Depending on the size of the class, the room should be arranged so that the interviews can take place in relatively private conditions – in far corners of the room, for example. The candidates should congregate in a different part of the room, or better still, in another room or in the corridor outside the room. Ideally, each panel would receive candidates in a different room, but this may not be possible to organize.

Equipment required

Access to photocopier *or* large sheets of paper, pinboard and pins.

Timing

To give a rough idea of how long each step should take, here is a suggested timetable for the simulation in a 90-minute lesson with about 12 participants, divided into 6 candidates and 2 panels of interviewers. This timing is given simply as a guide, and everything will depend on the time you have available and the number of participants.

A: 20 minutes– this should be done in a previous lesson, to allow a good 90 minutes for B1 to B5.
B1: 10 minutes
B2: 15 minutes
B3: 45 minutes (each panel conducts $6 \times 7\frac{1}{2}$ minute interviews)
B4: 10 minutes
B5 and Follow-up discussion: 10 minutes

Alternatively, you could do both A and B1 in one lesson and B2 to 5 in another.

Documents

To save having to circulate documents between groups, and to add to the realism of the simulation, it is desirable to quickly photocopy the advertisements that the participants compose in step A, and their letters and CVs after step B1. This is not absolutely essential, however.

■ DURING STEP B, THE CANDIDATES WILL BE USING THE CVs THEY WROTE IN 13.1, SO REMIND THEM TO BRING THESE TO CLASS WITH THEM.

Roles

In B, the participants will be playing the roles of interviewers or candidates:
The INTERVIEWERS are 'Consultants' who will work as a panel of three (or two) to choose the right person for the job on the employer's behalf. As the procedure is very thorough, each candidate may be interviewed by more than one panel. Each CANDIDATE has applied for one of the two jobs advertised.

Procedure

A   For this preparatory step, the class is divided into two groups – each will produce a different job advertisement. If you can't photocopy the completed job ads, ask students to use large handwriting, so that the ads will be easily legible when posted on the class bulletin board.

B ⬛

In the procedure given here, there is additional information for the teacher as the CONTROLLER of the simulations.

↓ Before step 1 ↓

CONTROLLER: Rearrange the class into two groups and assign roles – this should be done at random and the two groups should **not** be same as the ones in step A. There should be an even number of candidates; each interview panel will consist of three members, or possibly just two. If in doubt, have more interviewers than candidates.

1. Each panel of INTERVIEWERS discuss what they will be looking for and what questions they will ask.
   Meanwhile ...
   Each CANDIDATE writes an application letter.

↓ Before step 2 ↓

CONTROLLER: Collect the application letters and CVs and if possible, photocopy them so that each panel of interviewers has a complete set of these. If this isn't feasible, then circulate the letters and CVs between the panels until they've seen them all – in this case the candidates will have to take their own letters and CVs to each interview in step 3.

2. Each panel of INTERVIEWERS reads and assesses the application letters.
   Meanwhile ...
   Each CANDIDATE works with another candidate to prepare themselves for the interviews. They look again at the difficult questions in 13.7.

↓ Before step 3 ↓

CONTROLLER: Arrange the panels of interviewers and candidates in different parts of the room (or different rooms if possible, see above). The timetable should be announced and displayed, so that the interviewers know exactly how long they have for each interview. Ideally, each panel would every candidate, but if this isn't feasible, make sure each panel sees at least three candidates – and preferably each candidate should be interviewed twice.

3. Each panel of INTERVIEWERS receives a different candidate in turn. There is further guidance for the interviewers in File 89, where they are advised to assess each candidate's experience, personality and potential.
   Meanwhile ...
   The candidates wait to be called to one or another panel and, between interviews, sit silently or chat with other waiting candidates.

4. All the panels of INTERVIEWERS meet together in the same part
   of the room to discuss the various candidates for the two jobs and
   make a shortlist of three for both.
   Meanwhile ...
   The CANDIDATES meet 'in a café or bar' to discuss their own
   performance at the interviews and to decide which panel performed
   best.

5. The whole class reassembles for a feedback session: the Interviewers
   announce their shortlists and the Candidates announce their preferred interviewers.

Follow-up discussion

Find out how everyone felt at the different stages of the simulation:
relaxed, confident, authoritative, nervous, etc.

- What did you learn from participating in this simulation?
- How were any real interviews you've experienced different, easier or
  more difficult?
- If you could do the simulation again, what would you do differently
  as interviewer or as candidate?

Workbook

Contents of this unit:

13.1 Looking for a job	Reading aloud
13.2 Abstract nouns	Word-building
13.2 An interesting job	Writing
13.4 Relative clauses	Grammar
13.5 Vocabulary	
13.6 Who should we shortlist?	Listening 📼
13.7 Prepositional phrases – 3	
13.8 High flyers	Listening 📼

Background information: Working together

Work relations with other people at the place of work include relationships with fellow employees, workers or colleagues. A major part of work or job satisfaction comes from 'getting on' with others at work. Work relations will also include those between the 'boss' and yourself: management–employee relations are not always straightforward, particularly as the management's assessment of your performance can be crucial to your future career.

There will always be matters about which employees will want to talk to the management. In small businesses the 'boss' will probably work alongside his workers. Anything which needs to be sorted out will be done face-to-face as soon as a problem arises. There may be no formal meetings or procedures. The larger the business, the less direct contact there will be between employees and management. Special meetings have to be held and procedures set up, to say when, where, how and in what circumstances the employees can talk to the management. Some companies have specially organized consultative committees for this purpose.

In many countries of the world today, particularly in large firms, employees join a trade union and ask the union to represent them to the management. Through the union all categories of employees can pass on the complaints they have and try to get things changed. The process through which unions negotiate with management on behalf of their members is called 'collective bargaining'. Instead of each employee trying to bargain alone with the company, the employees join together and collectively put forward their views. Occasionally a firm will refuse to recognize the right of a union to negotiate for its members and a dispute over union recognition will arise.

Where there is disagreement, bargaining or negotiating will take place. A compromise agreement may be reached. Where this is not possible, the sides can go to arbitration and bring in a third party from outside to say what they think should happen. However, sometimes one of the sides decides to take industrial action. The management can 'lock-out' the employees and prevent them from coming to work. This used to be quite common, but is a method which is rarely used today by management because it does not help them very much.

The main courses of action open to a trade union in most democratic countries, where they are legally recognized, are the strike, a ban on working overtime, 'working to rule' (when employees work according to the company rule-book), 'go-slow' (employees may spend more time doing the same job) and picketing (employees stand outside the entrance to the business location holding up signs to show that they are in conflict with the management).

⟫→

Every country has its own tradition of industrial relations, so it is difficult to generalize. In some businesses unions are not welcomed by the management. But in some countries the unions play an important role both in the everyday working relations in individual companies and also in the social and political life of the country.

14 Working together

There are many occasions on which the question of relations between people in business are central to the actual job, in as much as one 'experiences' them on a day-to-day basis. But work relations are also a focal point as topics *about which* people in business may wish or need to talk.

This unit presents material to cover both aspects of interaction with others in business. It deals with how to ask for and give advice in a business setting between colleagues, as well as more work on progress interviews between manager and employee. Topics for discussion include the changing role of women in business and at work, schemes of flexible working hours and how the general atmosphere of office life varies from country to country.

14.1 Asking for and giving advice *Functions*

The important function of advising and asking for advice is the focus of this section. There will be many occasions in a business context in which students can be expected to employ it. It also tends to be a sensitive area of interpersonal relations. If one needs advice it is important that one strikes the right note or tone – otherwise the help or advice may well not be forthcoming. Likewise, when giving advice, it is important not to sound either too patronizing or over-familiar – otherwise one's advice may not be accepted. The forms presented and practised reflect these differences; it is often a matter of degree of indirectness versus directness or of familiarity versus formality.

Presentation

If possible, students should look at the presentation section *before* they come to class. This will give them a better chance of remembering the expressions, will save time in class and will lead to a more informed and interesting discussion of the topic in class.

Begin by getting the students to look closely at the examples in speech balloons. Discuss the points made in the text. Do a quick repetition exercise with the expressions, emphasizing the *tone of voice* that should be used: a friendly tone is to be preferred over a direct

267

tone. Ask the class to suggest how the incomplete sentences might continue.

The examples ('What ought I to ...', etc) are recorded so that students can hear as well as see the sentences that are used.

Exercises and activities

Make sure that any queries are cleared up before students begin step C – though it is to be expected that doing the exercise will give rise to further questions.

A Play the recording. It may be best to pause between each conversation so that partners can discuss their notes as they go, while they can still remember what happened in each part.

1

Man: I've seen the advertisement for the new costing clerk job. Do you think I ought to apply for it?

Woman: You'd better ask Madame Olivier what the chances are of getting it first.

2

Man: Do you have a moment please? I would appreciate your advice on this Johnson order.

Woman: Might it be an idea to deliver a week earlier than planned ... ?

3

Man: I should like to ask whether this pro-forma invoice is filled in correctly?

Woman: I would recommend you to check the details on the customer's account card first.

[Time: 35 seconds]

B For the next set of three dialogues, play the recordings and pause after each one. Give the pairs a chance to discuss their notes as they go. Then ask for suggestions as to what advice each pair would give. When this has been done play the rest of the dialogue and ask if the class agree with the advice given. Encourage them to say whether they agree or disagree with the advice given and why. If not, why not? How well do the people in the recordings know each other? What items of language make you think this/that?

4

Man: Look at this job advertisement. Do you think I ought to apply for it?

Woman: Yes, sure. Why don't you get you CV off as soon as possible?

5

Man: What ought I to do about Mr Benedetti? I didn't know he was going to be here tomorrow. I could see him about the Marseille project, couldn't I?

Woman: Well, if I were you, I'd get on the phone to him immediately and make an appointment to meet.

6

Man: Excuse me, could I ask for some advice on overseas payments? Which would you say is the safest method of payment if you are selling abroad?

Woman: I would advise you to use the letter of credit method. That way you can be sure of getting your money.

[Time: 55 seconds]

C [image] Rearrange the class into groups of four. With an odd number, or a class not divisible into four, groups of three are also possible. Student A should look at File 34, Student B at 29, Student C at 72 and student D at 27. Each student in turn describes to the others what their individual problem is. The task of the others is to give advice on how to solve the problem. After each student has had a turn at asking for advice, they are all directed to further Files with a second problem: Student A looks at File 83, B at 102, C at 93 and D at 4.

If there is sufficient time after the activity, students can be asked to discuss with others in the class how satisfactory or helpful they found the advice which was provided by their group. If you run out of time, you may ask them to leave out the second problem or else postpone it until the next session.

Workbook

Exercise 14.2 in the Workbook provides further practice on this function.

14.2   What next ... ?

This activity addresses the issue of staff – manager relations and looks specifically at the progress interview (see 13.8) from a slightly different point of view. While in the previous unit such interviews were dealt with in a general fashion, this activity treats them as examples of management–staff interaction. How both sides perceive the value of such interviews is here focused on. This serves as preparation for the role play activity in which students are expected to participate in a progress interview in a specific business situation.

Procedure

A   Students work in pairs. Before they begin reading the extract, read out the question for the first reading: 'What is the most important point, in your opinion?' Then tell the students to read the passage a second time and to answer the next question: 'What words are used to describe the procedure discussed?' Allow time for any queries to be raised.

Suggested answers:
- This approach is the core of its employee-relations philosophy.
- the staff reporting system

B Ask the students to recall the progress interview they did in 13.8 and what they did in the interview. Students should again work in pairs and read the list of comments on progress interviews from the point of view of the manager (8–14) and the employee (1–7) and put them in their own agreed order of importance. Point out that they may deal with each list separately, or combine the two into a single priority list from their own point of view. After they have done this in pairs, students should find a new partner and compare the list they have made. They should ask their fellow students for their reasons in making their particular choices.

C [🎦] Students work in pairs. Before you play the recording make sure the students have decided which department they are working in and have already looked at their individual Files. Student A looks at File 84, Student B at 54.

[📼] Play the recording. Students now have to continue the interview on the basis of the information they have in the Files.

Woman: Ah, come in. Please take a seat.
Man: Thank you very much.
Woman: Right, let's get straight to the point. I understand you would like to talk to me about the progress you've been making since you came to work with us 18 months ago.
Man: Er ... yes ... er ... that's quite correct ... er. Yes, I wanted to bring up the subject of my performance.
Woman: OK, so what's the problem?

Man: Oh, well, there are no problems as such. I, ... indeed everything seems to be working out fine from my point of view.
Woman: High job satisfaction, would you say?
Man: Yes ... oh ... um ... no ... um ... I mean, I ... um ....

[Time: 45 seconds]

After the activity you may wish to ask individual pairs to repeat their interviews for comments from the rest of the class. Allow time for questions and comments.

D Students work in pairs. They work together to draft a report of the interview from the perspective of the manager.

E When everyone has finished they show their report to another pair and look at the other pair's report and make comments and perhaps give advice on how to improve it. They discuss the questions listed in the Student's Book and ask another group what they discussed. What decisions did you come to? What experience do any of you have of such interviews? What is your opinion of them? How is progress watched in your country or company?

If time allows, students can draft a report from the perspective of the employee for his or her union representative.

What do the students think are the dangers and the strengths of progress interviews?

Leave enough time for the class to raise any questions concerning the discussion activity and any other queries they may have.

14.3 Women at Work!

The activity is concerned with taking in, extracting and processing information from written materials. The topic is the situation of working women and the kinds of jobs they are engaged in nowadays.

Procedure

The activities are clearly laid out in the Student's Book. Throughout the activity you should be prepared to allow questions and queries on vocabulary items and the comprehension of the written material which forms the basis of much of the activity.

A For this step students work in pairs.

B Re-arrange the class into groups of three or four so that the original pairs are not together. You may wish to let students discuss briefly as a class the differences agreed on and reasons given for the changes.

C Students again work in pairs. This is a reading for gist activity. After answering the questions students write notes which they can refer back to later. Once students have drawn up a list of improvements in the working conditions of women and have added points, they can again change partners or form groups of three or four and compare their results. The material in the book is intended to provide both authentic British and American sources on the topic. The matters considered are:

Promotion prospects of women compared with men, union membership in certain professions, the situation of pensions and social security for married women with and without children.

You should be prepared to answer queries on vocabulary during this step.

The activities in the Student's Book are straightforward: a preparatory task concerning deductions from wages or salaries, followed by reading tasks for the 'social security' extract.

The information about union membership concerns the Banking, Insurance and Finance Union (BIFU) in Britain.

The extract about social security is taken from a United States leaflet which is targeted specifically at working women published by US Department of Health and Human Services Social Security Administration.

Suggested answers:
benefits: amounts of money paid as a pension after retirement.
covered earnings: money earned, from which contributions to social security are deducted (thus earning 'credits').

D   This step using the cartoon is self-explanatory. Instructions in the Student's Book should be followed. It may be best to do this step in the class as a whole, possibly after students have had time to discuss it in pairs.

E   In this discussion, students should first work in groups. They should compare the list of items they made in step B. What similarities or differences do they now find? Can they agree on a new list of priorities?

Extra discussion activity

Depending on the kind of group you have, in a class with work experience it may be helpful to allow the class to discuss their own experience at work relating to some of the topics touched upon in this activity. Some additional questions:

* Should the law be strengthened to protect women's rights at work?
* Are salaries and wages fairly distributed between the sexes at work?
* Is equality of opportunity between women and men something to be aimed for or has it perhaps already been achieved?

14.4   Getting on together

This activity continues the topic of dealing with work-related problems – this time talking to superiors in the work context.

A   Students work in pairs. This step is a preparatory step for the listening activity to follow. Let the pairs compare their answers with others in the class before going on to B.

B   In this listening for gist activity, play the recording at least twice. Make sure everyone concentrates on this question for the first listening: What problems are being discussed? Play the recording a second time and tell everyone to concentrate on the next two questions:

Which speakers are friendly or unfriendly. Which are helpful or unhelpful? How do you think the situations will turn out? After hearing the recording, students should consider the next question in pairs:

How would you deal with similar situations? They should draft notes and compare them with another pair. They should share what sort of experience they have had in dealing with either superiors or juniors in the course of their working life. If only a few students have had work experience, they should be interviewed by the rest of the class for this activity.

First conversation

Superior: Now look, this stealing in your section has got to stop.

Junior: Yes, I'm doing my best to try and find out who it might be.

Superior: It must be someone from your section, mustn't it? Or do you imagine that it's people from somewhere else?

Junior: No, I'm sure you're right. It's someone who knows where the instruments are kept, of course.

Superior: Well. So you find out who it is and give them the sack.

Junior: It's not going to be easy, you know ... [fade]

[Time: 30 seconds]

Second conversation

Superior: I was expecting you back from holiday last Wednesday.

Junior: I know. I rang up last Monday to say my mother was ill.

Superior: But nobody told me. Nobody passed on the message to me. That's because nobody knew, did they?

Junior: But I spoke to the new girl on the switchboard. What's her name now?

Superior: Why didn't you ask to be put through to me?

Junior: She told me you were out.

Superior: Well you could have called later.

Junior: Well I did try again on Tuesday.

Superior: That's news to me.

Junior: I did try to get through, but your phone was engaged every time I tried.

Superior: Look this is not very convincing ... [fade]

[Time: 35 seconds]

Third conversation

Superior: How much money did you say he gave you?

Junior: 50 dollars. That's all.

Superior: That's all!

Junior: Yes, that's all.

Superior: That's far too much. It's 50 dollars too much, in fact.

Junior: Yes but everybody here does it.

Superior: Takes gifts from our customers, you mean? Has this happened before?

Junior: Yes. Last Christmas. We all got a present in purchasing.

Superior: Look, just because we buy our paper in bulk from them, doesn't mean it's a reason why you should accept any presents.

Junior: But other companies do it too.

Superior: Look, I don't care. As far as we are concerned, it's got to stop.

[Time: 35 seconds]

Fourth conversation

Superior: When did you say the operation was going to be done?

Junior: Well, it's due in May

Superior: So do you think you'll be able to work until then?

Junior: I don't see why not.

Superior: But look, I'll tell you what. You can take the morning off on Wednesdays.

Junior: But there's no need, I'm all right really.

Superior: No look, we never have anything to do anyway on Wednesdays, so ...

Junior: But I assure you, the doctors say there's no danger.

Superior: I know what doctors are like. But you do as I say. Take it easy on Wednesdays.
Junior: I don't really know how to thank you.

Superior: Don't bother, that's the best way ... [fade].

[Time: 40 seconds]

C   Students work in pairs for this step. They follow the instructions in the Student's Book. After drafting their letter they show it to another pair, acting the part of divisional manager. They themselves look at the other pair's draft and reply to it, giving suggestions as to what might be done.

At the end, allow time for feedback.

14.5   Flexible working hours

This activity consists of a case study and problem-solving activity based on the topic of flexitime in offices. In 11.1 the topic was encountered as one of the subjects discussed at a meeting. On this occasion, flexitime is dealt with in more depth within the context of staff needs and suggestions, thus allowing the students' own opinions and views to be brought into the activity.

A   Students work in groups of three or four. They read through the notes. If there are four people to a group they can share the task of gathering information by getting a different person to look at a different heading: *the facts, Management proposals, Staff suggestions, Staff requests.*

Remind them of their task: to work out an acceptable and suitable compromise with limits to flexitime for all staff *or* for certain staff members.

B   After they have worked out their compromise proposal the groups should draft a report in which they summarize their results. It should be formulated as proposals and recommendations to the Personnel Manager in the form of a memorandum. Students should then show their drafts to another group for their comments.

Allow time at the end for the groups to hear the reports of other groups and to compare the proposals they make.

Model:

[YOU MAY PHOTOCOPY THIS DOCUMENT]

MEMORANDUM

From: Romy de Bolero (PA)	*for*	*please*
To: Personnel Manager	*ACTION*	*DISPLAY*
	COMMENT	*FILE*
Date: 12 December 19—	*INFORMATION*	*RETURN*
	DISCUSSION	*PASS TO:*

Dept. Heads

Subject: Introduction of Flexitime ....

After closely studying both the staff requests and the
management proposals about flexitime working we would like to
present these preliminary recommendations for your consideration:
1. "Flexidays": Mondays, Wednesdays and Fridays. Offices
    could remain open from 8.30 am until 6 pm in certain
    departments.
2. Core time: all staff should be present between these
    times: 10am–1pm
             2pm–3.30pm
3. "Pairing system": We propose that two or more part-time
    employees are allocated to each full-time employee in
    each department, if possible. (Details about working time
    should be arranged with the departmental head in each case.)
4. Canteen opening hours: these should be changed to
    12.30 pm–2.15 pm. This would enable people working
    through their lunch hour to take an 'early' or 'late'
    lunch. (We are, of course, aware that this recommendation
    will require discussion with the financial department.)
Finally, we would be very grateful if you could pass on our
recommendations to the heads of department. It is evident
that in the end the system will only work to the full
satisfaction of all concerned, if the details are fully
worked out on an individual basis.

© Cambridge University Press 1989

Extra discussion activity

What do the class think about the system of flexitime? What do they
consider the advantages or disadvantages of the system to be? Students
who have experience of using the system should be interviewed by the
rest of the class.

Allow time for feedback and questions about any problems which may
arise.

14.6 Order of adverbs

Presentation

A First, with the whole class, look at the examples and discuss the concept of the 'comfortable' place of adverbs. Show that, for example, with the adverbs of time like *recently* or *yesterday*, the initial or fronted position tends to be used contrastively. End-position may also have an emphatic side to it, whilst mid-position would seem to be more 'neutral'. With an adverb like *certainly* end-position feels 'wrong' or 'uncomfortable'.

▣ The examples are recorded. They can be played to illustrate the important differences in emphasis which the changes of position bring about.

Exercises and activities

B Students should work in pairs and move the adverbs from the right of each sentence into the most 'comfortable' place in the sentence.

Suggested answers:
1. The corporate headquarters *recently* moved from Houston to Charlotte.
2. The company *very quickly* realised that it was a profit-making area.
3. Our staff worked *hard* the whole year.
4. The machine was *carefully* serviced by the engineer.
5. The production schedule will *probably* be achieved.
6. We are *currently* modifying our early retirement scheme.
7. They check their inventory *weekly*.
8. I'm sorry to say there is little we can *immediately* do.
9. The customer delivered the cargo *punctually*.
10. *Luckily* we have sufficient material in stock.

C This step deals with mid-position adverbs. First, with the whole class, look at the examples and point out the implications of the idea of mid-position when there is an auxiliary verb in the sentence. (The traditional concept of 'frequency adverbs' is an unhelpful one since it seems to include *twice* and *three times*, while excluding *almost*, *nearly*, etc. It makes better sense to exploit students' acquired knowledge and feelings for accuracy, than to attempt to categorize adverbs arbitrarily.)

D   Students should work in pairs for this exercise.

Suggested answers:
  1. There have *rarely* been disputes in our company.
  2. Last year there were *frequently* go-slows in the production plant.
  3. The company *nearly* went bankrupt as a result.
  4. Now our firm is *probably* going to open a European factory.
  5. We would *certainly* have accepted the offer.
  6. Workers can *hardly* expect the facts.
  7. You *obviously* don't know what we're talking about.
  8. Our subsidiaries *never* achieve essential production targets.
  9. Their operating expenses *apparently* remained low.
 10. The supervisor *completely* forgot to carry out an inspection.

Point out any other positions which might be 'comfortable'.

Extra activity

Either write up the following jumbled sentences on the board or
prepare an overhead transparency before class. Ask the students to
rearrange the words in each line. They can work in pairs for this
activity. As an added incentive, you can also ask them to try and work
out which unit in the book each sentence is from.

These are the jumbled sentences:

through you just put I'll.
the summarize single a report sentence in then.
office is Casagrande in working for now our Mr Kuala Lumpur.
of we irrevocable 60-day usually confirmed pay letter by credit.
you remind is may this we again that still overdue account.
yet order at has not the our arrived warehouse.
next forward USA going looking the to I'm to summer.
isn't a very Singapore for profitable us probably market.
everything covers well that I think.
find be fault to we'll perhaps able the.

Answers, together with the number of the unit each sentence is from:
  3. I'll just put you through.
  4. Then summarize the report in a single sentence.
  5. Mr Casagrande is now working for our office in Kuala Lumpur.
  6. We usually pay by confirmed 60-day irrevocable letter of credit.
  7. May we again remind you that this account is still overdue.
  8. The order has not yet arrived at our warehouse.
  9. I'm looking forward to going to the USA next summer.
 10. Singapore probably isn't a very profitable market for us.
 11. Well I think that covers everything.
 12. Perhaps we'll be able to find the fault.

There are further examples for practice to be found in *Use of English* (Unit 40).

Workbook

Workbook exercise 14.4 provides further work on this topic.

14.7   Information helps everyone

This activity deals with the issue of how much information about the firm should be given to the workforce within a company.

Procedure

A   For the reading activity, which is also preparation for the listening activity to come, students work in pairs.

Suggested answers:
Having information can help employees to identify with the company.
The company's policy on informing the workforce about developments.

B   Play the recording. You may need to play it a second time before the students can be certain what the answers are:

Um ... if I could just take this opportunity to ... to briefly summarize the company's attitude to the ... to the question of providing information for our employees. Well ... er ... we know that the majority of employees would like more opportunity to let the company know how they feel on ... on things that affect them. And certainly from the surveys that we've done, they seem to ... er ... emphasize the value of two-way communication ... er ... especially at a time of change and uncertainty within the company and ... and in the outside world. Anyway ... um ... action has been set in motion to increase ... er ... face-to-face communication between managers and staff and ... er ... and to improve the flow of upward ... upward ... um ... communication.

Um ... you also know how much we value consultation with our workforce and so we continue to provide training facilities to enable employees who are elected to consultative committees to perform effectively in their new role.

Now, when it comes to informing the workforce. Um ... well, employees, we believe, have a right to know the basic facts about the company. Er ... whether or not the information makes them more efficient.

And ... um ... and the 'Information Programme' makes this possible. Er ... well, let me just give you one example. Er ... supervisors, for instance, may need informing about new products before they go into production.

And supervisors should also be given some outline about a company's profit and ... and marketing objectives, and about its performance related to its competitors. At the same time, of course, we are naturally aware of the problems of giving too much information on future product plans. Well, the ... er ... the ... competition may get to hear about it too soon!

But ... um ... but in the end we shouldn't ignore the fact that ... that even if the management does not communicate with supervisors, that they and even the workers themselves will know a great deal about what is going on er ... even ... you know ... even if they haven't been told formally ...

[Time: 2 minutes 25 seconds]

Answers:

1. Points and procedures mentioned in the recording:
   use of the noticeboard
   one-way communication
   ✓ employees' right to have facts about the company
   ✓ informal information system
   ✓ profit and marketing objectives of the company
   ✓ information programme
   ✓ training for consultative committees
   ✓ employees' desire to express their opinions
   ✓ two-way communication
   the importance of the company newsletter

2. One might conclude from certain things the speaker says that the company is only grudgingly introducing their information programme. Consider the following points he mentions:
   They should be given information whether or not the information makes them more efficient.
   At the same time, of course, they are naturally aware of the problems of giving too much advance information on future product plans.
   And even if the management does not communicate with supervisors, they and even the workers themselves will know a great deal about what is going on.

C   Students work in groups of three or four and answer the questions in the Student's Book.

Extra discussion ideas

1 Compare the situation with other situations or companies with which you may be familiar in your country.
2 Is there a general philosophy in your country that workers and employees should be involved as much as possible?
3 Do you feel that workers work better or more willingly, if they know the objectives and the long-term plans of their managers?
4 Are short-term goals or long-term goals better for companies and their workforces, in your opinion?

Allow time at the end for the class to raise any queries on problems or
difficulties which may have arisen while doing the activity.

14.8   Working together in a company   *Vocabulary*

This exercise can be done by students working in pairs. It can be done
at any stage during the unit if you have time available, or done as
homework.

Answers:

1. negotiable	7. sacks
2. overtime	8. lay-off
3. reject	9. forced
4. industrial action	10. lump sum
5. arbitrate	11. redundant
6. mutual	12. drawbacks

Other important vocabulary is introduced throughout this unit and in
Workbook exercise 14.3.

14.9   Life in the office   *Listen and discuss*

This activity concerns the differences which are likely to be
encountered in different countries in everyday office practice. It is
centred around a listening activity in which the situation in the United
States is discussed.

Procedure

A   Students first work in pairs. They follow the instructions in the
Student's Book and mark the checklist of points they would mention.
This covers topics such as length of working hours, types of contracts,
company canteens, whether unions are recognized, etc.

B   Play the recording the first time and tell students to listen for
any points that were included in the checklist. Then play the recording
a second time after everyone has had time to read through the
statements. You may need to play through the recording a third time.
If you do play the recording a third time, you may find it helpful to
pause at specific points and ask individual students to repeat orally or

'shadow' what they have just heard or while they are still listening to it. The main points are <u>underlined</u> in the transcript.

Woman: First of all, when do people start work in American offices?
Man: Right, well the <u>official work day starts at 9.00 am.</u> This should really mean 9 o'clock — <u>not ten past or half past</u> nine.
Woman: Would you say that people work very hard in offices in America?
Man: Well I don't know about employees in your country. But some nations have a philosophy that you work when the 'boss' is around. And any time he's not there, one can relax by reading the newspaper or whatever one likes doing in a personal way.
Woman: And things are different in the States, you're saying?
Man: Well, in America one is being paid for your **time**. So employees are expected to find other work if their own desks are clear, or to help someone else with his or her work. <u>But you never sit idle, or doing nothing.</u>
Woman: Yes, as the saying goes: 'time is money'.
Man: Exactly. <u>Your employer 'owns' your time</u> while he is paying you for it. That is precisely what 'time is money' means. And anyway the boss doesn't ask more of you than he is doing himself: <u>he ... he will probably work through the lunch hour himself</u> and even take work home at night.
Woman: Talking about lunch hours. What about them? Do you have to take them seriously?
Man: Oh yes, sure, of course. The employee's lunch hour should be taken within the period allowed, unless you are officially discussing company business — say ... er ... on a business lunch. It's the same too with the end of the day. I mean ... work until the day officially ends at five o'clock, unless you are in an office where 'flexitime' is the accepted practice.
Woman: Oh, so you have the flexitime system, do you? I wasn't sure about that.
Man: Oh yes, sure. Flexible working

hours, that is, er ... starting or ending work earlier or later — <u>I ... I know that that is very common in Europe. But here in the USA it is still relatively new.</u> Certainly there are a million or so Americans on the system today. And the number is growing. Well for the same reasons as in Europe — to keep traffic and commuting problems down. And as more women now work it gives more family time.
Woman: Er ... could you say something about contracts of hiring in America, please?
Man: Well it's different in America from, say Asia, perhaps Europe too, I'm not sure. We are more democratic, I think. It means perhaps that we won't develop such a ... a permanent relationship between employer and employee. <u>I know that in some countries people relax when they have once got a job,</u> because they know they will almost never be fired — unless they do something awful.
Woman: You mean that your employer can just fire you in America?
Man: No, no, no. There are, of course, legal protections in the USA. So employees cannot be unjustly fired without good reason. Workers must do a good job, produce well, and get along with their colleagues — or they can be 'let go', as it is called.
Woman: From one day to the next, you mean?
Man: Well it's rarely done without warning, but it is important to remember that <u>in the United States you are a member of a business firm and not a family.</u> It makes a difference.
Woman: I wonder, is the physical or external appearance of office life different from European offices?
Man: Well, (coughs) I have heard people comment on <u>the informality found in American offices.</u> And this is certainly a little difficult for people who are more used to a hierarchical system to adjust to,

of course. But there are some very formal
offices, too, say, in ... in big banks, law
firms and major corporations. But in
many establishments the atmosphere is
loose and easy with a lot of joking, and
teasing, and wandering in and out of
offices among all levels of employees.

Woman: Well, that's about it, I think, oh,
except to briefly mention all those coffee
breaks I've heard about in the United
States.

Man: Haha, that's right. Nearly all large
offices have coffee wagons that circulate

for mid-morning and mid-afternoon
coffee breaks. But you should remember
that although 15 minutes are allotted
twice a day for relaxation and chatter,
many employees take coffee to their
desks and keep on working. In small
offices the coffeepot is often 'on' all day
and employees take coffee whenever they
like or they can make tea for themselves.
It all depends, I suppose....

[Time: 4 minutes]

Suggested answers (refer to the underlined parts of the transcript, if
necessary):
Only 3 is TRUE, all the rest are FALSE, according to the interview.

C   Students work in groups for this activity and make notes.

D   They then compare their notes as a class and see if they can agree
on the points of difference which they would perhaps emphasize to a
visitor from America or indeed elsewhere with differing office routines.

Extra discussion ideas

Students who have experience of working in more than one country
should be interviewed.

Students can be asked to share their own experience in their own
countries: there may be great differences in office life from company to
company. There may be similarities with the American picture in some
and vast differences in others.

Allow time for students to raise any specific or more general queries
they may have concerning the activity.

14.10   A consultative meeting

This activity practises holding a meeting dealing with industrial
relations. Students can be referred back to Unit 11 for the kinds of
language and ideas to be taken into consideration in holding meetings.

Procedure

The activity should be done in groups of four. In the case of odd groups of three, it is possible to drop a role – either the second staff representative or the second manager. If there are five in a group the fifth member can take the role of 'secretary' and take the minutes.

A [🗝️] Students decide who will be A, B, C, D by drawing lots, tossing a coin, etc.

Students read the agenda to see what the meeting is about. Any queries concerning the agenda are to be clarified at this point. Then Student A looks at File 95, Student B at 49, C at 85 and D at 110.

B After the meeting students work in pairs and draft a report or minutes of the meeting for their management or the people they represent; the two managers stay together and the two worker representatives stay together for the report writing.

C Students then show their draft report to another pair and check what they have written. They compare what important differences or similarities they find in each group's report or minutes. (If there was a group of five the 'secretary' should compare his or her minutes with another pair's report.)

Finally as a class, the differences or similarities between the reports can be commented on. Groups with items other groups do not mention should be asked why they included them and vice versa. Groups which left out points can be asked the reasons for leaving them out.

Allow time for feedback and queries. Perhaps ask students what they feel they have gained from this activity.

Workbook

Contents for this unit:

14.1 Prepositional phrases – 4
14.2 Asking for and giving advice   Functions 📼
14.3 Vocabulary
14.4 Order of adverbs   Grammar
14.5 Company training   Listening 📼
14.6 Unions and technological charge   Letters

15 A special project

This unit revises all the main areas of business that have been covered in the previous units, apart from Finance, which might be too much specialized information. It takes the form of a simulation which is spread over several lessons – each part of the simulation taking place in a different 'month'. Students will be working in teams, one based in the USA and the other in the UK.

The procedure for each step is described in the Student's Book and below, in more detail.

The revision includes using the basic business skills introduced in Units 1 to 4 as well as consolidating work done in other units:

January: Units 10 and 9
February: Units 5 and 14
March: Units 12 and 13
April: Units 6, 8 and 10
May: Unit 11

NOTE: There is further revision material in the Workbook, which can be used as a 'progress test' – see page 292.

Time

Each 'month' of the simulation will last about 90 minutes (i.e. five 'months' of 90 minutes each). If you have less time available, we have suggested how certain parts can be omitted or speeded up by using this symbol in the notes below: ¶

The real life needs of your students should be taken into account in deciding whether to omit anything, as it is not advisable to leave out any tasks or topics that are particularly relevant to the work they really do.

Class numbers

A class of eight to sixteen students should be divided into two teams of four to eight participants.

A larger class would be split into two groups, each subdivided into two teams, and at the very end the two groups would discuss what they each did and why they made the decisions they did. A smaller class should also be split into two teams, but in this case the April tasks can be done by everyone in a team, instead of subdividing the teams into two groups as suggested in the procedure below.

If there is another class in your institute using *International Business English*, the two classes could be combined for this simulation, thus making two separate rooms available and having two Controllers.

Photocopies and documents

You will need to make photocopies of the documents for this simulation, so that each team has at least one copy of the relevant documents. To make the photocopied documents look more authentic and business-like, it's best to trim the photocopies with scissors or a guillotine before handing them out to the class.

BUT, for heightened realism in the 'month' of FEBRUARY, you could use authentic literature about each of the sites that are recommended as possible locations: New York State, New Jersey, Telford and Wigan.

Perhaps write to the following addresses, requesting their 'Relocation Information Pack':

- New York State Department of Economic Development, Panton House, 25 Haymarket, London SW1, England. (Telex 912721 NYCOM G)

  or

  State of New York, Department of Commerce, Division of International Commerce, 230 Park Avenue, New York 10169. (Telex 969981 NYCOM)

- Industrial Development Manager, New York State Electric & Gas Corporation, 4500 Vestal Parkway East, Binghamton, NY 13903, USA. (Telex 932416 NYSEG)

- Governor's Special Trade Representative and Director, New Jersey Division of International Trade, 744 Broad Street, Suite 1709, Newark, NJ 07102, USA. (Telex 178089 NJDIT)

- Commercial Department, Telford Development Corporation, Priorslee Hall, Telford, Shropshire TF2 9NT, UK (Telex 35359 TELDEV G)

- Head of Economic Development, PO Box 36, Civic Centre, Millgate, Wigan WN1 1YD, UK. (Telex 677341)

The simulation would be tremendously enhanced by having colour brochures and additional pages of facts and figures to refer to. Alternatively, why not get members of the class to send a telex to each address, asking for the information pack?

January   This month consists of preparatory work: students are not yet in their teams or roles.

1. 🔲 Play the tape:

'... and I'd like to start by giving you a bit of background information. The first Spaghetti House restaurant opened in London in 1955. There's now a chain of 14 restaurants in the London area. Much of the products, in particular the pasta dishes are prepared in central kitchens, and the same items are on the menu in most of the restaurants. The chain has an excellent reputation and has managed to develop a product range that appeals to all ages and all income groups. In some of these restaurants they provide a ... take-away service for people who want to eat in their offices or ... or at home.

Well, a few years ago they launched a range of prepared pasta dishes which were designed to go on sale in supermarkets, so that the most popular dishes are now available to the public all over Britain. They have a nice slogan: "From our House to your Home" and a really nice colourful package with preparation instructions and so on.

Well, this launch was prompted by the success of another manufacturer's uncooked fresh pasta on supermarket shelves and by reque ... requests from their restaurant customers. Well, the Spaghetti House product is different from other products on the market in that it's a complete ready-to-cook meal for one or two people, no extra sauces or cheese are required. The product is designed to be microwaveable or cooked in a conventional oven and it's then ready to serve. The product is available in two versions: fresh and frozen. The fresh version is much more popular and available in a wider variety. The most popular varieties are Lasagne and Cannelloni. The shelf-life of the fresh product is about ten days, even though no preservatives are used, and most outlets are supplied once or twice a week.

Now, what I'd like to discuss with you is why you think this product has been so successful. So to begin with, I'd like you to exchange ideas in small groups, all right? So ... er ...'

[Time: 2 minutes]

2. Divide the class into small groups.
3. Go round the class while they are working on their brand names and packages.
4. Have each group do a short 'Presentation' of their product. The others should make notes and ask questions afterwards.
5. Take a vote or agree by consensus on one product range to deal with during the rest of the 'year'.
   For steps 6 and 7, it is not yet necessary to assign the participants to teams – the rubric in the Student's Book explains what will be happening later.
6. Students, working as a whole class or in groups, consider their criteria in choosing a location.
7. And they look at the maps to see which sites seem to fulfil their criteria – if you have large-scale maps of the areas that the class can consult, that would make the task more realistic.

February

1. The memo explains the parameters of the task.
2. Divide the class into two teams:
   the GB TEAM and the US TEAM.

   Give copies of February Documents (GB) and February Documents (US) to the appropriate team – these should be photocopied from pages 295 to 308. If the teams are small, one copy of each document should be enough and these can be circulated within the team – as if being circulated in the company.

   ¶ To save time the copies could be given out before the lesson, but in this case every student would need copies of the relevant documents.

   If you've been able to get real information packs about the four sites (from the addresses on page 285), now is the time to hand these out to the appropriate teams.

   NOTE: Participants can only use the information supplied in the documents and in the recordings. In a real-life situation, there would be hundreds of pages of documents and financial information to wade through and deal with, there would be experts and advisers to consult, there would be dozens or even hundreds of locations to evaluate and choose between, etc – what we're attempting to do here is to give a *flavour* of the real thing only.

   Participants who complain 'But there's some important information missing, we need to know so-and-so' may be placated with this advice:
   'Actually almost all the information you'd really need is missing – you'll have to make do with what you've got. I think you should assume that whatever's missing is the *same for each site.*'

3. ⊟ The teams get more information about the locations in recorded reports from a colleague 'on the spot'. The recorded reports should ideally be played to the separate groups in different parts of the room. If this isn't feasible, there's no harm in everyone hearing everything as it may help them to form a better impression of what the others are up to.

Reports on Telford and Wigan for the GB team

'Hello. I'm here inside the Shopping Centre at Telford New Town. In spite of the unemployment rate here, above the national average, there's an atmosphere of prosperity in the town. I was expecting this to be a bit of a concrete jungle, like some other new towns I've visited. But the mixture of housing, good roads, parks, and clean modern industry make this quite a pleasant place. Right here next to the indoor shopping centre is the Town Park and just up the road is some of the best scenery in England – and unspoilt countryside just outside the town boundary.
    Telford has the biggest concentration of Japanese companies in the UK: Seiko Epson

(they've invested £11m in a new plant manufacturing computer printers), NEC (they've just opened a £3.7m plant manufacturing videos and TVs, which will employ nearly 900 people), Hitachi Maxell have their European HQ here and make video cassettes and floppy disks, Ricoh manufactures photocopiers for sale throughout Europe. Also here are Tatung (from Taiwan) with 1000 workers making TVs, the French company Peaudouce making babies' nappies, and Unimation (part of Westinghouse) making robots.

Although Telford's quite a good place for sports and leisure – Telford even has its own dry ski slope – it's not too good for entertainments and cultural activities. You have to go to Birmingham 30 miles away for that kind of thing, but the shops here are good and this shopping mall I'm in now is quite impressive.

As you know, Telford has its own motorway, the M54 connecting it to the M6 but although it has a brand new Central Station, connections to London are not very regular or quick. Birmingham Airport and the National Exhibition Centre are 40 minutes away – if there aren't any holdups on the motorway!'

[Time: 2 minutes 20 seconds]

'I'm now sitting outside the Orwell Pub at Wigan Pier on the Leeds and Liverpool canal, having a drink. This is the place George Orwell wrote about during the Great Depression in the 30's and to me Wigan still had a bad image of being a run-down coal-mining and cotton mill town. This is the first time I've been here and I must say that I'm quite impressed. Although some of the mines are still operating, the town is surprisingly clean. You get the feeling that the people are proud of their history and are keen to make a visitor feel welcome. Lancashire people are famous for their hospitality.

Wigan itself is a down-to-earth, no-nonsense sort of town, many of the houses are Victorian and beginning to show their age, but there's been a lot of urban renewal with more modern houses outside the town and good sports facilities. Quite near are the Lancashire coast and the Pennine Hills, so it's quite easy to get away from the town by car and enjoy some fresh air and scenery. The shops are a nice mixture of the old and the new too.

You're also mid-way between Liverpool and Manchester, which both have fine theatres and symphony orchestras. The main line from London to Glasgow passes through Wigan, and you can be in London in under three hours. Manchester Airport is just 40 minutes away – with connections to all parts of Europe and even to Singapore and North America.

Wigan has a lot of modern industry: HJ Heinz have been here for many years canning baked beans, soups and so on. Also there's an ICI factory, GKN the engineering group, er ... and Nabisco making biscuits and breakfast cereals, and GUS, Europe's largest mail order house.'

[Time: 1 minute 50 seconds]

Reports on Binghamton and Trenton for the US team

'I'm here now in Binghamton, in Upstate New York. I'm sitting in Ely Park overlooking the city. This is a charming little city, it's safe and pretty – though maybe it's a little dull.

The people are kind of slow and hospitable and it's hard to believe that you're just a couple of hours from downtown Manhattan and that practically every city from Chicago in the west to Boston in the east and from Washington in the south to Toronto and Montreal in the north can be reached by overnight truck. In spite of the first impression you get of being in the heart of the country, there's plenty of high tech ... er ... industry here in town: there's a new IBM plant and Singer-Link make their famous flight simulators right here.

Here too there are plenty of people without special technical skills – one of the largest employers in the area is Fisher Price Toys whose workforce is largely semi-skilled. One thing that strikes me about the people hereabouts is that they are dependable and loyal and they're not afraid of hard work – indeed many of them come from farming communities where even the children have to work. One of the big attractions of the area is the beautiful scenery. The forests in the fall are glorious and in winter the main ski-ing resorts of the Eastern United States are just an hour's drive away. There are some lovely lakes too. People are moving out of New York City to get away from commuting and urban crime and to get closer to nature.'

[Time: 1 minute 55 seconds]

'I'm sitting beside the Delaware River in Trenton, New Jersey. I've just been finding out about the huge range of industry here in this state, which is the size of Wales but has about the same population as Sweden. New Jersey is one of most popular states for foreign companies to establish their headquarters: BASF, Mercedes-Benz, Volvo, Volkswagen, Toyota, Nissan, Fiat ... er ... all have their US headquarters here. Big foreign companies with factories here are Oki Data and Sharp from Japan and Samsung and Daewoo from Korea.

New Jersey is the number one state in the Union for pharmaceuticals with Hoffman-La Roche, Ciba-Geigy, Johnson & Johnson and Merck. Throughout the state each year $4 billion is being spent on research in academic and industrial R&D labs, including ... er ... Bell laboratories, ITT, AT&T, RCA. The people are very proud that 11 Nobel Prize winners live in New Jersey.

Here in Trenton I've been looking at the amazing DHC (district heating and cooling system) operating in our premises. Heating and cooling costs will be low because surplus heat generated by electric power stations is turned into steam, hot water and even cooled water for distribution by pipes to homes and industrial premises.

New Jersey calls itself the Garden State and it's true that once you get beyond the urban ... er ... areas of Newark and Jersey City, the countryside begins. One great plus is the Ocean – New Jersey has 127 miles of coast. And with the huge air network of Newark International Airport close, it's easy to get anywhere in North America and to anywhere in the world on a direct flight. From here it's just a short drive to Philadelphia or New York City.

Trenton itself is a pleasant city, though parts of it are a bit run-down. The people here are good workers and there's a long industrial tradition in the state. It's a nice place and not too large – it's quite a lively sort of place and there's a highly varied mixture of different races and nationalities.'

[Time: 2 minutes 45 seconds]

4. The two teams discuss the relative merits of the sites and when they've reached a decision, they report to the other team by fax, phone or in person. Students should decide on the most appropriate method, bearing in mind their own personal use of English for business purposes.

This step cannot be omitted or speeded up – it requires a good half hour.

5. Having informed the other team, the two teams make further decisions about the organization and staffing of their projected establishments. They inform their counterparts by role-playing a phone call.

¶ If time is short, this step could be speeded up or omitted.

6. Working individually, or as a team, they draft an outline of how they'll organize the business to foster staff motivation and efficiency.
   ¶ If time is short, this step could be speeded up or omitted.
7. At the end of the 'month' there is a meeting where the two teams exchange experiences.

March If time is limited the teams can subdivide into small groups to deal with the different tasks (steps 1, 2 and 3) in each smaller group. Alternatively, the teams can decide to devote themselves to accomplishing just **one** of the tasks (not necessarily the first). The GB team and the US team may decide to work on different tasks in this case. This needs to be discussed and agreed on before work starts on the tasks.
¶ This month can be omitted if time is short – but there won't be revision of Units 12, 10 and 13 if so.

1. To make sure everything necessary is done before the new location is opened, the various priorities are discussed. A fax is sent to the other team, to keep them in the picture.
2. To look after public relations and publicity, a press release is drafted for the local media. A copy is faxed to the other team.
3. To make sure the branch recruits suitable staff and managers, an advertisement has to be drafted. A copy is faxed to the other team.
4. Each team meets to discuss what individual members did this month.
   OR
   The two teams meet together to discuss what everyone did. (The wording in the Student's Book is deliberately ambiguous to allow for either alternative – the teams could decide for themselves which is preferable.)

April This month the GB team is divided into two groups: GB 1 and GB 2 and the US team is divided into two groups: US 1 and US 2. Each group will be dealing with a different aspect of the plans for relocating in their respective countries: 'Materials, supplies and distribution' and 'Marketing and sales'. Both groups will be discussing and making decisions, drafting letters *or* drafting outlines and an advertisement, and making phone calls.
   The sub-groups could be arranged according to the participants' real life expertise or interests – or in a high-level class, the groups could be arranged contrary to their real jobs.

NOTE: If one of these topics is of no interest to the class, the teams could continue working as large groups as they deal with the more relevant topic – the month will go more quickly but the phone calls will be less interesting and less crucial.

¶ In the unlikely event that nobody is terribly interested in either topic, this month can be speeded up — but *not* omitted altogether!

1. Give out copies of the Documents (on pages 309 to 310):

   Document 1 should be given to the members of groups GB 1 and US 1: one copy for each participant, or one copy to be shared between two participants. These sub-groups will discuss their policy on Materials, supplies and distribution.

   Document 2 should be given to the members of groups GB 2 and US 2: one copy for each participant, or one copy to be shared between two participants. These sub-groups will discuss their policy on Marketing and sales.

   |☎| At least twice during the month, a member of each group has to telephone his or her counterparts in the other countries. Inform the participants that the time has come for this by, for example, flicking the classroom lights on and off or making a suitable announcement. Designate one part of the classroom for the |☎| conversations to be made in.

2. The two sub-groups meet together to find out what the others have been doing. (US 1 meets US 2, while GB 1 meets GB 2.)
3. The US and GB teams meet to discuss what they did.

May In this part of the simulation, the teams discover that their months of planning may have been in vain — a not uncommon event in the real business world! From a language practice point of view the purpose of the work done in previous 'months' has been the *process* not the results, whereas in real life the results are all important!

This discovery is made by reading the memo (MAY Document 1). Only one copy of this is needed per team.

1. So that the surprise works realistically, get the teams to sit together in their by-now-customary places. Tell them to begin by reviewing what they did in April...

   Then deliver the memo for everyone to read. Be prepared for an angry reaction from some participants as the memo from head office rules that only one of the branches may be established — a meeting must be held to decide which one.
2. The memo has called for a meeting. The two teams draft their own agendas and decide who they will propose as chairperson. They also decide on their preferred venue.
3. The two teams exchange phone calls or faxes to negotiate the agenda and venue of the forthcoming meeting.
4. At this point the chairperson should be appointed from the two nominated by each team. To make this seem fair, a coin could be

tossed. The chosen chairperson is given a copy of MAY Document 2 – this document contains special instructions for the chairperson. Tell the chairperson what time the meeting should end, so that you have enough time after it for a debriefing / follow-up discussion.

5. THE MEETING is held. This is the climax of the whole simulation: allow 20 to 30 minutes for this step so that all the arguments can be presented and thrashed out.

    The two teams put forward their arguments and a final decision is reached, perhaps by voting or by consensus.

Debriefing / Follow-up discussion

At the end of the simulation, make sure there is time for participants to step out of role and analyse what they did. Ask these questions to stimulate a discussion:

- What happened in your team?
- What difficulties did you encounter?
- What was the most difficult part of the simulation for you?
- If you could do the simulation over again, what would you do differently?
- In what ways are real life situations similar to the events in the simulation?

Written work

Each participant should write a report of his or her work in the simulation. This may either be done 'in role' from the point of view of a member of the projected team, or it could be a report on the simulation written in retrospect.

Workbook

The Workbook exercises for Unit 15 consist of revision material, which can be used as a 'Progress Test' of the work that has been done while using *International Business English*.

If you wish to conduct a progress test of your students' oral work, you can supplement the written and recorded exercises in the Workbook with these two role play exercises, to be done in pairs. While your students are doing these, their proficiency can be assessed by yourself or by another teacher. Alternatively, you could get a student to play the longer role while you (or another teacher) play the shorter one in each role play.

[Photocopy this role information and give a copy to Student A or Student B, as appropriate.]

Workbook

Contents for this unit:

15.1   Grammar revision
15.2   Word-building revision
15.3   Prepositions revision
15.4   Vocabulary revision   Crossword puzzle
15.5   Functions revision
15.6   Midway International   Writing
15.7   The Peterborough Effect – 1   Reading
15.8   The Peterborough Effect – 2   Reading
15.9   The Nightingale Effect   Reading aloud
15.10 Franchising   Listening

1st Role play

A   You are on a visit to a foreign country and you have been unavoidably delayed because of a train strike. You have been invited to dinner at 8 pm. but now you won't be able to make it. Phone your host/hostess to explain the delay and apologize. The time now is 7.00 and the earliest you could get there would be 10 pm, which would be too late for dinner.

Tell your host/hostess that . . .
- You'll arrive at the factory tomorrow morning at 8 am – or will that be too early for your host/hostess?
- You're catching the 17.30 plane tomorrow, so the meeting will have to be in the morning.
- You're staying at the Sheraton Hotel – phone number 44 76 18.
- You've booked a table at the Excelsior Hotel for lunch for your host/hostess and colleagues at 12.30 tomorrow.
- You'll phone your host/hostess from the station when you finally do arrive.

B   You are expecting a visitor from abroad as your guest of honour for dinner. The visitor is due to meet you and your colleagues formally tomorrow afternoon at the factory. You have invited several colleagues who will be arriving at 7.45. The time now is 7.00.
   Answer the phone. Make a note of any information you are given.

2nd Role play

A   You are expecting a visitor from abroad who is coming to your office. Your assistant has already left for the airport to meet the visitor when his or her plane arrives at 12.00. The time now is 10.00.

Answer the phone. Make a note of any information you are given.

B   Your flight to a foreign country is delayed and you're waiting at the airport for it to leave. Your host/hostess is going to meet your flight when it is due to arrive at 12 noon. Phone your host/hostess and explain that you'll be late and he or she shouldn't come to the airport to meet you. You will make your own way to the office when you eventually arrive. The time now is 10 am and the plane isn't going to leave till about 11.00.

Tell your host/hostess that ...
- You'll need photocopies of the technical report for the meeting tomorrow morning.
- Your boss (Jean du Maurier) is calling you at 1 pm – can your host/hostess take a message?
- You'll be staying at the Metropole Hotel, near the station – phone number 80 18 29.
- Your return flight tomorrow is at 15.30, so you'll have to leave straight after lunch – will there be enough time to settle everything by then?

© Cambridge University Press, 1989

February Documents (GB)

One copy of each document can be circulated within the team —
though a large team may need more than one copy of each document.

I am pleased to report that we have found suitable
buildings in two locations. The two sites are Bradley
Hall Trading Estate, Standish, in Wigan (Greater
Manchester) and Stafford Park Industrial Estate in
Telford (West Midlands). There are suitable buildings
available at both sites that are ideal for our
purposes, providing excellent low-cost industrial and
office accommodation.

    Wigan is mid-way between Liverpool and Manchester.
Its population is over 300,000.
    Telford is a New Town to the west of Birmingham
with a population of about 110,000.
Both are well-sited for the motorway network: Wigan is
close to the M6 and Telford is connected by the M54 to
the M5 and M6. They have good access to all the major
British markets and also to ferry ports for access to
markets in Ireland and Northern Europe. From this
point of view, both would make ideal bases for
shipping our product all over the United Kingdom — a
growing market with a population of 55 million.

    Our own research and advice from local consultants
suggest that cost-wise there is nothing to choose
between the two sites: both offer the same corporate
taxation incentives, and government grants are
available at each location for setting up a new plant
and training staff are available. Labour costs and
power costs are similar in both sites.

    I will be visiting both sites soon and I will send
you a cassette giving you my personal impressions of
both locations.

    In the meantime, I enclose some background
information about each place.

With best wishes,

Leslie Maxwell

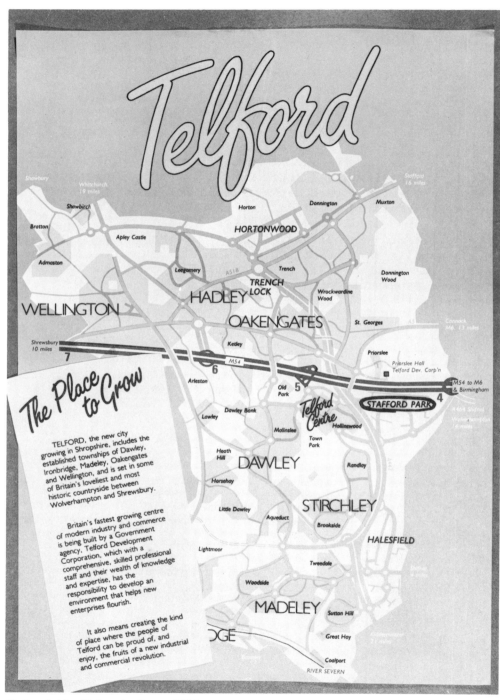

Mr. R. Daffern
Managing Director
BAT Building and Engineering
Products Ltd

"We were one of the first companies to move on to the Halesfield Industrial Estate in Telford and the ready availability of industrial land and buildings has allowed us to expand from an original workforce of 20 to 180 today."

Mr. G. Webster
Managing Director
Martin Industries Ltd (USA)

"Telford's location, with its excellent communications, is ideal for our development and expansion plans and as a base it will serve both the UK and Europe, which is why Telford was our first choice."

Mr. K. Markham
Managing Director
Debenhams PLC

"Over the last four years we've seen Telford grow dramatically in terms of retail development, services and recreational activities. This, coupled with the positive attitude shown by Telford Development Corporation, means there is still temendous potential for growth for both old and new businesses."

Mr. J. Jamieson
Managing Director
Merlin Gerin

"During our ten years in Telford, the ability to add more space without the need to move has been a very important factor in helping us to achieve dramatic growth. We now employ more than 53 thousand square feet."

Mr. J. Bowett
Managing Director
Lindemann Machine Co Ltd.

"In the ten years since we moved to Telford, thanks both to the efforts of our employees and the co-operation of Telford Development Corporation, we have enjoyed a growth of 1000%."

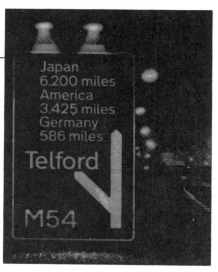

*W*hen *Bischof and Klein, the West German plastic
materials manufacturers, opened up in Telford
they were over 580 miles from home.*

*Unimation, a robotics firm from Connecticut and
part of the mighty Westinghouse Group, have ventured
even further afield. They're now over 3,400 miles from
their base.*

*And should anyone from Maxell want to pop back
into head office, then the company car would have to
clock up a staggering 6,200 miles.*

*But no matter how far they've come, all these com-
panies have found that there's something in Telford to
remind them of home.*

*For the Germans, inventors of the autobahn, there's
Telford's own motorway, the M54. It links up with the M6
giving easy access to all Britain's major ports and bringing two thirds her population within four hours' drive
by heavy goods vehicle.*

IF YOU'RE WORRIED ABOUT MOVING YOUR COMPANY A FEW MILES THINK HOW THE GERMANS, AMERICANS AND JAPANESE FELT.

*For the Japanese, who value the virtues of hard work so highly,
there are the hard working local people of Telford.*

*And for the Americans, for whom the maxim "time is money"
is almost gospel, there's an attitude of mind that proves that
Britain's get up and go, hasn't got up and gone. As they've discovered,
in Telford things get done with the minimum of fuss and the maximum of efficiency.*

*As for something to make the British businessman feel at home,
there's the area itself.*

*Telford lies among some of Britain's finest countryside and includes within its boundaries
the historic town of Ironbridge – the Birthplace of the Industrial Revolution.*

*But perhaps what's more important is how welcome the people of Telford will make you,
and your business, feel.*

*Should you decide to come, Telford Development Corporation will do everything they
can to make your move as smooth as possible.*

*They'll find you the site that best suits your needs. They'll make sure you get the most
out of all the grants and loans that are on offer. They'll even help you and your staff find
somewhere to live. And they'll do much more besides.*

*If all this has made you want to find out more, then ring Chris Mackrell on 0952 613131.
Or better still just drive up the M6 and turn left at the M54.*

*But if you do end up having to ask for directions don't be surprised if the reply you get
comes back in Japanese.*   TELFORD DEVELOPMENT CORPORATION, PRIORSLEE HALL, TELFORD, SHROPSHIRE TF2 9NT

The success story continues.

Introduction

This may not be the first industrial development document you have read recently. But the area it concerns may well prove to be the most surprising.

How else would you describe a community traditionally associated with coal and cotton, whose interests these days include everything from man-made fibres to food processing, engineering and plastics?

An area which in a mere 77 square miles (199km²) has 10 substantial townships. Yet retains considerable tracts of farm land, open country and sites of special environmental interest.

A district which to the outsider may conjure up images of streets of terraced houses, but which, in fact, has larger and more varied housing stocks than a great many other parts of the country.

A place rightly celebrated for brass bands and rugby league, which has two major symphony orchestras on its doorstep, four leading football clubs, and a host of other activities in the arts, sport and entertainment.

The community in question is Metropolitan Wigan. It has a population of over 300,000, a potential workforce of more than 140,000, and within 50 miles a market of 9.6 million.

Its communications, by road, rail, air or sea, are by any standards remarkable. It has an impressive range of industrial accommodation in both ready-built factories and greenfield sites, and a wide-ranging portfolio of grants, loans and incentives.

It also has something of a

reputation for taking a very positive and energetic approach to industrial development. Which may explain its increasing popularity as a base for businesses both large and small; for new enterprises and expanding established companies.

This document will give you the facts about Metropolitan Wigan and although much of what it has to say may indeed come as a surprise, rest assured, the surprise will be entirely a pleasant one.

Location

Probably more than any other single factor, the key to Metropolitan Wigan's value as a venue for industrial growth lies in its geography.

In the County of Greater Manchester, it sits midway between Manchester and Liverpool, in the part of the country where industry first began.

At a glance, there may seem to be nothing remarkable about its location. But look again.

The triangle of motorways that surrounds it is part of the densest motorway network in Europe.

To the south, the M62 runs

coast to coast, taking in Liverpool, West Yorkshire and Humberside.

To the west is the M6, the main route to Scotland, the Midlands and London.

Manchester, too is directly accessible by the M61 motorway (in under half an hour), as are Chester and North Wales via the M56.

Wigan is on the main London to Glasgow railway (the capital being less than three hours away), and there are direct rail links to the Midlands, excellent local services and rail container transport.

The motorways bring the port of Liverpool within easy reach, with the giant Seaforth Container Terminal, the Freeport and also the east coast ports, with access to Europe.

Air travel is similarly well served.

You can be at Manchester International Airport within 40 minutes, with the London Shuttle, routes to North America, the Far

East, Australia, most major European cities and the largest air freight facility outside London at your disposal.

While Liverpool's Speke Airport in the main provides a useful second link, for domestic and Irish flights.

The proximity of Liverpool and Manchester has other advantages.

Manchester, in particular, is Britain's second commercial city, with the regional offices of insurance companies, the Stock Exchange, merchant and foreign banks, newspaper offices, TV and radio stations, advertising agencies and the local branches of government departments, including the Department of Trade and Industry and the Small Firms Information Centre.

All of which should make one thing abundantly clear. Thanks in part to its geography, Metropolitan Wigan is a surprisingly easy place in which to get business moving.

Summary

When you weigh up all the arguments, there can be few places in Britain with quite so much to offer as Metropolitan Wigan.

Thanks to its unique position on the motorway network, it has communications which are unequalled anywhere in the country.

After years of being dependent on a few large employers and two major industries, it has successfully built a new and increasingly diverse industrial base.

There are great opportunities for new factories, warehouses and offices, and acres of space for expansion.

To encourage new business to start up or move here, all manner of help is available, and there is nowhere in the region, and only a handful of areas elsewhere, which can match it for grants and incentives.

Every bit as helpful is the attitude of the Council, which is a very positive one, and this is matched by that of the workforce, whose adaptability and record of industrial relations speak for themselves.

Finally, as you've just seen, through the quality of its education, housing, services, shopping and leisure facilities it offers a good quality of life.

The facts about Metropolitan Wigan often come as a surprise, not only to the people reading about them, but even to those who have made the considered decision to do business here.

As a director of one company new to the area once said, you have to "come and see Wigan for yourself."

In the circumstances, we could hardly offer any better advice.

To arrange a visit or find out more about Metropolitan Wigan and any of the organisations mentioned in this document, speak to the Head of Economic Development. He'll be more than glad to help you.

Contact: The Head of Economic Development,
Wigan Metropolitan Borough Council, Civic Centre, Millgate,
Wigan WN1 1YD.
Telephone: 0942 44991
Telex: 677341

Acknowledgements
We would like to thank those many individuals and organisations for their co-operation in the preparation of this document. Pictures by Photofit Photography Ltd of Stockport, Wigan MBC, and organisations throughout the Borough. Published by the Economic Development Unit of Wigan MBC, produced by Grove Advertising Services Ltd of Stockport and printed by Collins and Darwell Ltd of Leigh. 10M8/86.

February Documents (US)

One copy of each document can be circulated within the team –
though a large team may need more than one copy of each document.

I am pleased to report that we have found suitable
buildings in two locations. The two sites are Interstate
Industrial Park in Binghamton, NY and Delaware Corporate
Park in Trenton NJ. There are suitable buildings available
at both sites that are ideal for our purposes, providing
excellent low-cost industrial and office accommodation.
> Binghamton is in Upstate New York. It has a
> population of 55,000 and good communications by
> interstate highway to all parts of the East Coast and
> Mid-West.
> Trenton is the State Capital of New Jersey, with a
> population of 110,000. It is mid-way between
> Philadelphia and New York City on the banks of the
> Delaware River and also well-sited for communications
> by truck or automobile.
Both places seem to be equally well-sited for easy
overnight access by truck to major markets in the Eastern
Seaboard area and Canada. Over 50% of the total population
of both the USA and Canada are within 750 miles (over 130
million people) – the most extensive and affluent consumer
market in the Western Hemisphere. So although the
competition here is very fierce, the potential is
enormous!
   Our own research and advice from local consultants
suggest that cost-wise there is nothing to choose between
the two sites: the tax advantages of New Jersey are
balanced by the lower power and labor costs in Upstate New
York. Grants are available at each location for setting up
a new plant and training staff.
   I will be visiting both sites soon and I will send you
a cassette giving you my personal impressions of both
locations.
   In the meantime, I enclose some background information
about each place.

Best,

Lee Carter

© Cambridge University Press, 1989

302

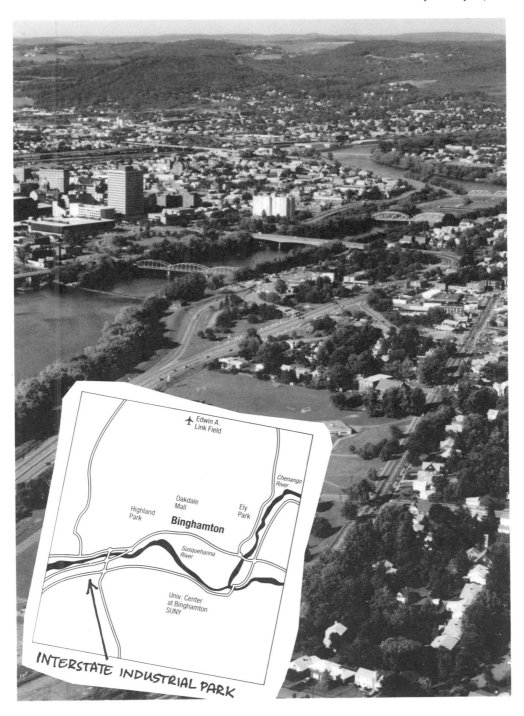

Edwin A.
Link Field

Chenango
River

Oakdale
Mall

Highland
Park

Ely
Park

Binghamton

Susquehanna
River

Univ. Center
at Binghamton
SUNY

INTERSTATE INDUSTRIAL PARK

© Cambridge University Press, 1989

Living Environment

Something for everyone in a state almost the size of England.

An environment of the highest quality
New York State is a place of amazing diversity. But whether you choose the big city or the countryside, suburb, or small town, the State has carefully preserved a high quality of life for those living and working within the State.

Outdoor recreation
85% of New York State is rural, wild, or forested. 150 State parks afford magnificent walking trails and facilities for camping, swimming, and, in winter, skiing. The State has about 4,000 lakes, including Lake George, Oneida Lake, and the famous wine-growing region of the Finger Lakes. Fast-flowing streams yield trout and other game fish. Grouse, partridge, pheasant, wild duck and wild geese are plentiful, as well as whitetail deer in many parts of the State.
On Long Island, you can roam along more than 100 uninterrupted miles (161 km) of sandy beach. Long Island Sound has many beautiful harbors and great conditions for sailing.
The state has 4 thoroughbred and 7 harness racecourses, 736 golf clubs, 65 skiing centers, 9 hunt clubs, innumerable riding schools, squash and tennis courts.

A full range of cultural activities
A host of private cultural organizations, as well as the New York State Arts Council, sponsor opera, theater, ballet and orchestral performances in communities throughout the State. They also organize exhibitions of art, architecture, film and photography as well as lecture series. The Metropolitan Museum of Art, the American Museum of Natural History, and some of the world's most famous galleries, museums and performing arts centers are to be found in the State. The Rochester and Buffalo Philharmonic orchestras, the Saratoga Performing Arts Center, and Lincoln Center (home of the Metropolitan Opera, the New York Philharmonic Orchestra and the New York City Ballet) are among the outstanding cultural attractions.

Bright lights and excitement
New York State is the home of Broadway, Off-Broadway, Off-Off-Broadway, glittering nightclubs and glamorous revues.
It's also a great place to be a supporter of major-league sports. Take the children to a baseball game – it's an afternoon event, and your neighbors in the stands will be happy to explain.
American football combines skillful strategy with physical prowess, but be warned: it's addictive. And during the winter, take in a fast-moving indoor soccer or hockey match.

Nostalgic touches
It's easy for an international business executive to feel at home in New York State. The seasons revolve in a familiar cycle, with an accent on sunny skies. Once you get outside New York City, you'll be surprised how quickly the hubbub dies down. Food, prices, and style of life tend to be comfortably traditional. You'll soon feel at home with friendly neighbors and familiar pursuits.

Case Studies

Success stories: They're showing up all over New York State.

PHILIPS CABLES LIMITED

When Philips Cables, Canada's leading manufacturer of wire and cable, chose Watertown, New York, as the base for its entry into U.S. markets, it found ready assistance and cooperation from the local and State authorities. The costs of setting up a new manufacturing plant for Philips, a subsidiary of BICC of the U.K., were held well within the limits specified by the board, with the help of a financing package put together by the New York State Department of Commerce and the Industrial Development Agency of Jefferson County.

An issue of tax exempt bonds arranged by the IDA on Philips' behalf, together with a loan from the Urban Development Authority, reduced interest charges significantly.

The State Department of Commerce provided funds for an on-the-job training scheme which helped assure Philips an adequate supply of skilled labor during the start-up period of the new plant.

Mr J. Leroy Olsen, President and Chief Executive Officer of Philips Cables, pays tribute to "the excellent help and cooperation given by officials in the Watertown area, which have considerably eased our entry into this new venture."

INTERKNITTING, LTD

The first links in the chain which drew Interknitting, the West German textile firm, from its home base to a new operating venture in Cobleskill, New York, were forged in the European office of New York State's Commerce Department.

Now, after eight years, Interknitting, a subsidiary of Paul Hoffman K/G of West Germany is soundly established in Cobleskill on a site originally found for it by the Commerce Department. The location included an existing textile plant, and offered an experienced labor force and close proximity to both suppliers and market outlets.

A substantial start-up cost was lifted from Interknitting's shoulders when the Commerce Department helped eliminate a required deposit from the local power utility.

Other valuable help came from the Schoharie County Industrial Development Agency which purchased the factory building and then leased it to Interknitting, which will eventually acquire ownership.

Since opening for business in Cobleskill, the German firm has increased its work force nearly tenfold, helped by on-the-job training funds from the State authorities.

LAZZARONI SARONNO, LTD

After nearly fifty years of selling its high quality pastries in the U.S., D. Lazzaroni of Saronno, near Milan, decided it could best serve its American markets from a manufacturing facility close to the New York City Metropolitan area. Lazzaroni wanted to be near its major customers, but also wanted to take advantage of New York's business network and of New York State's business tax incentives.

Lazzaroni Saronno, the new U.S. subsidiary, achieved these goals when it opened for business in 1981 in Rockland County, just one hour from Manhattan. From the new plant, the company expects to establish new markets in Canada as well as attract new business in the U.S.

Lazzaroni was helped by the New York State Commerce Department which arranged the issue of industrial revenue bonds to meet the initial $2.25 million investment cost.

Moreover, Lazzaroni qualified for a reduction of 95% of its New York State corporation income tax.

New York State was not the only venue considered for the new development by the Italian group. But Paolo Lazzaroni, chairman of the parent company, said, "the personal contacts and warm relationships" tipped the balance in the decision in favor of New York State.

QUO VADIS INC.

The opening in 1983 of its new printing and production facility near Buffalo in Hamburg, New York, by Quo Vadis was the culmination of more than two years of planning by the company and the State Commerce Department.

Quo Vadis, whose parent company is based in Marseilles, obtained a financing package covering the total cost of the new facility which will handle production of its business diaries and desk calendars for markets throughout the U.S., as well as Canada, Australia and the U.K. The financing was put together with the help of the Erie County Industrial Development Agency and the New York Job Development Agency.

The New York State site location office helped the French firm find a suitable site to replace the small sales office originally opened eight years earlier, and put the company in touch with the local agencies which arranged the financing.

As a final touch, Quo Vadis expects to qualify for relief for at least 90% of its New York State corporate income tax under the Job Incentive Program.

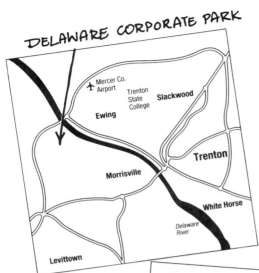

DELAWARE CORPORATE PARK

The State has attracted the top talent in business and industry because it is a good place to work and live, and it is a great place to play!

It is one of the most beautiful states in the nation; there are breathtaking beaches, farms, mountains and pinelands. Of the State's total of 5 million acres, 2 million acres are in woods and forests and more than 1 million acres are under cultivation. State forests and parks account for over 25,000 acres with more lands being conserved under the Green Acres Program. You can ski, sail, horseback ride or beachcomb all on the same day. New Jersey has 218 golf courses and has hosted the U.S. Open and many other major golf tournaments. The national headquarters of the United States Golf Association is located here, too. And, with 127 miles of ocean front, the shore area has attracted many who want it "all" including rapid accessibility to New York and Philadelphia.

Some of the most beautiful suburban areas in the country are found in New Jersey. An excellent highway system and ample public transportation have helped create a "commuter class" who work on Wall Street or Madison Avenue in New York City or work in nearby Philadelphia but want to enjoy the suburban New Jersey lifestyle.

NEW JERSEY HAS IT ALL . . .

- a location in the heart of the world's largest concentration of market wealth
- an international business environment of diverse industries
- a large pool of highly qualified professionals and technical specialists
- a close link between academia and new technology/research industries.

- a state government committed to business growth
- a large roster of innovative financial institutions with resources earmarked for new and growing business
- a transportation network ideally situated and equipped for international trade and for rapisly reaching a part of the United States
- a high quality of life featuring an unmatched diversity of cultural, recreational and entertainment facilities – all within close proximity of each other.

We Wouldn't Have Such A Good Climate For Working If We Didn't Have Such A Good Climate For Playing.

For some people New Jersey is high, rolling hills and tranquil valleys.

For others it's picnicking, camping and fishing in Worthington State Park, where twice a year you can watch the sun go down in the center of the Delaware Water Gap.

Golf lovers can take their pick of over 200 courses. Music lovers can choose from over 50 musical groups. And the more scholarly have their choice of over 60 museums. You can stroll through one of our quaint, historic villages where you'll make an interesting discovery. Some of the nicest New England Villages aren't in New England.

They're in New Jersey.

To a lot of families, New Jersey is white sand beaches and quiet seashore towns like Avalon and Mantoloking. Or the excitement of the boardwalk casinos. (Did you know that the first boardwalk in the country was built in Atlantic City? All 6 miles of it.)

But that's not all.

The Meadowlands Sports Complex is home to two pro football teams — the NFL's Giants and Jets — plus the pro basketball Nets and the pro ice hockey Devils.

And just a trot away is thoroughbred horse racing.

In New Jersey, you can ride down a winding country road. Drive through a safari park at Great Adventure. Or schuss down a ski slope.

As you can tell, we feel strongly about our state.

We think you will too.

It's Been Said There Are Three Important Things To Consider When Choosing A Business Site.

Location, Location, Location.

The business community in New Jersey is a study in diversity.

We have a wide range of businesses doing everything from manufacturing pharmaceutical products to harvesting cranberries.

Not to mention all the service industries that a business community like ours attracts.

But, with all their diversity, our businesses share one important thing.

A terrific location.

Every one is situated right in the heart of the Northeast Corridor — the richest market in the world.

In the world? In the world.

Within a 250-mile radius, (the distance of an ordinary overnight truck delivery), are 12 states and 60 million consumers.

That's one out of every four Americans.

And right across the Hudson River are the international banking centers of New York City.

We have 35,000 miles of highway and more railroad track per square mile than any other state.

The international airport in Newark is one of the most modern, efficient and fast-growing in the United States. And, besides Newark, there are 11 other New Jersey airports capable of accommodating business jets.

The Port of Philadelphia, incorporating many of the ports on the Delaware River, comprises the nation's second largest foreign trade port.

And Port Newark/Port Elizabeth has earned the distinction of being named "the container capital of the world," handling more than 12 million long tons of cargo annually.

Oh, and there's one more thing our extensive transportation system has earned us.

Lots of new business.

April Document 1   (1 or 2 copies for the relevant sub-group)

Supplies, materials, and distribution

1. SUPPLIES
   You'll have to invite tenders from companies in the locality to
   supply you with office equipment, furniture, stationery, catering,
   cleaning, etc.
   - What kinds of firms will you need to contact?
   - What other specialized services will you need to obtain locally –
     advice on taxation, translation services, etc?

   Draft a standard letter to be sent to establish contact with companies who may be able to supply you with goods or services.
   Send a copy of this to your counterparts in the other country.

2. MATERIALS
   You will need to obtain the basic ingredients for your manufactur-
   ing process locally.
   - Will you set up a warehouse or rent warehouse space?
   - Can you employ JIT ('Just in Time') methods – does your
     operation have enough influence to rely this much on suppliers?

   Draft a standard letter that you can send, inviting prospective
   suppliers to contact you.

3. DISTRIBUTION
   Your product will be delivered directly to the catering trade and
   store groups. You estimate that 45% will sell to the trade (hotels,
   restaurants and canteens), 35% to store groups and 25% to
   independent retailers.

   - Will you use your own fleet of trucks or use trucking contractors
     to ship goods to customers?
   - Can you supply direct to independent retailers, or should you
     deal through a wholesaler?
   - How much warehouse space will you set aside for goods ready
     for dispatch?
   - Will this be a completely separate building or area?

   Draft a standard letter that you can send, inviting prospective
   transport firms to contact you.
   Send a copy to your counterparts in the other country – and ask
   for their comments.

☎ KEEP IN TOUCH WITH YOUR COUNTERPARTS IN THE OTHER
COUNTRY BY PHONING THEM AT LEAST TWICE TO EXPLAIN THE
DECISIONS YOU HAVE MADE SO FAR.

April Document 2   (1 or 2 copies for the relevant sub-group)

Marketing and sales

What are the main differences between this market and the market in your own country?

PRODUCT
- Is your brand name suitable for this market?
- Will the product need to be changed at all to suit customers' tastes?
- What age groups and income groups will be your customers?
- Will the product be bought by families or single people?

PRICE
- In this market, what is your customers' attitude to high prices? What is their attitude to low prices?

PLACE
- In what kinds of retail or catering outlets should the product be available?
- Is there any chance of exporting the product from this base to neighbouring countries?

PROMOTION
- Are packaging and design more important in this market than in the home market?
- What methods of promotion can be used for this kind of product?
- What are the best ways of informing (a) trade customers, (b) retailers and (c) end-users about the product?

1. Using your answers to the questions above, devise a marketing strategy for your product.
   Draft an outline of your marketing strategy. Send a copy to your counterparts in the other country – and ask for their comments.
2. What will be your sales strategy? Will it be product-oriented or customer-oriented? Will each rep deal with a different territory, or will different reps deal with the trade, with retailers and with key accounts?
   Draft an outline of your sales strategy. Send a copy to your counterparts in the other country – and ask for their comments.
3. Draft an advertisement for the trade press describing your product, informing retailers and caterers when it will be available in their area and how you will be promoting it.

☎ KEEP IN TOUCH WITH YOUR COUNTERPARTS IN THE OTHER COUNTRY BY PHONING THEM AT LEAST TWICE TO EXPLAIN THE DECISIONS YOU HAVE MADE SO FAR.

May document 1

(one copy per team)

To: Special Project Team
From: Frank Miller, Head Office.

The board has looked at your plans for the new plant. They
are very impressed with the thoroughness of your
arrangements.

Unfortunately, in view of the firm's poor results for the
first quarter of the year, it is now clear that the firm's
original expansion plans were too ambitious. The start-up
costs for the two projects are much higher than the board
foresaw. Consequently, I regret to inform you that we
cannot go ahead with both of these projects.

However, it has been decided that one of the plants can be
set up. A meeting will be held in July to discuss and
decide whether this is to be the location in the USA or in
the UK.

All members of both teams will attend this meeting.

Franke Miller

© Cambridge University Press, 1989

May Document 2

(one copy for Chairperson)

YOU WILL BE CHAIRING THE MEETING BETWEEN THE TWO TEAMS:

1. Read out the agreed agenda at the start of the meeting.

2. Tell everyone at what time the meeting will finish.

3. Announce that there will be a vote at the end to decide which location is to be chosen.

4. To prevent any one person from dominating the meeting, anyone who wishes to speak must raise their hand and wait to be named by you. Inform everyone of this procedure.

5. Make sure both teams have the same amount of time to put their case.

Acknowledgements

The authors and publishers are grateful to the authors, publishers and others who have given permission for the use of copyright material identified in the text. In cases where it has not been possible to identify the source of the material used the publishers would welcome information from copyright owners.

Page 141 invoice form © Simplification of International Trade Procedures Board (SITPRO); page 297 Telford Development Corporation; page 299–301 Wigan Metropolitan Borough Council; pages 303–308 New Jersey Division of International Trade, New York State Department of Economic Development, New York State Electric and Gas Corporation (NYSEG).

Artwork by Ace Art, Peter Ducker, Hard Lines and Wenham Arts. Book designed by Peter Ducker MSTD